Trend Trading

FOR

DUMMIES®

A Wiley Brand

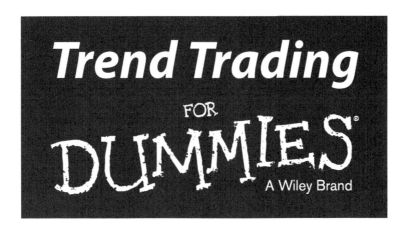

Trend Trading

FOR

DUMMIES

A Wiley Brand

by Barry Burns

FOR

DUMMIES

A Wiley Brand

Trend Trading For Dummies®

Published by: **John Wiley & Sons, Inc.,** 111 River Street, Hoboken, NJ 07030-5774, www.wiley.com

Copyright © 2014 by John Wiley & Sons, Inc., Hoboken, New Jersey

Published simultaneously in Canada

For general information on our other products and services, please contact our Customer Care Department within the U.S. at 877-762-2974, outside the U.S. at 317-572-3993, or fax 317-572-4002. For technical support, please visit www.wiley.com/techsupport.

Wiley publishes in a variety of print and electronic formats and by print-on-demand. Some material included with standard print versions of this book may not be included in e-books or in print-on-demand. If this book refers to media such as a CD or DVD that is not included in the version you purchased, you may download this material at http://booksupport.wiley.com. For more information about Wiley products, visit www.wiley.com.

Library of Congress Control Number: 2014931921

ISBN 978-1-118-87128-7 (pbk); ISBN 978-1-118-87136-2 (ebk); ISBN 978-1-118-87140-9 (ebk)

Manufactured in the United States of America

10 9 8 7 6 5 4 3 2 1

Contents at a Glance

Table of Contents

Introduction

*M*y beloved father, Patrick F. Burns, started trading stocks when he was 18 years old. Every day on his lunch break, he'd take his sack lunch and walk to his broker's office and sit in front of the *tape* — a series of wide blackboards that listed the most popular stock symbols. One man's job was to manually update the prices of those stocks, from left to right, across the blackboards.

My dad started teaching me about trading the markets when I was about 8 years old. He'd sit me down at our dining room table, lay out the portfolios of five stocks (which I'm sure he prescreened for me), and ask me which one he should buy. I'd ask some questions, he'd explain as best he could, and then I'd pick a stock. He'd buy that stock, and then together we'd watch all five stocks and how they progressed over time. We did this for years.

When I left home at 18, I left the markets behind as well. I pursued an education that had nothing to do with finance, got a job, and later started several businesses. And although I enjoyed running a business, and I became very successful, I started to resent the long hours, the unreliability of employees and vendors, the increasingly burdensome amount and complexity of government-mandated paperwork and taxation, and the never-ending need to adapt my business to a changing world.

I decided to make a major change in my life and do something new. I evaluated every career and business I could imagine. My criteria included the following:

- ✔ It would be a simple business where 90 percent of my activity would directly result in income. (I was tired of spending so much time on paperwork and record keeping.)
- ✔ It would provide me time flexibility so I could work when and if I wanted. I could also take time off whenever I chose.
- ✔ My financial results would be a direct result of my personal achievement. I wouldn't be dependent on vendors or employees.
- ✔ I could work at home so I could have a great family life and not be married to my job.
- ✔ It would have the potential to make huge amounts of money and become independently wealthy.

After reviewing all of my options, I saw only one that met all my criteria: trading! My dad was my first mentor, so I called him up to re-educate me. I then hired several other mentors and eventually branched out from trading stocks to also include futures, forex, commodities, and options.

The accumulation of all this education and experience resulted in designing my own personal trading method — the five-energy trading method — which I share with you in this book.

About This Book

I wrote *Trend Trading For Dummies* to be a no-nonsense, real-world guide on how to make money in the markets. You can find plenty of books on market theory, and they make for fascinating reading and intellectual stimulation. There's also a plethora of get-rich-quick trading schemes marketed online. They are a shame to the trading profession, and I take great offense at them.

I've been studying trading off and on for 47 years and can guarantee that nothing is easy about trading and shortcuts to success don't exist. Well, let me qualify that last statement. This book is actually designed to be a shortcut in the sense of helping you avoid wasted time looking in the wrong places.

Trend trading is a subset of the larger topic of trading, and therefore I assume that you have some knowledge of trading before picking up this book. However, I know that won't always be the case so I make a conscious effort to accommodate the beginning trader as well.

In this book, I introduce you to some basic concepts about trend trading, its benefits, and its risks. I share with you how I measure trends with objective indicators so you don't have to rely on your own subjective discretionary observation.

Trend trading, as powerful a technique as it is, shouldn't be conducted in isolation. Therefore, I also reveal other market "energies" to be used in conjunction with the trend, namely momentum, cycles, support/resistance, and scale (using multiple charting time intervals). Used together, these energies help you create a probability scenario that can put the odds of success on your side.

To ensure a well-rounded and realistic approach to trend trading, I provide strategies to help you determine the best markets to trade at any given time, managing the ever-present risk of trading, and practical exercises to improve your trading skills.

Foolish Assumptions

Given that you've picked up a book on trend trading, I assume you know enough about trading to know what a trend is and that it's one of the most popular and profitable approaches to trading. On the other hand, you may have simply heard that trend trading is a good approach to trading, but you're not familiar with the details of it. You may be asking questions such as these:

✔ How do I know for certain which way the market is trending?

✔ What are the risks of trading with the trend?

✔ Is trend trading enough, or do I need to consider other factors?

✔ What chart time intervals are best for trend trading?

✔ What markets are best for trend trading?

✔ How can I add trend trading to my current style of trading?

✔ How can I improve the trend trading I'm already doing?

Don't worry: I've got you covered. I answer all of these questions and a lot more through the pages that follow. Every chapter includes information for the beginner who needs the foundational concepts. Then I develop each of those concepts to a level that even advanced traders can find some precious gems to improve their trading, even if they're already profitable.

Icons Used in This Book

Icons — little pictures you see in the margins of this book — highlight bits of text that you want to pay special attention to. Here's what each one means.

Paragraphs marked with this icon provide unique insights and applications that go beyond basic trading principles and concepts.

This icon makes reference to trading information that you'll want to tuck away for later reference in your trading endeavors.

Take this icon seriously! It highlights issues to avoid at all costs and common mistakes traders make.

This icon flags information that is interesting but not essential to your understanding of the topic. Feel free to skip paragraphs marked with this icon.

Beyond the Book

In addition to the abundance of information and guidance on trend trading that I provide in this book, you also get access to even more information at dummies.com. Go to www.dummies.com/cheatsheet/trendtrading for a free cheat sheet that accompanies this book. It includes info on why and how trend trading is so effective, what's required to be a successful trend trader, and tips for managing risk.

You can also head to www.dummies.com/extras/trendtrading for some free supplemental articles that will help you as you begin your journey of trading with the trend.

Where to Go from Here

Although I think every word in this book is valuable, if you're not sure where to start reading (and don't have time to start at the beginning and read through the end), check out the Table of Contents to get an overview of the book and look for topics that catch your eye. Or, depending on your level of knowledge and trading experience, take the following approach:

✔ If you're new to trading, you may find it best to begin with the first chapter and read through the entire book from first page to last. However, you can also just pick a chapter that interests you and begin reading there.

✔ If you're an intermediate trader, you're welcome to skip some of the more basic topics and simply focus on the topics you need to expand upon your current trading knowledge. Especially draw your attention to Parts III and V. Part III introduces you to my five-energy trading methodology. Part V focuses on the real-world topics and practices that separate profitable traders from unprofitable traders.

✔ If you're an advanced trader, I encourage you to especially focus on Part III. Although you may be familiar with the various topics covered in that part of the book, the trading methodology revealed therein may provide that one new distinction in your trading that results in thousands of dollars of newfound profits.

Happy trades!

Part I

Getting Started with Trend Trading

In this part . . .

- ✔ Find out what exactly trend trading is and how it works.

- ✔ Gather the necessary tools, including charting software and a reliable Internet connection, to get started on the right foot.

- ✔ Become aware of risks of trading so that you begin with your eyes wide open.

- ✔ Realize that no trading method is perfect, and consider both the pros and cons of trend trading.

Chapter 1

What Is Trend Trading?

*T*rend trading is taking trades in the direction the market is moving. That sounds very simple, but it's deceivingly difficult. Many factors determine whether your trade in the current direction of the market will become successful. The important issue isn't whether you're taking a trade in the current direction of the market but whether the market will continue to move in your direction after you place your order.

In this chapter, I explore how to determine the trend, clue you in to the importance of the trend, and show you why trading with the trend is so profitable.

Figuring Out What the Trend Is in the First Place

Trend trading begins with determining the trend. The *trend* of the market is defined as the long-term direction of the market. But how do you determine what that direction is?

You can look at a chart, such as the one in Figure 1-1, and see that from the left side of the chart to the right side of the chart, the market has been moving up. Based on that observation, you may say that the trend is up.

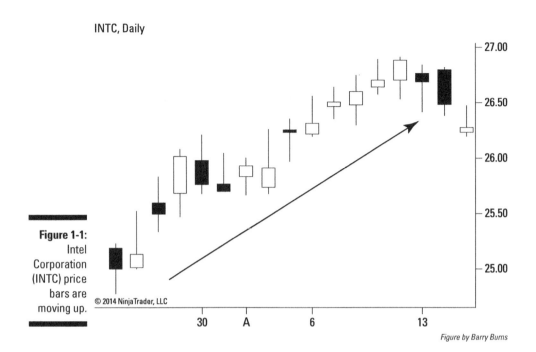

INTC, Daily

© 2014 NinjaTrader, LLC

Figure 1-1:
Intel
Corporation
(INTC) price
bars are
moving up.

On the other hand, if you look at that same market but change the beginning point of the chart to include more history, such as illustrated in Figure 1-2, you may say that the market is actually in a downtrend.

Looking at the direction of the market on these two charts illustrates two points:

- ✔ **Trend is always relative to the scale of the chart.** No one trend exists for any market.

- ✔ **Determining the trend can be very subjective.** You need a tool to measure trend for you to make the determination of the trend an objective measurement, not a subjective personal evaluation.

In Chapter 6, I share with you several objective tools for measuring trends, specifically the ADX indicator, Bollinger Bands, and moving averages.

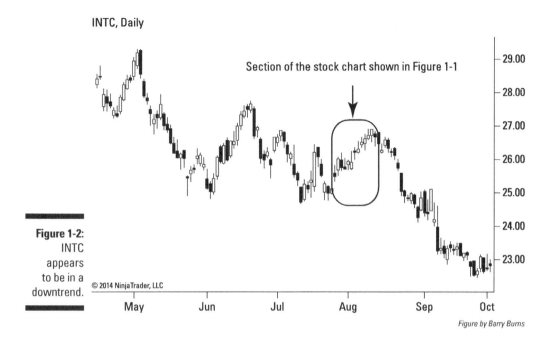

INTC, Daily

Section of the stock chart shown in Figure 1-1

— 29.00

— 28.00

— 27.00

— 26.00

— 25.00

— 24.00

Figure 1-2:
INTC
appears
to be in a
downtrend.

© 2014 NinjaTrader, LLC

— 23.00

May   Jun   Jul   Aug   Sep   Oct

Figure by Barry Burns

Knowing Why the Trend Works

Trend trading is one of the most popular approaches to trading. It's been around for decades because it's a proven approach to making money in the markets.

Understanding why trend trading works may give you more confidence in trading the trend. Trend trading has a rationale behind it that has its roots deep in human psychology. I explore those roots in the following sections.

Being a follower by nature

Human beings are naturally social creatures. Part of what comes with that is developing social structures to get along and function as a group. For the sake of organization and to prevent chaos in the group, people naturally tend to set up leaders (the minority) who guide the rest of the group (the majority).

This dynamic finds its way into chart patterns as well. The financial markets move because people are buying and selling. That buying and selling is based on people's ideas, beliefs, and feelings. Therefore, the patterns you see in the charts are maps of human nature.

Following the leader

The nature of the masses is to follow, so most traders are waiting for someone to initiate a move in the market. Then and only then will they jump onboard. After the leaders (the professional traders) make their commitment to buy or sell the market, the masses have a tendency to follow them, further pushing the market in the direction of the professionals' trades and creating a trend.

Although many people may not like the idea of being followers, there's nothing wrong with this in trading. The average retail trader simply doesn't have enough financial clout to begin a trend. Large institutions often start trends by trading enormous volume, taking positions, and continuing to add to them. That creates a momentum that can start a sustainable trend.

Jumping into a trend established in this way can be a great way to trade because a high probability exists that the large commitment of money made in a given direction will create momentum for the market to keep moving in that direction for the long term. You want to join that trend as soon as possible because a trend can end at any time.

Understanding Why You Should Trade with the Trend

Because this book is about trend trading, it seems appropriate to ask why the topic is relevant and important. The rationale to trend trading is if the market is already moving up, it's given at least some evidence of its bullish bias so it makes sense to follow that.

For this reason, trend trading is also called "trend following" because instead of guessing which way the market is going to move, you wait for it to establish a direction. After that's clear, you simply jump onboard and follow the trend that has already begun.

Trends make your life easier

"An object in motion tends to stay in motion" is part of Newton's first law of motion. You can certainly argue that such a law of physics doesn't directly apply to the financial markets. However, when large financial institutions managing enormous amounts of money make a commitment to a market, that market will indeed often continue in that direction.

Such institutions aren't able to bring all of their financial power into a market at one time without disrupting the pricing structure of that market. In other words, if they were to use all of their buying power at once, it would create such a demand versus supply imbalance that the price of that market would skyrocket. The institution would have to pay exponentially higher prices as the asks evaporated and the bids moved up in an almost parabolic fashion.

Everyone wants to buy at as low a price as possible, so institutions leg into a position slowly over time in an effort to hide their intentions and keep the prices they have to pay for that market low.

The best time to enter a trend is as early in the trend as possible. The famous saying, "the trend is your friend," is countered by, "the trend is your friend until the end."

Identifying a trend is one of the easiest chart patterns to recognize. You can clearly look at a chart and see whether the market is moving up or down. As opposed to more sophisticated and complicated chart patterns, a trending market is the easiest pattern to spot.

Trend trading is also simple for traders. In assuming you've correctly identified a long-lasting trend, there isn't much for you to do after you've entered the trade. Trends are long-term moves, so the best thing you can do as a trend trader is to hold tight and enjoy the ride. You don't need to micromanage the trade.

Trends can make you more money

Trend trading is a good style of trading, not only for its simplicity but also for its profitability.

To evaluate the effectiveness of my trading, I measure the following ratios:

- ✓ **Win/loss ratio:** The number of my winning trades divided by the number of my losing trades
- ✓ **Risk/reward ratio:** The amount of money I initially risk on a trade (from my entry to my stop loss) versus the amount of money I make on a trade

Of course, I like to have more winners than losers. But I also want to make more money on my winning trades than the amount I lose on my failed trades. When you're winning trades make a lot more money than your losing trades, it makes the losing trades much easier to handle.

Because trends are long-term moves, the rewards of successful trend trades are much bigger than the amount of risk taken on the trade. This is good for you both financially and psychologically.

The psychology of trading is a vital aspect to being successful. Losses can be hard to take and can create a distressing emotional state in which it's hard for you to trade with a clear mind. On the other hand, the perfect trade method doesn't exist, so all trading methods experience losses. How you mentally handle those losses is a vital part of determining whether you'll survive and thrive as a profitable trader.

Figure 1-3 illustrates an example of the small risk compared to the potential large reward of a successful trend trade.

ES 06-14, 5 Min

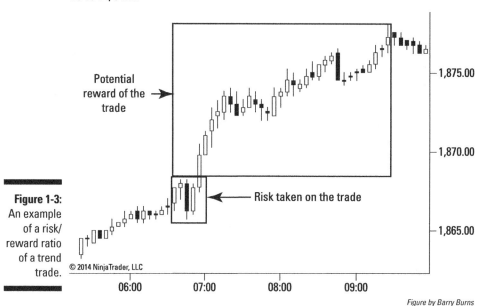

Figure 1-3:
An example
of a risk/
reward ratio
of a trend
trade.

© 2014 NinjaTrader, LLC

Figure by Barry Burns

Trend Trading as Part of a Complete System: The Five-Energy Methodology

As simple and profitable as trend trading can be, profitable trading includes much more than simply watching which way the market is moving and placing a trade in that direction. That's a good place to start. In fact, that's always the first thing I look at when I analyze a chart.

The thing to keep in mind is that even though the market is moving in a particular direction now, nothing guarantees that it will continue moving in that direction after you enter the market. In addition, entering the market in an uptrend that follows through can still be a challenging position for you to hold if the market goes down short-term after you enter.

One of my mentors told me that "traders are often right but at the wrong time." By that, he meant that traders can read the direction of the trend, but if they entered at a high price in the trend and then made a significant retrace so they saw their position move into the red more deeply than they're comfortable with, it would be psychologically difficult for them to hold onto the position.

Many students have shared with me similar sentiments of buying the market then getting stopped out, only for the market to then subsequently turn back up in the original direction of their trade. This illustrates the importance of not only trading in the direction of the trend but also knowing the best time to enter that trend.

To add more sophistication to a simple directional trend trading approach, I created the five-energy methodology, which I discuss in detail in Part III of this book. It incorporates the energies of momentum, support/resistance, cycles, and scale to the energy of trend to create high-probability trading opportunities.

How losing trades taught me to be profitable

A few years ago, I conducted an experiment that changed my trading forever and provided me with a skill set that remains with me to this day. During this experiment, I joined amateur live trading chat rooms during market hours and listened to the discussions of the traders. I wasn't interested in participating in chat rooms that had professional traders commenting on the market or teaching their system. For this exercise, I was specifically and only interested in listening to losing traders.

I pulled up the same charts the amateur traders were trading (market and time interval) and listened to them talk about it as they traded. The idea was to hear their thoughts and feelings as the markets were moving in real time and forming certain patterns. I wanted to get inside the head of the losers (I don't mean that in a derogatory sense but in the literal sense of traders who were losing money).

Knowing that human beings are creatures of habit, what I was especially curious to discover was whether these traders were making certain repeatable patterns of mistakes. If they were, my goal was to (1) avoid making those mistakes myself, and (2) perhaps trade the opposite direction of them when I saw those chart patterns.

I engaged in this exercise for about six months, and sure enough, I witnessed losing traders making several patterns of mistakes over and over again. I listened to them analyze the market and share their thoughts and feelings, and then I looked at the chart to see what would happen after their comments. It was fascinating to see them make the same mistakes repeatedly and expect different results. They probably weren't aware of their bad habits, but I was documenting them and had the statistics of their trades!

The patterns were so frequent and consistent that after a few months I was actually able to do the reverse. Instead of listening to their comments and then seeing the chart pattern that developed (which most often went against their trade), I was actually able to look at a chart pattern and hear what the losing traders were saying about it in my mind without even being in the chat room! The "scripts" of their voices and analyses were embedded in my brain!

One of the most common of those patterns is what one of my mentors later called the "kamikaze trade." Essentially, this behavior involves trading in the opposite direction of a strong trend.

In an uptrend, the amateurs in the chat room would say, "This market can't go up any higher, I'm going short now." Inevitably, the market would fill their order and then back up to make a higher high, stopping them out in the process. The market would go higher, and the same person would say, "Okay, now this is way overbought. This is crazy; it has to go down now. I'm shorting again." They'd get filled, and the market would go up, stopping them out yet again. "Ugh, this is so frustrating. Okay, *now* the market is beyond sustainable levels. There's absolutely no way the market is going higher. This is a sure thing. I'm shorting with more size on this one." They'd get filled, and you guessed it, the market made a higher high and stopped them out for yet another loss, only this time a bigger one. "This market makes no sense today. I'm going to play golf."

For some reason, this type of behavior is one of the most common trading mistakes amateurs make. It's the opposite of trend trading. That's one reason I wrote this book — to help you avoid that common mistake.

Chapter 2

Gathering What You Need to Get Started

In This Chapter

▶ Assembling the right trading tools

▶ Being ready in case of emergency

Before you begin trend trading, you need the right tools. Now isn't the time to be frugal. Your trading tools can be the difference between making money and losing money. You need an edge over your trading competition, and one area in which you can get an edge is by using better tools than your competition.

In this chapter, you discover the essential tools you need to put together to be a successful trend trader. You also find out how to prepare for any emergencies that may occur that could hinder your trading efforts.

To be successful at trading, you must treat it like the profession it is. And professional traders need professional tools.

Creating Your Trend Trading Toolbox

The world is evolving fast, especially when it comes to technology. To be successful, you must stay on the cutting edge. Let your competitors lag behind because they're too set in their ways to adapt to new information, too lazy to keep up with the latest education, or too cheap to invest in the latest technology.

Trading is a competition, and some of your competition is extremely proficient. Trading firms, funds, and other large financial institutions seek out the best and brightest people in the areas of mathematics, computer programming, and finance to trade their money. Some of these people are literally geniuses.

You may never be able to compete against the best of them. The good news is that you don't have to. There's more than one winner in the markets every day. Your job is to rise above the average amateur trader and be one of the winners.

The professionals have the best tools available. Most amateur traders don't. Having excellent tools is one simple way to set yourself above the amateurs. Keep that in mind as you assemble the trading tools I discuss in this section.

Choosing the right broker

Your brokerage firm is the company that facilitates the transaction between the buyer and seller through a stock or futures exchange. It usually takes a commission for its service. However, the spot forex market doesn't have a central exchange to match orders, so your brokerage firm may make its money on the *spread* — the difference between the bid price and the ask price of the market you're trading.

For example, if the bid for EUR/USD is 1.4185 and the ask is 1.4188, that means buyers are willing to buy at 1.4185, and sellers are willing to sell at 1.4188. Thus, there's a three-pip spread between the bid and ask. (A *pip* is the smallest move that a forex pair can make.) Those three pips are the profit made by the broker (and any other liquidity providers involved in the trade).

Brokerage firms typically supply other services to their clients, such as education, news feeds, advice, and recommendations. Generally, the more services a broker provides, the higher the commissions you'll pay. These full-service brokers provide value by supplying more services and hand-holding, which may be useful for a new trader or investor. For investors, full-service brokers may provide valuable services.

Discount brokers typically charge much lower commissions, providing significant savings to a self-sufficient trader who doesn't need much personal attention.

If you're a day trader, you should be actively trading only if you're well educated and self-sufficient. Because day traders execute a large number of trades, it's important to keep your commissions as low as possible.

Picking the right trading hardware

The trading hardware you require depends on the type of trading you're doing. In this context, *hardware* refers to your computer, monitors, network, power supply, and so on.

Be sure to check the hardware recommendations of your trading software provider to see the minimum computer requirements for using its software.

If you're simply investing for long time periods, the type of computer you use and the type and number of monitors you employ aren't as important as for short-term traders. You can often get by with a single monitor and use websites, rather than software, to analyze the markets and execute trades.

Day traders require the most robust hardware configuration. The type of software used for charting, running quote screens, scanning markets in real time, and executing trades is resource-intensive.

Day traders often use more than one monitor. For example, I use seven monitors for my day trading. I dedicate five monitors to charts of the five markets I like to trade most frequently, I use one monitor for watching the overall market signals (net volume, advancing/declining issues, $TICK index, and the net gain/loss of the major sectors), and I reserve the final monitor for my trade execution platform.

As a short-term (day) trader, investing in a computer designed specifically for that task optimizes you for day trading. It provides proper memory allocation, the processor type and speed you need, and the absence of a lot of extra software programs that often come with most retail computers. Search online for trading computers and/or call computer retailers. Tell them the type of trading you'll be doing and the charting software you'll be using. They can give you specific recommendations based on your needs.

Exploring trading software options

The trading software you use depends on many variables, including your own personal preference. Your broker will often have charting software available for free that may or may not fit your needs. Generally, you'll have to pay for more sophisticated software, or its cost may be built into the commission structure charged by your broker.

Some of the considerations in choosing trading software include the following:

✔ Whether you're investing, swing trading, or day trading

✔ Which indicators you prefer to use, and if you want access to proprietary indicators

✔ If you want fundamental analysis as well as technical analysis tools

✔ The type of price bars you want (candlesticks, point and figure, renko, tick bars)

✔ Scanning capabilities

✔ Operating system (PC, Mac, mobile apps)

✔ Options analysis

✔ Back testing

✔ Brokerage firms supported

✔ Whether it holds historical data on your hard drive or you have to be connected to the Internet to view charts

✔ Ability to use a simulator so you can practice trading without putting real money at risk

Deciding on your Internet access

Your Internet connection is vital to your trading success. Because day traders are in and out of positions quickly, the speed and reliability of the connection are critical.

Broadband Internet is the norm now, and dial-up connections have become rare (which is a good thing!). The most common type of Internet connections are DSL and cable. I have both DSL and cable connections for my computers (in case one goes down), and they both work well.

✔ DSL is only available if your location is within a certain distance of the DSL Access Multiplier, and the farther you are from it, the lower the data rate. On the other hand, DSL can be more secure than cable Internet because it isn't a shared connection.

✔ Cable Internet signals can be sent long distances without much signal degradation. However, cable Internet is a shared connection, so during peak usage times in a given neighborhood, you may find your Internet speed slowing down.

In my area with the services I use (results will vary on your location and service provider), DSL is more consistent in the sense that service rarely goes down. I experience more service interruptions with cable Internet, but even those interruptions are rare.

Beware of satellite Internet services. Although they can be fast and provide accessibility to locations that may not be serviced by DSL or cable, satellite Internet often has latent signals, meaning that the data isn't streaming in real time. This may not matter for most Internet uses, but for a day trader who's placing quick, in-and-out trades requiring the best price for entries and exits, those signal delays are intolerable.

When shopping for Internet service, always check the upload speed and download speed. Both are important for different reasons. When you ask your provider for the speed of its service, you'll often get an answer like, "as fast as _____ megabits per second." This number is usually the highest number possible (which is rarely ever realized) and refers only to download speed.

For day trading, both upload and download speed should be as fast as possible.

- ✔ The *download speed* determines how fast the data comes from the exchange or your broker to your computer. You want that to be fast so you're seeing prices in real time — a price at which you can actually buy the market now, not one second ago. Because market prices move so fast, even a second delay may mean it's showing you a price you can no longer get. Fast download speeds also ensure that you're seeing your charts updating in a timely manner.

- ✔ The *upload speed* determines how fast your order goes from your computer to the exchange to be filled. Again, if the speed is even a second too slow, it may mean that you won't get filled at the price you intend.

So what is a good speed, you ask? Because technology changes so fast, including a number here won't be useful. My rule is to get the fastest upload and download speeds available in your area.

Getting the best connection to the exchange

Speed in technology is critical for a day trader. It determines whether you can get the entry and exit price you want and even whether your trade gets filled at all.

Your order can route through one of the following three pathways from the time you execute your trade to the time it gets filled:

- **Your order resides on your computer after you place it.** When the market hits the price you designated for your order, your order is sent to your broker's server. From there, it's immediately sent to the exchange (if you're trading a market that has a central exchange, such as stocks and futures), where your order is matched with other orders, generally on a first-in, first-out basis.

- **Your order resides on your broker's server.** After the market hits the price you designated for your order, your order is then sent to the exchange (if you're trading a market that has a central exchange), where your order is matched with other orders, generally on a first-in, first-out basis.

- **Your order resides on the exchange's server.** When the market hits the price you designated for your order, it's matched with other orders, generally on a first-in, first-out basis.

Although the time that elapses between these three scenarios may not be long, it's clear that having your order sit on the exchange's server is the fastest way to get your order in the *queue* so it's filled quicker than orders that reside on your computer or on your broker's server.

Orders are typically filled on a first-in, first-out basis (often referred to as *FIFO*). This means that if your order resides on your computer before it's sent to the exchange, it will be placed behind all the orders of traders who have had their order sent directly to the exchange. So even though you may have placed your order on your computer before them, because their order got in line at the exchange before yours, yours will actually be filled after theirs. This can adversely affect you in the following ways:

- If the price of your order is just "touched" by the market but doesn't go through the price, your order may not get filled, whereas those orders that were earlier in the queue will get filled.

- If the market moves quickly through your price, your order may get filled at a worse price than you intended because all the offers were filled by those in the queue before you, and your order isn't filled until the price moves to the next price level of offers.

In day trading, time is money, so this small difference in the speed of your order being filled can have a large cumulative effect as you trade day after day, week after week, month after month.

Always Preparing for an Emergency

As a day trader (and even as a swing trader) for several decades, I've seen a lot of problems arise that were beyond my control but that lost me thousands of dollars, which I later had to make up through the hard work of trading. Most of those problems were due to a failure of power or technology. For that reason, I've added safeguards against such mishaps in the future. I discuss those safeguards in the following sections.

Using a battery backup

One of the most common problems I've encountered is a power outage. When the power goes out unexpectedly and you're in a trade, it can be very nerve wracking!

You have a live position in the market, but without electricity, you can't see your charts because your monitors turn off; you can't tell whether the market is going in your direction or against your position; and you can't get out because your computer shuts down.

You can mitigate this problem by getting one or more battery backups (often called a UPS, which stands for *uninterruptible power supply*). A UPS is superior to a simple power strip that you use to protect your computer from power surges. A battery backup keeps your computer running for a certain period of time while you experience a power outage in your home or office. This extra time allows you to exit your trade and turn off your computer to avoid damage.

Keeping that cellphone handy

If you're in a trade and your computer shuts off or your Internet connection goes down, you're blind to what's happening to your trade (and your money). In such a situation, I call my broker and ask him to get me out of the trade.

If your electricity goes down, many phones won't work. That's why God created cellphones! Have your broker's number programmed in your address book and assign it a speed dial button so you're able to reach your broker quickly.

Making the call in an emergency

If there's an emergency and you aren't able to exit an open order with your computer, you need to call your broker on the phone. Now, you not only need the technology to help you, but you also need to know what *exactly* you want your broker to do, which I learned the hard way.

I experienced a power outage and called my broker to get me out of my live order, which he did. However, at the end of the day, I downloaded my daily trading statement and found that I had an open order in the market that I didn't remember making. The market was closed, so the order would be live until the market opened the next morning, exposing me to overnight risk and also affecting the margin requirements of the trade (margin requirements overnight are often different than they are during market hours).

How did this happen? I had left an open order active in the market that hadn't been filled. When I entered the trade (which I later had my broker exit for me), I had also placed a stop order and a profit target into the execution software, neither of which had been filled when the power went out and I called my broker to get me out of my live position.

My broker had simply sold the shares I had bought. This made me "flat" the market, meaning I didn't have any money involved in a trade in the market at that time.

What I had forgotten, and my broker didn't address, was the two orders I had placed that weren't yet filled at the time of the phone call. Before the end of the trading day, the market moved to the price of my target order and it got filled, thus putting my money back into the market without me realizing it. So when I looked at my daily trading statement, that order showed up to my surprise and horror. I didn't intend for that order to be an entry but rather an exit because it was a profit target.

Additionally, I didn't intend to hold any trades overnight, because my analysis, and the basis for the trade, was dependent on my intraday analysis. I hadn't done any multi-day analysis to create a basis for taking a swing trade. This led to a very sleepless night!

Sometimes, it's possible to execute a trade (in this case, to exit the trade from the previous day) premarket the next morning. But such price valuations can be highly volatile at that time and liquidity can be prohibitive for making a large trade at a good price.

The best practice is to first of all be aware of all trades you have in the market, whether they've been filled yet or not and make sure your broker closes all of those orders. When you call your brokerage firm, tell your broker that you want to be "flat and working nothing." This means that you want any *active orders* to be closed and any *working orders* pulled. (*Active orders* are orders that have been filled and placed your money into the market. *Working orders* have been submitted into the market but haven't yet been filled because the market hasn't reached the price you stipulated for the order to be filled.)

When you call your broker's trading desk, be clear, succinct, use the terminology he's used to, and get off the phone. Have your trading account number handy because it's the first thing your broker will ask for. Better yet, give it as part of your greeting. When you call, simply say, "This is [name], account number [###], and I want to [purpose of your call]."

Don't expect your broker to be personable or friendly, and don't take it personally when he talks in a matter-of-fact tone of voice. Don't engage in small talk or ask him how his day has been. The trading desk is there to make orders happen quickly and to help as many people as quickly as possible, especially during busy times.

Having a non-AC-powered landline

If you don't have a cellphone or you have one but can't use it for some reason, you may want to have access to a non-AC-powered landline.

Today, most phones require an electrical outlet. However, some phones don't; you simply plug them into a phone jack. These phones tend to be simple without many features. The one nice feature they do have is that if you suffer from a power outage, you can still use them to call your broker!

When calling your broker during such emergencies, you want to ask him to get you out of any live trades you have. In other words, you want to "go flat."

I emphasize putting your broker's number on speed dial for an important reason. If there's an emergency that affects a lot of other traders, they'll all be calling their brokers — your broker — at the same time. To get your open position closed as quickly as possible, you want to reach your brokerage firm before it's inundated with massive phone calls after which you'll be put into a waiting queue.

Speed of execution is critical for day traders. Although the difference between various speeds of bandwidth and where your orders are held may often amount to only a second or two, it's actually deceptively important.

Just like football is really a game of inches, even though it takes place on a 100-yard field, so is day trading a business of seconds. In football, the team that's more willing to fight for every inch is the one that wins. In day trading, you must have the tools that put every second, even every millisecond, on your side.

Chapter 3

Considering the Risks of Trading

. . . .

In This Chapter

▷ Understanding the biggest risk of trading

▷ Working with leverage and margin

▷ Avoiding the overnight gap

▷ Taking a stance against technology and exchange-based risks

▷ Being prepared for trading crises

. . . .

*T*rading is risky. You've probably seen (and hopefully actually read) disclaimers when you signed up for a brokerage account, trading software, educational courses, data feeds, and so on. Such statements are so prevalent that they're almost impossible to ignore, yet many people don't take them seriously. You should definitely take them very seriously.

Being fully aware of your risks in trading at all times is absolutely critical. A common sentiment in the trading world is that amateurs focus on making money, while professionals focus on managing risk.

In this chapter, you discover some of the most common risks of trading and what to do about them.

Acknowledging the Ugly Truth about Trading

Although you may not want to hear it, traders lose money — and that's the honest truth. I've personally experienced that fact while working with traders and have seen many reports that show this fact as well.

It bothers me when I receive emails or see advertisements that use hype to promote the sales of trading courses, software, or services. The companies promoting such exaggerated claims make trading sound like a get-rich-quick scam.

I can tell you from my personal experience, as well as that of my students, that trading is a profession that takes time to master. Becoming a professional trader takes years of education, dedication, disciplined skill development, and the gaining of experience over time.

The consensus among my colleagues has been fairly consistent: Becoming a successful trader generally takes about three to five years (about the same time it would take to get a college degree).

One of the most famous studies (though on a small sample of traders) was conducted by Ronald L. Johnson who randomly chose 30 short-term trading accounts at a retail day trading firm.

Disclaimer statements to watch for

Following are some trading disclaimer statements to watch for:

✔ "Trading and investing involves substantial risk."

✔ "Consider carefully whether trading is appropriate for your financial situation."

✔ "Past performance is not necessarily indicative of future results."

✔ "The risk of loss in trading can be substantial."

✔ "Only use risk capital (discretionary money) when trading."

✔ "Financial loss, even above the amount invested, is possible."

✔ "Seek the services of a competent professional person before investing or trading with money."

✔ "Hypothetical or simulated performance results have certain inherent limitations. Unlike an actual performance record, simulated results do not represent actual trading. Also, because the trades have not actually been executed, the results may have under- or overcompensated for the impact, if any, of certain market factors, such as lack of liquidity. Simulated trading programs in general are also subject to the fact that they are designed with the benefit of hindsight. No representation is being made that any account will or is likely to achieve profits or losses similar to those shown."

Here's the conclusion of the study:

> *If this analysis is representative of short-term public trading, the individual and cumulative results show that most public traders will lose money attempting to short-term trade.*
>
> *In fact, this study shows that 70 percent of the public traders analyzed will not only lose but almost certainly lose everything they invest.*
>
> *Only three accounts of the 26 analyzed (11.5 percent of the sample) illustrated trading results and techniques sufficient to profit from short-term speculation.*
>
> *In sum, based on these findings, the vast majority of retail public investors (88.5 percent) would be best advised to refrain from short-term speculative trading.*

You can read the entire study by going to `www.nasaa.org/wp-content/uploads/2011/11/Day_Trading_Analysis.pdf`.

Being Aware of Leverage and Margin

One of the secrets to wealth is the use of *leverage* (which I address in detail in Chapter 16). In short, the principle of leverage, as applied to making money, is to use a small amount of money to control a large asset.

In this section, I explore leverage and how it relates to and differs from the margin made available to you by your brokerage firm.

Leverage: A double-edged sword in the battle for wealth

A common example of using leverage is when you buy real estate. You're able to control an expensive piece of property with a small down payment. Because you're investing only a small amount of your own money, you're able to use the balance of your remaining cash to invest in other financial vehicles and, thereby, expand the interests of your investments far beyond what you could if you had to pay the full amount for each investment.

It's similar in the trading world. I like to trade futures and forex because they often give me 20-to-1 or even 50-to-1 leverage. Controlling a large amount of money by investing only a small amount of money allows me to make more money faster.

As an example, if you place an order for one lot on a forex pair that's worth $100,000, you may be able to open that order by investing only $2,000; however, you can make money based on the $100,000 value of the currency pair. On the other hand, you can also lose the amount of money based on the $100,000 value of the currency pair! That's exactly what the saying, "Leverage is a double-edged sword," means.

Margin: The requirements for the privilege of using leverage

In keeping with the comparison to buying a house using a mortgage (from the preceding section), to open a leveraged position in the market, you're required to make a down payment. Brokerage firms operate a little differently than buying a house in that you're not actually putting down a small percentage of the value of the real estate to one day own it. When trading, you put up a percentage of the financial vehicle's value to control the full value you're buying. This is called *margin,* which functions as a "good faith deposit." The margin requirement is the amount of money a trader is required to have in his account to control a certain order size. It's based on a percentage of the value of the entire order.

With stocks, the margin requirement is typically 50 percent (or 25 percent for qualified day traders). With futures, the margin requirement is often around 5 percent. With spot forex, the margin requirement is at most 2 percent in the United States (and can be lower in other countries).

If you're losing money and the value of your open positions (the money you still have invested in the market) goes below your margin requirement, you may receive a *margin call.* When this occurs, your broker will typically close the position you have open in the market unless you add more funds to your account.

Leveraged investments can be riskier than those that aren't leveraged because the balance of the money you're controlling, minus your "down payment" (margin), is borrowed money. If the market were to tumble catastrophically, beyond your down payment, you'd owe the full amount (plus potential interest on the borrowed money).

Be sure to talk to your broker and ask about your maximum risk exposure based on your account. Some brokers offer technology that attempts to limit your maximum loss to the funds in your brokerage account. However, exceptional situations can make that difficult; I touch on these situations in the rest of this chapter.

Going Broke While You Sleep: Overnight Gaps

Overnight risk refers to the risk of what happens to the markets while you're sleeping or while the exchanges are closed and you're not able to exit your positions. During this time, your money is exposed, and if you're trading on margin, you're exposed to a margin call (see preceding section for a definition).

Some markets, such as forex, trade around the clock, so the nature of their overnight risk is different. However, even forex closes for the weekend, at which time you're exposed to dramatic market movements.

You may place a stop-loss order to help limit your risk. Placing such an order is as simple as executing any other order through the order execution software provided by your broker. Then if your position moves against you to a certain level you designate, your broker will close your position. However, if the exchange is closed, it's possible that the market can gap through your stop, and your position won't be closed at the price you designated with your stop-loss order.

For example, if you buy a stock at $20 and put in a stop-loss order with your broker to sell at $18, your position would normally close at, or near, $18 when the stock reaches that price. You'd put this stop-loss order in if you wanted to risk on the trade to $2 per share. But the next morning, you could find that due to some catastrophic event, the stock opens at $5! In such a case, your stop-loss order won't be executed at $18, thus giving you a loss of $2 per share, but instead it will be filled at about $5 per share, so you'll now have a loss of $15 per share!

And even then your order may or may not get filled depending on whether your stop-loss order was a *limit order* or a *market order:*

- ✔ A *stop-limit order* is where you set the price range at the point you're willing to execute the trade. For example, if you place a limit order to sell between $17.50 and $18 and the market gaps the next morning, you wouldn't be taken out of your position because the stock had moved beyond your limit high or low range for the order.

   You wouldn't be selling the stock at a low price you may not want to accept (such as $5), but your loss — called an *unrealized loss* because you haven't sold your stock and locked in your loss (because your stock position is still open and the price can still go up or down before you sell) — is still very real in the sense that it has reduced your overall wealth.

✔ Unless designated as a stop-limit order, a regular stop order is a *market order*, in which your order will be filled after the market reaches the price you designate; however, you have no guarantees at what price your order will be filled. For example, the next morning, you're taken out of your position around $5, thus locking in your $15 per share loss.

Dealing with Technology Errors

Although technology makes our lives easier in many ways, it's also prone to failure. Any of the following errors can occur at any time:

✔ The electrical power to your house or office can go down, thus leaving you without power to watch the market or execute trades.

✔ Your computer can crash, or your monitor can fail, not allowing you to watch a crucial trade that you've executed and is now live in the market.

✔ Your Internet service can go down, or your software can freeze, leaving you blind to what's happening to your trades.

✔ Your phone line can go dead, thereby cutting you off from quick communication with your broker in case of emergency.

✔ Your broker's data feed can slow down or disconnect, or his server can fail, leaving you without the ability to get out of your position if the market turns against your trade.

Although you can't completely control these risks, you can do some things to mitigate them. In Chapter 2, I outline how to create redundancy in your trading room to help minimize your risk in these situations.

But what happens if the technology error occurs with your broker? As one of my friends told me when something similar happened to me, you should always have at least two accounts with two different brokerage firms. That way if you get stuck in such a situation, you can place an option trade to help hedge the risk of the initial trade.

Trading the opposite side of a market in one brokerage account against a trade in another brokerage account may have legal ramifications. It may violate wash-sale rules. Such rules can change from time to time, so if you plan on doing this, make sure you check with a professional first.

Trading Halts, Suspensions, and Curbs

Another area of risk is at the exchange itself. Some of these situations are rare, but they can and do occur (I've experienced them all personally).

- ✔ One of the more common exchange-based risks is the *trading halt,* which occurs when the exchange stops a stock from trading for a short period of time. You aren't able to enter or exit that stock until the halt is lifted by the exchange. Trading halts are imposed for various reasons, such as the following:

  - Important company news may dramatically impact the valuation of its stock. The purpose of the halt is to allow the public to digest the news and avoid an emotional knee-jerk reaction in trading.

  - Delayed opening of a stock when a critical imbalance exists between buy and sell orders (often caused by unexpected news announced after the close of the previous trading day).

- ✔ A *trading suspension* of a stock occurs when the Securities and Exchange Commission (SEC) determines that the trading public is at risk due to inaccurate or missing information filed by the company. The SEC can suspend a stock from trading for a longer period of time (up to ten business days) than a trading halt.

- ✔ When a stock or the entire market makes dramatically large moves in a short period of time, the exchanges may exercise *curbs* in an attempt to protect investors from such volatility. Curbs are now commonly referred to as *market-wide circuit breakers.* The exchanges stop trading if the market experiences such a dangerously fast and deep price drop as to come close to threatening the liquidity of the market.

  These circuit breakers can be set at several levels, based on a percentage of the loss of value from the previous day's close.

Knowing What to Do When (Not If) a Crisis Occurs

Problems are part of life. They're also part of trading. Many beginner traders fail to take into consideration the crises that rarely occur that could devastate their entire account or their entire financial life.

Such people naively think that disasters that wreak havoc in the markets will never happen to them. Or they believe that the chances are so remote that they aren't worth taking into consideration.

They couldn't be more wrong. Although crises are rare, they're part of the very fabric of the nature of the universe; therefore, you should expect and be prepared for them. In the following sections, I share with you some of these crises that are beyond your control so you're not completely taken off guard when they occur.

Economic disasters

The economy experiences normal cycles of prosperity and stagnation (or worse, poverty). What makes these cycles even more challenging now is that the world has become more codependent, so the economics of one country affect other countries more than it did 100 years ago.

You can prepare yourself for economic disasters by being aware of scheduled economic news announcements that are released most every day. At those times of day, be especially aware that the market can make significant moves depending on the nature of the news release and the degree to which the announcement is a surprise.

A few of my favorite sites to consult for each day's schedule of economic news announcements that affect stocks are the economic calendars at the following websites:

- ✔ Barron's: `online.barrons.com`
- ✔ Bloomberg: `www.bloomberg.com`
- ✔ Yahoo! Finance: `finance.yahoo.com`

For forex, check out the economic calendars at the following sites:

- ✔ FXStreet: `www.fxstreet.com`
- ✔ DailyFX: `www.dailyfx.com`
- ✔ Forex Factory: `www.forexfactory.com`

Markets often make extreme moves when economic news at one of the scheduled times surprises the market participants or when economic news is released as a surprise without a scheduled time.

Broker problems

In addition to potential technical problems with brokers (which I discuss earlier in this chapter), some people have had to face a much bigger problem with their brokers. In recent years, some brokers have gone out of business, with their clients' money caught in the shutdown. And I'm not talking about just small firms; even large, big-name firms and their clients have been affected by these situations.

Unfortunately, the cause of such meltdowns is often mismanagement of funds; poor investments; risky, overly leveraged positions; failure to segment clients' funds; and even fraud. In such situations, clients are unable to get access to their funds, often having to wait for lengthy legal proceedings, including bankruptcy filings. At the end of the process, there may not be much, if any money, to return to clients.

Sometimes, it's difficult to know whether your brokerage firm is on the verge of bankruptcy, so be sure to keep your funds diversified among several brokerage houses.

Fat-finger trades

Although there have been times when my own fat fingers got in the way of a trade and I placed a market order to buy well above the price of the market by mistake by hitting the wrong key on my keyboard, or I placed an order for more contracts, lots, or shares than I intended to, *fat-finger trades* typically refer to those errors made during the execution of a trade. Such an error can occur regarding the price of a trade, or more commonly, the size of a trade.

The more significant type of fat-finger trade is the mistake made by a large trading institution where it isn't buying 1,000 shares instead of 100 but rather buying 1 billion shares instead of 1 million! Such a high-volume order can certainly cause a spike in the market and spook retail traders, or worse, affect its own trading by moving the market with such volatility as to hit its open buy/sell orders.

An example of such a fat-finger trade occurred in January 2014 when a trader caused a 10 percent jump in price (within 30 seconds) of Europe's largest bank, HSBC. Not only did it have an effect on the stock, but, being such a large company, it also affected the entire FTSE 100 index.

Brokerage firms and exchanges have safeguards in place to help prevent such drastic mistakes. For example, the London Stock Exchange had a "circuit breaker" programmed that kicked in to temporarily suspend HSBC stock from trading until an orderly market could be regained.

Chaos unleashing on the markets

The markets can become chaotic, erratic, and directionless for short or even long periods of time. Such chaos makes it difficult, if not impossible, to trade.

In trading, you look for some type of order in the market to create high-probability scenarios for trading rules. Here are two schools of thought:

- ✔ Some people believe that the markets are completely chaotic at all times, and they point to such books as *A Random Walk Down Wall Street*, by Burton G. Malkiel (W. W. Norton & Company) to support their claims. They believe in the *efficient market hypothesis* — that the price of markets already reflect the previous information and doesn't contain any forward-looking information. If this hypothesis is true, then it's impossible to consistently outperform the market.

- ✔ Others contend that the markets have an internal natural order (often with a mathematical basis) and are, therefore, very predictable. People in this camp often cite W. D. Gann, who claimed to be able to predict stock and commodity major highs and lows in the distant future of the market. Gann's fame began when he increased his trading account 1,000 percent in one month in 1909 as documented by *Ticker Tape Magazine* (one of the most popular financial magazines of the time).

Decades of observation of the market and of watching various traders in the market has led me to believe that both of these opinions have merit. To make money in the market consistently, you need repeatable patterns upon which you can base a probability scenario. I've seen many traders, who have set rules, be consistently profitable trading year after year. However, most people who attempt trading aren't profitable. As I watch those who don't succeed, the commonality I witness is impatience, overtrading, and lack of psychological discipline.

The market rotates in a cycle between being orderly and chaotic. Profitable traders are patient and wait until the market begins an orderly cycle, where the market moves in a structured manner that provides a high-probability trading opportunity. Amateur traders aren't aware of this cycle, or they're too impatient to wait for the market to enter an orderly cycle, and they trade through both cycles, orderly and chaotic.

The market is an untamed beast

I'll never forget the day I woke up to a horrific surprise. I had placed a swing trade for a high-flying technology stock. It was a company that everyone was excited about. "This is an entirely new paradigm of technology, so normal price valuations don't apply to it," was a common comment.

The company was on the cover of all the major news magazines, and stories about it were constantly in the newspapers. It had the best management, the best ideas, the best business model, and the best technology. This company was literally changing the world!

"Buy and hold until you die" people were telling me. I had waited nervously on the sideline before buying the stock, thinking surely this is too good to be true. So finally I decided I'd buy on a dip in price. But it never made a substantial dip. It just kept going up and up and up.

This was an exciting "sure thing," and I didn't want to be left behind while everyone else made fistfuls of dollars. So I finally decided to

just jump in and invested a huge percentage of my account in the stock, and it did well for a while. Then one morning I got up and checked my position. While I was sleeping, the stock had gapped down nearly 50 percent from the previous day! I felt a hot flash of panic rush through my body. It seemed surreal. How could this happen? This was impossible!

Oh, no. It was possible. It was a fact. And I lost nearly half of my money on a "sure thing" in my sleep. Lesson learned.

Now I never place a large position on any one stock. I don't keep all my money in any one brokerage firm. I hedge my positions with options. I have redundancy on all my technology.

I may seem a bit paranoid to some, but this wasn't the only disastrous event I've had in trading. Through experience, I've learned to focus on managing my risk, because those huge losses can wipe out a slew of diligent trading wins and take a long time to recover from.

This leads to a common experience a lot of traders complain about: "I make some money, but then the market took it all back, and more." In other words, they're making money during the orderly cycle when the market moves in a rhythmic, structured manner, and then they give it all back (and more) when the market enters a chaotic cycle. This happens for several reasons, including the following:

- Chaotic cycles last longer than orderly cycles, thus they're placing more trades during chaotic cycles.
- The money they make during orderly cycles can make them overconfident to the point where they even increase their trading frequency and/or the size of their trades.

The natural follow-up question is how to know whether the market is in a chaotic or orderly cycle at any given time. In Part III, I reveal my five-energy methodology that I use for high-probability trading. I consider the market to be in an orderly cycle when the five market energies align for a buy or sell signal.

Chapter 4

Understanding the Advantages and Disadvantages of Trend Trading

In This Chapter

▷ Seeing how trend trading can be profitable

▷ Avoiding the dangers of trend trading

*T*rend trading is a two-sided coin. It's definitely a valid approach to trading that's been used by professional traders throughout the history of financial trading. However, although it can be traded profitably, it has some inherent shortcomings.

This chapter explores some of the advantages and disadvantages of trend trading. Being armed with the knowledge of trend trading's strengths and weaknesses is the best way to become successful.

Discovering the Advantages of Trading with the Trend

Trading with the trend has several advantages that are important to know so you can capitalize on the strengths of your trading approach. The most basic advantage is this: By trading with the trend, you're trading in the direction of the market. And because trading in the direction of the market just makes sense, trend trading has an inherent rationale.

The following sections explore specific benefits that come with trading with the trend.

Getting big, winning trades

One of the most important advantages of trading in the direction of the trend is that when done correctly, your winning trades are much bigger than your losing trades. This advantage is stated right in the definition of the word *trend* — "to extend in a general direction." The terms *extend* and *general direction* reveal that trends are long-term moves. When trading market trends, you're making money on the long-term moves of the market and, therefore, making large profits.

The potential for large profits in trend trading is due to the price structure of a trend itself. The market tends to make bigger moves (covering more price range) and spend more time in the direction of the trend than it does during the correction phases against the trend, as illustrated in Figure 4-1.

CL 06-14, 500 Tick

Figure 4-1: In an uptrend, price makes bigger moves and spends more time going up than it does going down.

© 2014 NinjaTrader, LLC

Figure by Barry Burns

Making a lot of money with your winning trades has a clear psychological value: It's both fun and encouraging to make a lot of money on each trade — the more the better! It also has a mathematical value: When your winning trades are bigger than your losing trades, you can have as many losing trades as winning trades and still make a net profit.

Having some losing trades is inevitable. At times, you'll even have a signifi-cant series of losing trades (such events are called *drawdowns* in the trading community). Drawdowns are normal and expected.

The important factor in being able to successfully weather these natural draw-downs is to keep your losing trades smaller than your winning trades. Trend trading, by its very nature, is designed to help you do that.

Avoiding choppy, chaotic market movement

Amateur traders often complain that they make some money trading and then they soon give it all back (and sometimes give back more than they made). This seesaw effect of making money and losing money over and over is common for many traders because, for example, markets aren't always trending in a clear direction up or down. Markets typically spend long peri-ods of time making choppy, chaotic price movements, which occur when the market participants don't have a consensus among themselves as to whether a given market is undervalued or overvalued, or whether it's a great opportu-nity or a bad one.

During such times, the market doesn't exhibit any type of predictable pat-tern. It's simply gyrating around randomly without any clear direction up or down. It can be characterized by high volatility or low volatility (wide-range price moves or low-range price moves), but the one defining characteris-tic is a lack of clear, long-term direction up or down, such as the pattern in Figure 4-2.

Some people believe that the markets are by nature unpredictable and some-what random. The extreme adherents to this view often cite the famous book *A Random Walk Down Wall Street,* by Burton G. Malkiel (W. W. Norton & Company), and claim that all information that's publicly known is already priced into the market; therefore, no current information can lead to future predictions of market movement. This view is referred to as the *efficient market hypothesis.*

One of the problems with this view is that many investors and traders (though still small by percentage of total traders) do make money consis-tently. Even Warren Buffet, one of the most famous consistently successful investors, disagrees with the efficient market hypothesis.

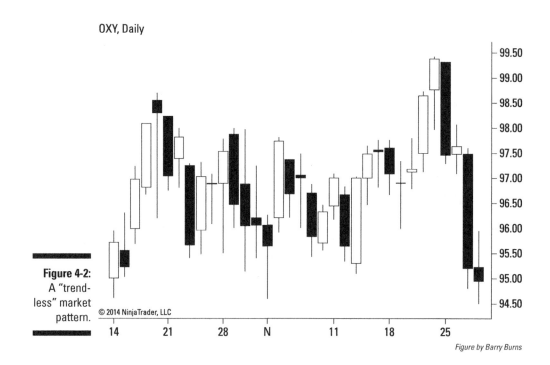

OXY, Daily

© 2014 NinjaTrader, LLC

Figure 4-2:
A "trend-less" market pattern.

Figure by Barry Burns

Another group of people assert that the market is perfectly orderly and predictable. They often cite the works of W. D. Gann who used both mathematics and astrology to predict market movements years into the future.

My personal belief is that both theories continue to have followers because both have validity, just at different times. Based on my decades of observing the markets, along with my historical research of charts, I've come to the conclusion that the markets cycle between times of being orderly (providing high-probability trade opportunities) and chaotic (not providing high-probability trade opportunities).

Being aware of this cycle, and being able to identify it, is critical to success because then you can trade only during orderly cycles and stay out of the market during chaotic cycles, thus allowing you to minimize the dynamic of making money in the markets, only to give it all back later. Figure 4-3 illustrates a chaotic cycle ending and an orderly (trend) cycle beginning.

$USDJPY, 500 Tick

Non-trending, chaotic
price movement

Trending, orderly
price movement

© 2014 NinjaTrader, LLC

Figure 4-3:
Coming out
of a chaotic
cycle and
entering
an orderly
cycle.

Figure by Barry Burns

Having confirmation before entering

It's often said that trend trading gets in "late to the party" because trend is a lagging indicator. That statement definitely holds some truth. Amateurs often hear the term *lagging indicator* and run for the hills as though it's an obscene term.

One of my teachers early in my trading education would tout the advantages of using a lagging indicator, and I thought he was bonkers! It took me a few months of experience using his techniques before I understood why anyone would want to use a lagging indicator.

The bottom line is this: Lagging indicators are lagging because they take more time to provide a signal. During that time, they're accumulating data that they'll (eventually) use to give a signal. Because they calculate more information before giving a signal, they tend to be more accurate than so-called *leading indicators,* which often give signals based on less data crunching (and therefore are less accurate).

No indicator can predict the future with certainty. Some indicators will at times signal a turn in the market before the price patterns indicate a turn in the market (which is why they're called leading indicators). These leading indicators aren't always accurate, especially when used without other confirming factors (find out more about using confirming factors in Chapter 14).

My favorite potentially leading indicator is momentum (which I discuss in detail in Chapter 12). It's notoriously difficult to determine where a market will top out before falling significantly or bottom out before rising significantly. In other words, it's extremely challenging to call where exactly an up- or downtrend will end and a new trend in the opposite direction will begin.

Using a lagging indicating (whether an actual mathematical indicator formula or a price pattern) provides more information for you to use to determine a trend change. It supplies you with some confirmation of that change instead of simply trying to guess which high will be the final high in an uptrend.

Figure 4-4 shows a high in an uptrend. Do you think this is the final high before the trend reverses? How would you know?

As you may have guessed, the high in Figure 4-4 wasn't the final high in the uptrend, as you can see by looking later on the same chart in Figure 4-5.

SCHW, Daily

Figure 4-4:
A high in an uptrend.

Figure by Barry Burns

SCHW, Daily

Now will this be the highest high
before the market turns back down?

No, that high was not the
end of the uptrend.

Figure 4-5:
The market
went up
and made
another
higher high.

© 2014 NinjaTrader, LLC

Nov   Dec   14   Feb

Figure by Barry Burns

Realizing the Disadvantages of Trend Trading

Trading with the trend seems like an obvious choice for a trading methodology. It seems easy enough, but it's deceptively difficult to do.

Of course, if it were easy, everyone would be doing it. The problem arises in not only determining the trend at the time you enter the market but also establishing a probability scenario indicating that the market will continue to trend in the direction of your trade after you enter.

To be a successful trend trader, you need to be aware of some of the challenges you'll encounter before you start. Following are some of the more notorious obstacles you'll face.

Having more losers than winners

People who are pure trend traders may find that they have more losing trades than winning trades. One reason for this is that by many estimates, markets trend only approximately 20 percent of the time.

Trying to catch the beginning of a new trend can be very difficult. Because the market is moving chaotically most of the time, timing the end of a chaotic cycle and the beginning of a trend cycle can result in a lot of false signals before you catch one of the 20 percent opportunities. This may contradict the principle of a lagging indicator being more accurate (which I discuss in the earlier section "Having confirmation before entering"), but it's accurate at the cost of giving a late signal late.

So how can pure trend traders make money if they lose more trades than they win? Here's how:

- ✔ They're very good at cutting their losses quickly when they're wrong, thus making sure their losing trades are very small.
- ✔ They're excellent at holding onto their winning trades for the big profits that a long trend will supply them.
- ✔ They offset their negative win/loss trade ratio with an excellent risk/ reward ratio.

 Personally, I'm not comfortable having more losing trades than winning trades. Therefore, even though I love trend trading because of the big winners and small losers, I also watch the energy of *momentum* (the strength of the trend; check out Chapter 12 for more details). It's a potentially leading indicator, which when used along with the lagging indicator of trend, provides a better win/loss ratio than depending on trend alone.

Getting bored

In the previous section, I mention that it's commonly accepted that the market trends only about 20 percent of the time. That can lead to a psychological challenge of boredom because traders like to trade! As a trader, you want to be involved in the market and make money. Sitting around and waiting when there aren't any high-probability trades isn't fun.

Getting bored is especially challenging for day traders who sit in front of computer screens for hours every day. Hours can go by, and even entire days, when the market is in a chaotic cycle, not providing any high-probability trading opportunities.

This constant waiting can lead a day trader to distraction. You may start checking your emails, texting, watching the news, sports, or a movie . . . and then when you look back at your screen, you may find that you just missed a great trade setup by a minute.

 Missing a great trade is a difficult issue for anyone to handle, so here's how I deal with it, whether I'm day trading or swing trading: I always watch several different types of markets concurrently, actively seeking an opportunity for a trending market. As a saying among traders goes, there's always a bull market somewhere and there's always a bear market somewhere. Markets I typically watch are equities, oil, gold, real estate, bonds, various currencies, international markets, emerging markets, frontier markets, and various sectors within the equities.

The grass is always greener on the other side

One of the biggest and most common mistakes I see new traders make is trading against the trend of the market. Essentially, they're trying to trade the final high of an uptrend or final low of a downtrend. If you could do this consistently, you'd have the best risk/reward ratio trade. However, this also often proves to be the worst win/loss ratio trade because it's impossible to call the very top or bottom of a trend with consistency. Interestingly, some strong, driving urge in human nature makes people want to try to trade the tops and bottoms.

I saw this behavior in myself first, and one of my dear mentors helped cure me of the bad habit. When I became a trading teacher, I saw that same behavior in student after student. Out of curiosity, I started attending several free trading chat rooms (the ones that amateurs attended) and sure enough, I witnessed traders there attempting to do the same thing, with the same consistently losing results.

Do yourself a favor: Trade with the flow (trend) of the market instead of trying to buck the trend. You can't fight city hall, and you can't fight the dominant direction of the market.

Not getting the earliest entry

Trend indicators are lagging indicators, but their lagging nature carries a benefit. They're waiting for the accumulation of more information before they give a signal, and that tends to make them more accurate than so-called leading indicators.

That accuracy does come with the price of the lag, though, so by the time the signal is given, the trend may be close to an end. Whether the trend continues long after the trend indicator provides the signal, it will never provide you the earliest entry.

Trend indicators provide new trend signals only after the market has already been moving in the direction of the trend for a certain period of time (depending on the trend indicator you use and the settings you employ). A common trend indicator is the *50-period simple moving average (SMA),* which draws a line on your chart that represents the average closing prices of the last 50 bars (or periods). An uptrend is indicated by an upward angling 50 SMA, and a downtrend is indicated by a downward angling 50 SMA.

Figure 4-6 illustrates how the 50 SMA begins indicating an uptrend only after the price bars on the chart have already been moving up for a period of time.

$AUDJPY, Daily

© 2014 NinjaTrader, LLC

The 50 SMA starts angling up here.

Figure 4-6: The 50 SMA angles up after the price bars have been going up for a while.

Figure by Barry Burns

Part II
Essential Trend Trading Strategies

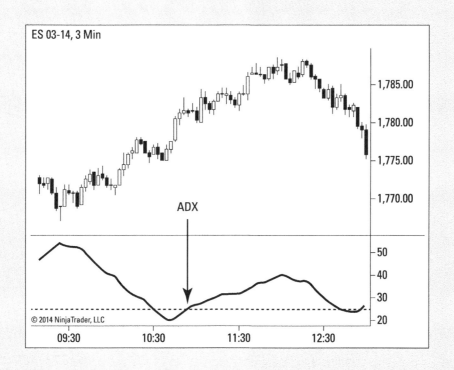

Want to be able to find the trend of any market at any time? Head to
www.dummies.com/extras/trendtrading to find out how!

Part II

Essential Trend Trading

Strategies

In this part . . .

✔ Make a serious profit surfing price waves.

✔ Find out how to use indicator tools to measure trend.

✔ Use broad market indicators to determine the market "big picture."

✔ Pick the time to trade that's best for you.

✔ Find out how to make money regardless of whether the market is going up or down.

Chapter 5

Price Waves You Can Surf to Profits

. . . .

In This Chapter

▷ Seeing how the markets move in waves

▷ Realizing the downsides to subjective wave counting

▷ Following an objective approach to wave theory

. . . .

*T*rend trading is a beneficial way to make money in the markets because it allows you to make big profits while risking a small amount of money.

As I mention throughout this book, trend trading is trading the long-term moves of the market. However, the market doesn't trend straight up or down during those long-term moves. On its way up or down in the direction of the trend, it wiggles or oscillates.

Chart analysts call these oscillations *waves* because they form short-term crests (highs) and troughs (lows) as the market moves in its long-term direction. This is similar to how the ocean makes a series of waves as the water moves toward the shore.

An uptrend typically forms a pattern of higher highs (wave highs) and higher lows (wave lows) in its long-term ascent. A downtrend typically forms a pattern of lower highs (wave highs) and lower lows (wave lows) in its long-term descent.

In this chapter, I explore the basics of wave theory, from Elliot waves to Fibonacci levels, and all the related rules. I then introduce my theory for measuring cycles and waves.

Grasping the Basics of Wave Theory

On a chart, you see the price pattern of a stock, commodity, or currency make some short-term moves against the long-term moves of the trend. This oscillating pattern is akin to the human experience of moving toward a long-term goal, but on the path, people often make reference to taking "three steps forward and two steps back."

Figure 5-1 gives a typical example of this oscillating trend pattern. The extended general direction of the market is up, but short-term moves occur against the trend.

CL 06-14, 5 Min

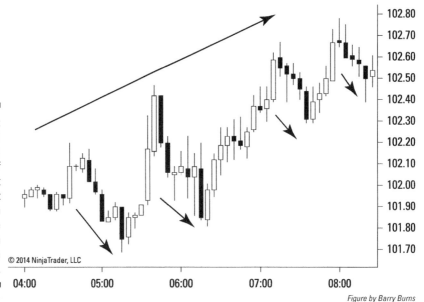

Figure 5-1: The general direction (trend) of the market is up, but short-term moves are going down against the trend.

© 2014 NinjaTrader, LLC

Figure by Barry Burns

These fluctuations in the trend occur because the people trading the markets fluctuate in their optimism and pessimism based on the two primary emotions traders experience: fear and greed. Traders generally buy into a market because they're optimistic and have a degree of confidence that they'll make money. The more the market moves in their direction, however, the emotions of fear and greed begin to creep into their thoughts — *fear* that the market may turn against them and they'll lose their money, and *greed* regarding the money they've already made and want to now take out of the market and put in their pocket.

After the market moves up for a while, many traders will sell all or part of their position. They want to lock in some profits and reduce their risk by reducing the amount of money they have exposed in case the market turns against them.

Other traders will feel, for a variety of reasons, that it's time for the market to go down. When they see the market stalling out because people who bought into the market are now selling, they take this opportunity to short the market, thus adding more volume to the downside and pushing the market down against the trend.

Shorting the market refers to the practice of selling before you buy. Instead of buying low and selling high, you reverse the order. For example, if you believe the market is going to go down, you can sell first at a high price and then buy back the position later at a low price. You're still buying low and selling high but in reverse order! This may seem strange, but it's a common practice. In the stock market, you borrow the stock through your broker (and usually pay a fee to do so) and also post margin (collateral).

After the market moves down a bit, the traders who are still convinced that the market is in a long-term uptrend will come back in and buy because they're getting a lower price. This can cause the short-term move down (called a *correction*) to stall and the market to begin going up again with a new impulse move. *Corrections* are price moves against the trend; *impulse moves* are moves in the direction of the trend.

This is a simplification of what causes the oscillations of price action as markets trend. Figure 5-2 provides a visual reference for impulse and correction moves.

In the following sections, I take you deeper into more specific applications of wave patterns in trends. I introduce *Elliott waves,* the most well-known approach to wave counting, and *Fibonacci numbers,* the most popular approach to measuring the mathematical movements of waves.

Elliott waves for fun and profit

The term *waves* is most often associated with *Elliott waves.* Ralph Nelson Elliott developed the Elliott wave theory and wrote about it most comprehensibly in his book *Nature's Laws: The Secret of the Universe* (Snowball Publishing).

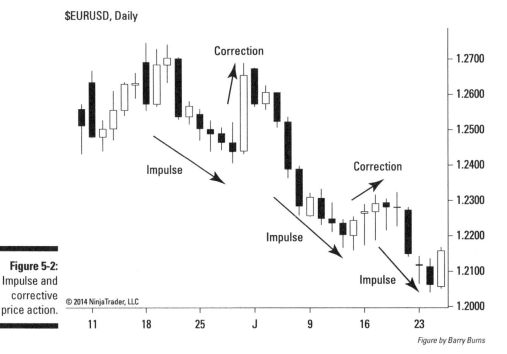

$EURUSD, Daily

Correction

Impulse

Correction

Impulse

Impulse

© 2014 NinjaTrader, LLC

Figure 5-2:
Impulse and
corrective
price action.

1.2700
1.2600
1.2500
1.2400
1.2300
1.2200
1.2100
1.2000

11   18   25   J   9   16   23

Figure by Barry Burns

Elliott wave theory can be very detailed in its rules and complicated in its application. My intention is not to explain all those details but simply to introduce you to the general concept to help you understand why markets move the way they do.

The alternation of optimism and pessimism among the masses of traders creates the waves in the market.

Traditional Elliott wave theory declares that every trend has five waves: three impulse moves and two corrective moves. Each impulse move has unique characteristics with regard to the actions of market participants:

✔ The first impulse move is difficult to spot until after it's over. Prior to this impulse move, the market had been trending in the opposite direction, and for that reason, sentiment is still generally bearish (assuming the market is starting a new wave of an uptrend).

✔ The second impulse move is normally the longest of the three impulse moves. As it begins to gain steam, sentiment begins to change, and eventually the masses begin to get onboard (normally after the market breaks the high of the previous impulse move).

✔ The third and final impulse move is characterized by very positive senti-ment among traders. It's during this third leg up that many retail traders buy in because now the uptrend is very clear. However, like many things in trading, by the time everything is obvious for all to see, you are late to the party. This move is typically shorter in duration and price range than the second impulse move.

Elliott waves take the general information about the mass psychology of waves and apply more strict and specific rules. Here are three hard-and-fast rules that determine which impulse and corrective waves are Waves 1, 2, 3, 4, and 5:

✔ Wave 2 can't go beyond the beginning of Wave 1.

✔ Wave 3 can't be the shortest of the three impulse moves.

✔ Wave 4 can't go beyond the end of Wave 1.

Figure 5-3 provides a visual guide to these three rules.

SBUX, Daily

Rule 1: Wave 2 can't go beyond the beginning of Wave 1.

Rule 3: Wave 4 can't go beyond the end of Wave 1.

Rule 2: Wave 3 can't be the shortest of the 3 impulse moves.

© 2014 NinjaTrader, LLC

Figure 5-3: The three rules of identify-ing Elliott waves.

Figure by Barry Burns

Elliott waves: A road map to where?

During my years trading Elliott waves, I had ups and downs. At the beginning, I was excited to have a road map for my trading. I thought that someone had figured out the secret "code" of market movement. The promise of certainty was intoxicating, and I was excited to learn all I could.

After a period of study, I found myself doing pretty well, and it was fun to see the five-wave pattern work so well. Other times I thought I was confident of my ability to predict the markets' future based on Elliott waves and Fibonacci, only for the patterns to completely disintegrate before my eyes.

When I showed these failed patterns to a teacher, I was normally told that I had counted the waves incorrectly. After a while, it seemed that whenever I made money, I was told that I counted the waves correctly, and when I didn't make money, I was told I didn't count the waves correctly.

Eventually, I bought software that counted the waves for me. To my dismay, when trades failed, the software would automatically change all the wave counts it had previously plotted on the chart!

At the same time, I was following an Elliott wave technician predict the future movement of the market. His prediction failed dramatically, and he then recanted his predictions later saying that he had counted the waves incorrectly and then provided the "correct" count in hindsight, saying "see, Elliott waves still work!"

I'm not arrogant enough to dismiss anyone who trades using Elliott waves. Some people trade them and probably make money consistently. My opinion is that they can be used as a methodology for trading successfully along with good risk and money management. But I caution against attributing to them (or any other trading method) magical powers of flawless prediction.

Fibonacci levels – trading the golden mean

After developing his Elliott wave theory, Ralph Nelson Elliott observed that the wave patterns relate to the *Fibonacci sequence*.

The *Fibonacci sequence* is a series of numbers created by adding the sum of the previous two numbers to create the next number in the sequence:

$1 + 2 = 3$

$2 + 3 = 5$

$3 + 5 = 8$

$5 + 8 = 13$

$8 + 13 = 21$

$13 + 21 = 34$

Thus, the beginning of the sequence is 1, 2, 3, 5, 8, 13, 21, 34. . . .

In trading, Fibonacci ratios are more commonly used than the Fibonacci numbers themselves. You create these ratios by dividing one number in the sequence by another. The most significant of those ratios is the *golden ratio*, which you get (or get very close to) by dividing any number in the sequence by the number immediately preceding it. For example, 34/21 = 1.619. The actual golden ratio is 1.618.

You use the Fibonacci ratios in conjunction with Elliott waves as potential price levels for impulse and correction moves to begin and end.

The most common Fibonacci ratios used in trading are

0.236

0.352

0.500

0.618

0.786

You use these ratios to measure corrective movements. Figure 5-4 demonstrates how these ratios help find a support level for a corrective move before the next impulse move begins.

For impulse moves, you use those same ratios, but you add a 1, 2, or 3 in front of them:

1.236

1.352

1.500

1.618

1.786

These ratios help measure impulse waves. Figure 5-5 shows how these ratios find potential resistance for the end of an impulse wave.

FDAX 06-14, 5 Min

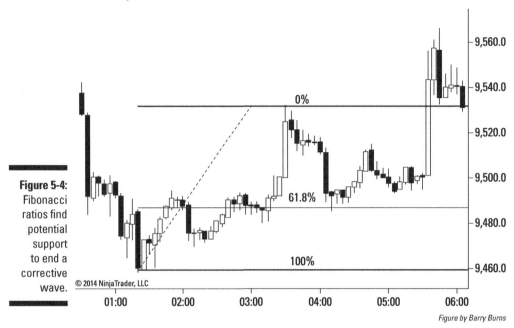

Figure 5-4:
Fibonacci
ratios find
potential
support
to end a
corrective
wave.

© 2014 NinjaTrader, LLC

Figure by Barry Burns

FDAX 06-14, 5 Min

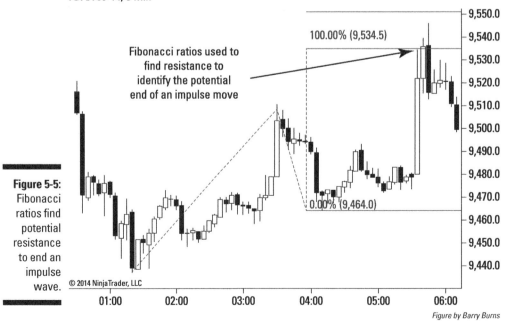

Fibonacci ratios used to
find resistance to
identify the potential
end of an impulse move

100.00% (9,534.5)

0.00% (9,464.0)

Figure 5-5:
Fibonacci
ratios find
potential
resistance
to end an
impulse
wave.

© 2014 NinjaTrader, LLC

Figure by Barry Burns

Looking at the Limitations of Subjective Wave Counting

Although I traded Elliott waves for a few years and still appreciate the theory of waves, I became disillusioned by the subjectivity required to interpret Elliott waves. For example,

- In addition to the three rules (see earlier section "Elliott waves for fun and profit"), using Elliott waves also includes guidelines, but those guidelines aren't required and exceptions are allowed for them, making clarity and objectivity illusive.

  To make things even more complicated, and open to a variety of inter-pretation, each wave is made up of *fractals* — a pattern that exhibits the same, or very similar, structure on all scales.

- In Elliot wave terms, each impulse wave has a five-wave fractal inside of it on a smaller scale. Each corrective wave has a three-wave fractal inside of it on a smaller scale.

  To make things even more interesting, inside each smaller scale impulse wave, there's yet another five-wave fractal inside of it on a smaller scale! This pattern continues to nine scales of waves within waves within waves . . . as you can see, it can get very complicated!

  My observation over my years of trading is that the markets aren't as neat and tidy as to make five wave patterns in every trend.

Nothing is wrong with having theories to work with, but it's a mistake to hold on to a theory so tightly that you try to force it on the market.

Trading isn't about trying to prove a theory or prediction right. It's about having a probability scenario you can follow (that has objective rules) and trading that with the realistic expectation that your rules will put the odds on your side but won't always lead to winning trades. Therefore, risk manage-ment and money management are crucial for those times when the market doesn't do what you think it's supposed to do.

Objectifying Waves for Trading Clarity and Confidence

I appreciate the theory of the market moving in waves and agree that it's a valid and useful concept to keep in mind. Personally, I prefer to trade with completely objective rules, so I developed my own method for measuring waves. It doesn't impose a five-wave maximum rule for each trend (as the Elliot wave theory does; see previous section). It simply defines a mathematically objective definition for what a wave is and allows a trend to have as many waves as it decides to make.

My theory isn't predictive in nature. It's simply a method to develop reference points and also provide a sense of how early or extended a trend is at any given time.

Even though I use the angle of the 50 simple moving average (SMA) as my trend indicator, it does just that — it indicates. In my methodology, I don't consider a trend confirmed until three full waves are completed.

Some traders may argue that you don't know whether you have a trend until after the fact. They're exactly right. I don't believe in being able to predict the future of the market accurately because I've never seen anyone do it consistently.

Trading isn't about knowing the future. It's about looking at the indications (evidence) available at the time and using them to determine when you have a probability scenario that favors you entering a successful trade.

When you understand that the very nature of a probability implies that any given trade won't always work out the way you want, it becomes clear that the risk-management techniques of using stops, hedging, and money management are paramount to your trading success.

Trading is an inherently risky profession. You don't want to make it even riskier by working with trading rules and principles that are subjective and open to interpretation. Therefore, I developed very objective rules for measuring cycles and waves so that my trading decisions are based on a perfectly clear analysis of the chart.

Measuring cycles

I use the term *cycles* to reference highs and lows the market makes as it oscillates during its longer-term moves into the future, up, down, or sideways. The way I measure cycles is very specific and measurable based on objective mathematical rules.

To measure cycles, I use the stochastic indicator, but I change the default settings (see Chapter 10 for more on the stochastic indicator):

 Period D (%D): 3

 Period K (%K): 5

 Smoothing (average): 2

A *cycle high* is the highest high on the price bars after %D gets above the value of 50 and before %D gets back down to the value of 50. A *cycle low* is the lowest low on the price bars after %D gets below the value of 50 and before %D gets back above the value of 50. In Chapter 10, I take you into the world of cycles in a more detailed manner.

Figure 5-6 illustrates how to identify cycle highs and lows, using this method.

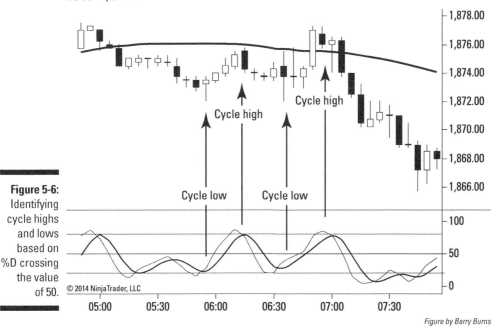

Figure 5-6:
Identifying cycle highs and lows based on %D crossing the value of 50.

© 2014 NinjaTrader, LLC

Figure by Barry Burns

Cycles and waves are different but related. Cycles differ from waves in that cycle highs can be higher, lower, or equal to previous cycle highs in an uptrend. However, a high is considered a wave high only if it's higher than the previous wave high. In this way, every wave high is a cycle high, but not every cycle high is a wave high.

Measuring waves

With my wave theory, you measure waves in an uptrend, using the following rules:

- ✔ The 50 SMA must be angling up for all of the waves in an uptrend.
- ✔ Impulse waves:
  - • Wave 1 is the first cycle high after the 50 SMA begins angling up.
  - • Wave 3 is the first cycle high where the open and close of the current bar is above, or equal to, the high of the previous wave high (in this case, Wave 1).
  - • Wave 5 is the first cycle high where the open and close of the current bar is above, or equal to, the high of the previous wave high (in this case, Wave 3).
  - • You apply this same rule for every wave high after that.
- ✔ Corrective waves:
  - • Wave 2 is the lowest low between Wave 1 and Wave 3
  - • Wave 4 is the lowest low between Wave 3 and Wave 5.
  - • You apply this same rule for every wave low after that.

Chapter 6

Looking at Chart Indicator Tools

*U*nderstanding the concept of trend is easy. In its simplest terms, *trend* is the long-term direction of the market. The trend can be up, down, or sideways. But although the idea is simple, the implementation may be deceptively difficult. Ten traders may eyeball a chart and come up with various answers to what they see the trend of the market to be because each is using a different and subjective criteria.

This is where indicators are helpful. Indicators are mathematical formulas that objectively measure market movement. They're so precise that they're programmed into computer formulas and give exact readings so you don't have to depend on subjective misinterpretation.

The objectification of the trend is also critical because you need a set of objective rules that you combine to create a trading methodology that isn't subject to individual interpretation. If the rules aren't static and measureable, you can't test the methodology for its consistency and reliability into the future.

The creation of a consistently measureable definition of trend is also helpful when communicating and sharing ideas with other traders. All debate begins with an agreement on defining terms so you're speaking the same language.

In this chapter, you discover some of the most common indicator tools.

ADX Indicator: Finding Strong Trends

The average directional index (ADX) was developed by J. Welles Wilder, author of *New Concepts in Technical Trading Systems* (Trend Research). Although the indicator was introduced a long time ago, it's still very popular among traders because it not only indicates trend, but it also focuses on finding strong trends. This potentially increases the probability of profitable trades because a strong trend is more likely to continue to follow through in the direction of your trade than a weak trend.

In the following sections, I show you how the ADX measures the trend and how you can use it to trade.

Staying on the right side of the market with the ADX

ADX measures trend strength by calculating a *moving average* (typically the 14-*period* moving average) of price expansion, using *average true range*. I define these terms in the following list:

- A *moving average* is the average of the closing prices of a set number of previous bars. For example, to calculate the average of the last 14 days of a market, you simply add the closing price of the last 14 days and then divide by 14. To create a moving average, you calculate the average of every day and plot the series of those values on the chart. The result is a line on the chart as price continues to move into the future with each new day.

- A *period,* with reference to a moving average, is the time interval of each bar you've selected for that chart. A 14-period average on a daily chart (each bar representing one day of price action) is the average of the closing price of the last 14 days. A 14-period average on a five-minute chart (each bar representing five minutes of price action) is the average of the closing price of the last 14 five-minute bars.

- *Average true range* measures price volatility over a period of time or stated number of bars (a typical default is 14 bars). Volatility measures the range of market moves from high to low but doesn't directly reference the direction of those moves.

J. Welles Wilder suggests that the objective signal for a trend, using ADX, is when its value is above 25, but some traders prefer to use a value of 20. This signal doesn't indicate whether the market is in an uptrend or a downtrend, simply that the market is in a strong trend. Thus, the indicator is popular for being simple, objective, and easy to interpret.

Figure 6-1 shows the ADX line providing clear and objective readings for a strong trend (up or down) when it crosses above the value of 25.

ES 03-14, 3 Min

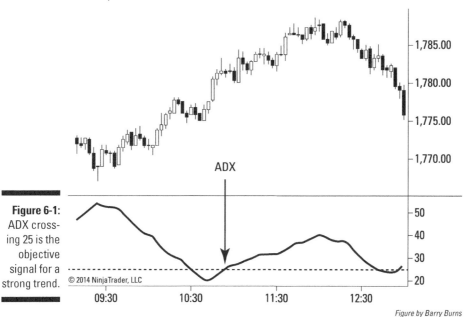

Figure 6-1: ADX crossing 25 is the objective signal for a strong trend.

Figure by Barry Burns

Trading the ADX indicator

Two other elements to the ADX indicator that help determine whether the market is trending up or down are *plus directional movement* (+DM) and *minus directional movement* (–DM). These two elements indicate trend direction:

✔ When +DM is above –DM, trend is up.

✔ When –DM is above +DM, trend is down.

ADX measures the strength of either the uptrend or downtrend.

One approach for trading the ADX indicator is to wait for ADX to get above a value of 25 (or 20 if you want to be more aggressive) and then buy when the +DM line is above the –DM line. Figure 6-2 illustrates an example of this (ADX is the thickest line, +DM is the second thickest line, and –DM is the thinnest line).

ES 03-14, 3 Min

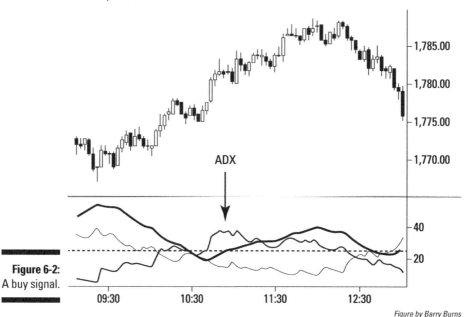

Figure 6-2:
A buy signal.

Shorting the market involves waiting for the ADX to get above a value of 25 (or 20 if you want to be more aggressive) and then short when the –DM line is above +DM line. Figure 6-3 illustrates an example of this short signal.

I was introduced to the ADX indicator by one of my personal trading mentors. He loved it and used it throughout his trading career. He didn't employ it alone but would always use it in conjunction with other indicators and price patterns (a common practice among those who use the indicator).

Although the ADX indicator is a popular tool and can be used effectively, after the ADX line crosses above 25, it often moves back against the direction of the trend while the price bars continue in the direction of the trend. When this occurs, it's not a clear signal whether the trend is reversing, simply slowing down, or consolidating. Therefore, it's very difficult to use it in determining when the trend is ending, as demonstrated in Figure 6-4.

To further complicate matters, an uptrend can turn into a downtrend as seen on the price bars. But it won't be signaled on the ADX indicator until it returns all the way back down to 25 and then crosses above it, thereby giving a very late signal for trend reversals, or even trend continuations, as seen in Figure 6-5.

CL 03-14, 3 Min

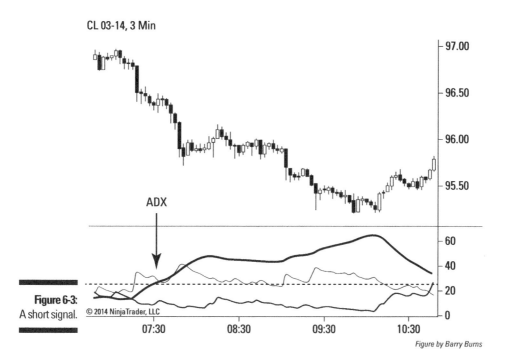

ADX

07:30   08:30   09:30   10:30

Figure 6-3:
A short signal.

Figure by Barry Burns

INTC, Weekly

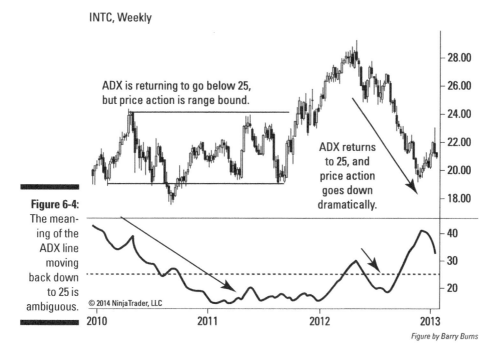

ADX is returning to go below 25,
but price action is range bound.

ADX returns
to 25, and
price action
goes down
dramatically.

2010   2011   2012   2013

Figure 6-4:
The mean-
ing of the
ADX line
moving
back down
to 25 is
ambiguous.

Figure by Barry Burns

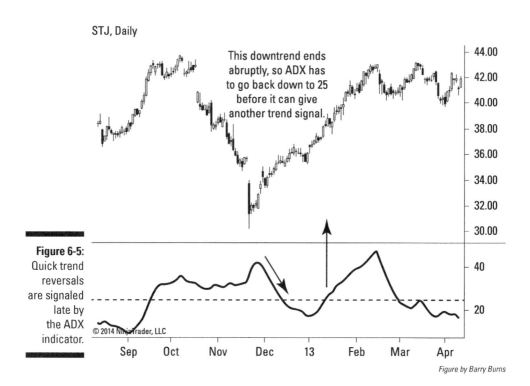

STJ, Daily

This downtrend ends abruptly, so ADX has to go back down to 25 before it can give another trend signal.

© 2014 NinjaTrader, LLC

Figure 6-5:
Quick trend reversals are signaled late by the ADX indicator.

Figure by Barry Burns

Bollinger Bands: Seeing Both Trend and Volatility in One Tool

Bollinger Bands were created by John Bollinger in the 1980s, trademarked by him in 2011, and have enjoyed a wide following by many technical analysis traders. You can use them to help determine trend, strength, and *volatility* — the variation of the price of a market over time — in a dynamic, adaptive manner. A market that has high volatility makes a large price movement in a given period of time. A market that has low volatility makes a small price movement in a given period of time. I personally find Bollinger Bands to be very useful in identifying price patterns that would otherwise be hard to spot.

In the following sections, I demonstrate how Bollinger Bands are calculated and how to trade them.

Getting a clear signal

Bollinger Bands are one of my favorite tools. They're easy to read, provide meaningful signals, and measure both trend and volatility in one tool. Bollinger Bands consist of three elements:

- **A simple moving average, usually of intermediate length:** A simple 20-period moving average is often the default setting. You can use this average for measuring trend and to calculate the other two elements of the indicator (see the following bullets).

- **The upper band:** The upper band is a standard deviation above the simple moving average used in the indicator. Two standard deviations is often the default found on most charting software.

  Note: Standard deviation is the measurement of how far the current price is deviating from an expected norm. In the context of Bollinger Bands, the standard deviation is drawn as lines above and below the expected norm, which is the moving average. In this way, it measures the volatility of the market and strong moves in one direction or another.

- **The lower band:** The lower band is a standard deviation below the simple moving average used in the indicator. Two standard deviations is often the default found on most charting software.

Unlike the ADX, which is plotted on a sub graph below the price graph, Bollinger Bands are plotted on the same graph as the price bars and thus give clear signals of price bars interacting with the indicator. In addition to providing indications of direction and volatility, Bollinger Bands are often used to visually show contracting market conditions, which many traders use to anticipate large breakout moves.

Figure 6-6 shows a *squeeze* where the Bollinger Bands contract, signaling a low volatility cycle, after which traders look for a breakout of the narrow range of trading.

FDAX 03-14, 5 Min

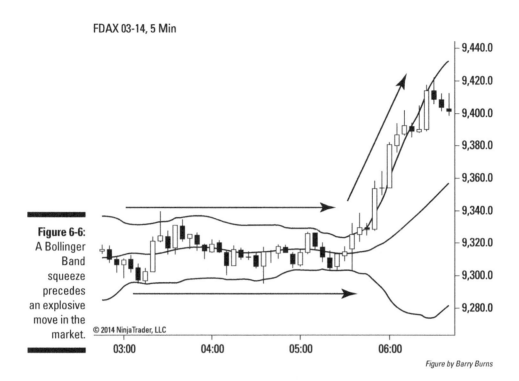

Figure 6-6:
A Bollinger
Band
squeeze
precedes
an explosive
move in the
market.

© 2014 NinjaTrader, LLC

Figure by Barry Burns

Trading Bollinger Bands the right way

You can choose from many rules and signals when trading Bollinger Bands. To keep within the topic of trend trading and the scope of this book, in this section, I focus on one signal that indicates a new trend may be starting: waves.

When the market makes relatively larger moves (in both time and price) in the direction of the trend, such moves are called *impulse moves*. When the market makes relatively smaller moves (in both time and price) against the direction of the trend, such moves are called *corrective moves*.

Bollinger Bands provide a way to objectively measure impulse and corrective waves:

 ✔ When price bars move far enough to reach the upper or lower Bollinger Band, you may consider that an impulse move, providing evidence of strength in that direction and therefore an indication that a trend may be starting.

  ✔ The corrective move against the trend often retraces back to the moving
    average used in the indicator but definitely shouldn't move so far as
    to touch the opposite Bollinger Band. If it does, then it indicates you
    have an impulse wave in the direction of that move, and it negates the
    impulse move in the previous direction.

Figure 6-7 provides an example of an impulse move that reaches the upper
Bollinger Band, a corrective leg against the trend that doesn't reach the
lower Bollinger Band, and another impulse move that again reaches the
upper Bollinger Band.

FDAX 03-14, 5 Min

Figure 6-7:
Price bars
reaching the
Bollinger
Band signal
a potential
trend in that
direction.

© 2014 NinjaTrader, LLC

Figure by Barry Burns

Moving Averages: Charting the Markets

Moving averages may be the most common type of indicator used for charting the markets. Like Bollinger Bands, they're plotted on the same graph as
the price bars and provide not only an indication of the trend of the market
but also *support* or *resistance* barriers as price moves into the moving average

lines. (Support and resistance are price levels in the market that price bars may have trouble moving through and therefore often bounce off of them. See Chapter 11 for details.)

In the following sections, I show you how the moving average is calculated and how to use it for trading signals.

Following the closing price

Each type of moving average has its own unique variation of how it calculates the average of closing prices over the past. For measuring trend, I prefer to use the simplest of the moving averages, not surprisingly called the *simple moving average* (SMA).

The SMA is the average of the closing price for a certain number of bars. It's called a "moving" average because this process is repeated with each new bar, thereby creating a line that continues to move forward with each new bar plotted on your chart.

Like most things in trading, moving averages work because a lot of people use them. The more people use an indicator and respond to it, the more it will have an impact on the movement of the market itself. It's a self-fulfilling prophecy.

Trading moving averages

The most common moving average is the 50 SMA. The second most common moving average is the 200 SMA. Professionals have used these two moving averages for years.

I use the 50 SMA as the trend indicator on all my charts for two reasons:

- ✔ It's very popular, so masses of people respond to it.
- ✔ The period of 50 bars fits the definition of *trend,* which is "to extend in a general direction." Based on this definition, trend is a long-term move; therefore, you wouldn't want to use a short-term moving average.

Moving averages are among the most simple of the trend indicators to use. Typically, the trend is considered up when the price bars are above the moving average and the moving average is angling up, as shown in Figure 6-8.

Trend is considered down when the price bars are below the moving average and the moving average is angling down, as shown in Figure 6-9.

FDAX 03-14, 5 Min

Figure 6-8:
Uptrend:
Price above
an upward
angling
50 SMA.

© 2014 NinjaTrader, LLC

Figure by Barry Burns

The trend is your friend . . . until the end

One of my mentors told me the story of a trader at a large firm who impressed everyone with his hugely successful trading record for a number of consecutive years. As is typical in such circumstances, everyone pushed him to reveal his secret to success, but he kept it to himself. After a few years, his performance dropped dramatically, and he started losing money. Finally, he revealed his secret to my mentor. He used a simple moving average crossover system.

Using two moving averages, whenever the shorter-term moving average crossed above the longer-term moving average, he'd buy. It was a long-only trading system, so when the shorter-term moving average crossed below the longer-term moving average, he'd get out of the market until he got another buy signal.

What's remarkable is that this is one of the most basic trading approaches that all seasoned traders are familiar with, but none of them could figure it out. They had all evolved to such complicated systems that they never thought to try something so simple. However, no one simple technical system like this will succeed forever. It worked well at the time because the markets the trader was trading were trending dramatically for several years. As soon as the dramatic trends ended, so did the success of that simple system that worked well for trending markets but not for choppy or consolidating markets.

FDAX 03-14, 5 Min

Figure 6-9:
Downtrend:
Price below
a downward
angling
50 SMA.

© 2014 NinjaTrader, LLC

Figure by Barry Burns

Chapter 7

Understanding Broad-Based Market Indicators

....

In This Chapter

▷ Keeping your eye on volume patterns and the advance/decline line

▷ Putting the price and volume indicator together in one

▷ Taking a consensus of sectors and industries

▷ Getting sentimental about the market

▷ Influencing the future

....

*I*n Chapter 6, you explore indicators that measure the trend on any one given market (stock, commodity, or currency). In this chapter, you look at *broad market indicators,* which measure the energy of a large group of stocks combined into an *index.* (An index is calculated from the prices of a select group of stocks, such as those in the S&P 500, the NASDAQ, or the DOW.)

Just as you apply indicators to individual markets, you can also apply indicators to indexes and then compare the market you're trading to the broader market it's a part of.

The benefit of comparing a stock to its broader index is that traders look at the broader market for clues as to how the individual markets should be trading, especially in terms of direction (trend). Therefore, the broad market influences the movement of the individual markets of which it's comprised.

Seeing What Others Can't: Volume Patterns

Because trading is a business of probabilities, it's important to have an advantage over other traders, usually in the form of you seeing something they don't see. I refer to this type of advantage as an "invisible edge."

Volume is closely related to trend because for the market to make a strong sustained move in one direction, it requires a lot of trading activity in terms of shares, lots, and contracts (volume). So if the market moves up but then a dramatic amount of shares start selling against that move, the market will have a difficult time following through to the upside.

In my opinion, seeing volume patterns that others don't see is the best advantage you can enjoy.

In this section, I gift you with one of the most powerful tools I've ever discovered for day trading: comparing the broad market's up volume to down volume.

Going up with the buying volume index

One volume index tracks the amount of *up volume* or *buying volume* of the various markets (most notably the NYSE and the NASDAQ). You can plot the up volume on your chart by simply plotting its symbol on your chart as you would any stock symbol.

This index isn't an indicator as such, so don't look for it in your indicators list (a common misunderstanding among traders). The symbol for this index can vary from one data provider to another, so request the symbol for up volume from the company that provides data for your charts. A common symbol for the NYSE up volume is $UVOL, and for the NASDAQ up volume, it's $UVOLQ, but yours may be different. *Note:* The dollar sign at the beginning of such symbols indicates that it's an index. Your data provider may use another symbol, such as ^.

Coming down with the selling volume index

Another index tracks the amount of *down volume* or *selling volume* of the various markets. You plot the down volume on your chart by plotting its symbol on your chart.

Just as with the up volume, the symbol for this index can vary, so request the symbol for down volume from your data provider. A common symbol for the NYSE down volume is $DVOL, and for the NASDAQ down volume, it's $DVOLQ.

Focusing on the difference between the up/down volume indexes

Now here's the secret that's going to give you an edge over other traders. You're not interested in looking at the up volume or the down volume index individually. You're interested in the difference between the up and down volume indexes.

Some data providers have a symbol that plots the difference between those two indicators for you. If your data provider doesn't, then you simply plot both indexes on the same chart and then apply an indicator that measures the difference, or spread, between two symbols on your chart.

If your charting software doesn't have such an indicator, check the forums for your software to see whether anyone has created one, or ask someone to do so for you. It's an easy indicator to create, and you'll find that most forums have programmers who create and give away indicators freely.

Though this process may seem a bit involved, the reason this approach is so powerful is because it gives you an edge over other traders because many don't know about it, and those who do aren't willing to go through the small, one-time inconvenience of putting this together. Do what they aren't willing to do, and you'll make what they aren't able to make — profits!

Volume is a primary driver of market direction and strength. Keep the following in mind when looking at the up/down volume difference:

✔ When the up/down volume difference is moving up, the market is bullish, and you should favor long trades.

✔ When the up/down volume difference is moving down, the overall market is bearish, and you should favor short trades.

✔ When the up/down volume difference hovers around the 0 line, the overall market is neutral, and you should either stay out of the market or trade short-term oscillations in a channel.

Figure 7-1 shows an example of how the broad NYSE market up/down volume started the day rather neutral (hovering slightly above the 0 level) and then began trending down. Seeing this downtrend begin, I'd favor short trades only in whatever individual stock I was trading in the NYSE.

^UVOL, 2 Min

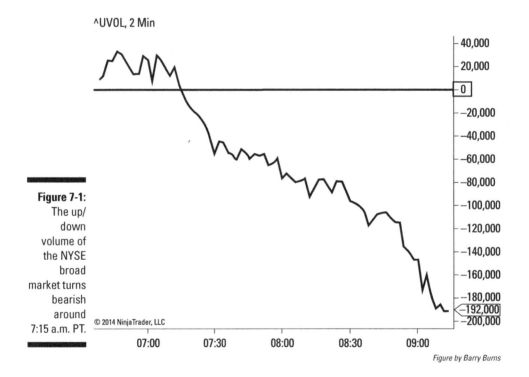

Figure 7-1:
The up/down volume of the NYSE broad market turns bearish around 7:15 a.m. PT.

© 2014 NinjaTrader, LLC

Figure by Barry Burns

Looking Behind the Scenes: The Advance/Decline Line

Although my favorite broad market indicator is the up/down volume index (discussed in the previous section), another good one is the advance/decline line. This index provides indications of what the market you're trading may do.

Like the up/down volume index, the advance/decline line measures the difference between two indexes. Instead of volume, however, it measures the number of issues moving up and down. (An *issue* in this context is a symbol, such as a stock.)

In the following sections, I show you a broad market index I use in conjunction with the up/down volume. Instead of measuring volume, this index measures the number of stocks moving up or down.

Advancing issues versus declining issues

When charting *advancing issues,* you're simply charting how many stocks are currently moving up. The advancing issues index can move in the same direction or a different direction than up volume because the group of stocks moving up includes different sizes (number of shares traded).

You can have more stocks moving up, but if they're all small caps, then the up/down volume index can be moving down because although fewer stocks are moving down, they may trade more volume than the stocks moving up.

The *declining issues* index measures the number of stocks moving down at any given time, again regardless of the volume of those stocks.

The difference between the advancing and declining signals

In the same way you get signals from the up/down volume indexes by measuring the difference between them, you also get signals from the advancing and declining issues by measuring their difference.

Generally, the advance/decline line has more up and down swings than the up/down volume index. I like to plot it as bars and apply a 20-period *exponential moving average* (EMA), which gives more weight to the most recent prices in calculating the average. (The *period* just refers to the number of bars on the chart used to calculate the average.) I then use the angle of that average as my reference as to whether the advance/decline index is moving up or down.

Many data feeds have a single symbol for the advance/decline line. It may be something like ^ADD or $ADD. Ask your data provider for the symbol it uses.

Figure 7-2 is an example of the advance/decline line (plotted with candlestick bars) with the 20-period EMA. Based on this chart, I'd favor long trades until about 12:00 and then favor short trades after that when the 20 EMA of the advance/decline line turns down.

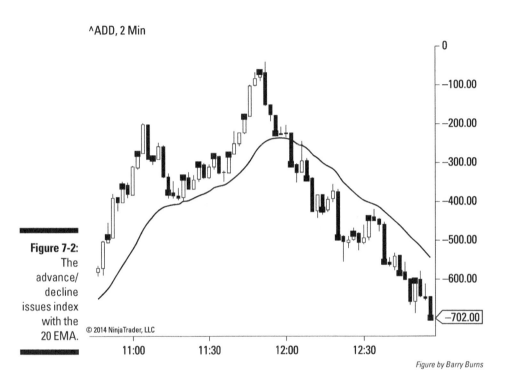

^ADD, 2 Min

© 2014 NinjaTrader, LLC

Figure 7-2:
The advance/decline issues index with the 20 EMA.

Figure by Barry Burns

One of my favorite setups is to wait for the up/down volume index and the advance/decline index to diverge. Then I look to take a trade in the direction of the up/down volume index when the advance/decline index starts moving back in the direction of the up/down volume index. I do this because I consider the up/down volume index to be the dominant energy of the market the entire day, so I always like to trade in its direction.

Figure 7-3 illustrates one of these situations. Here, the pattern sets up between these two indexes, and the market creates a trend against the direction of the up/down volume index, allowing for a high-probability trend reversal trade (which is the highest reward-to-risk setup but generally has a low win/loss ratio).

(a)   ^UVOL, 2 Min

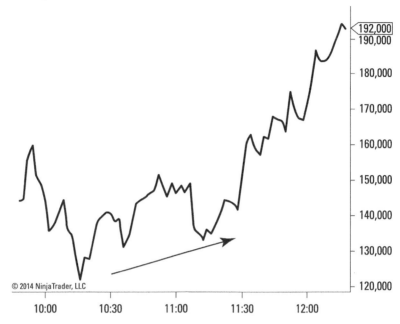

(b)   ^ADD, 2 Min

Figure 7-3:
After the
two indexes
diverge,
trade in the
direction
of up/down
volume.

Figure by Barry Burns

TRIN: Combining Price Action and Volume

The TRIN, or Arms index, was created by Richard W. Arms Jr. and combines the difference between the advancing and declining issues, with the difference between the volume of advancing issues and the volume of declining issues. Therefore, it combines everything introduced so far in this chapter into a single indicator, thus making it much more efficient and effective.

Ironically, when TRIN gets below a value of 1, it's considered bullish. And when it gets above a value of 1, it's considered bearish, thus the index moves inverse to the market.

The TRIN index is an oscillator and can be quite choppy, so some traders use a 10-period SMA of the TRIN to smooth it. Other traders look for extreme highs and lows to find overbought and oversold levels for trading.

Personally, I haven't found any of these approaches to be to my liking, but because the index is popular and is often used to identify the direction of a trending market, I introduce it to you here. Although you may be tempted to combine advance/decline and up/down volume, I find it actually more telling to watch them individually and look for times when they diverge.

Trading with Market Consensus

Another way to evaluate the condition of the broad market on any given day is to open a quote screen and enter the symbols for a variety of *sectors* and *industries.* (Find a list of sectors and industries at `biz.yahoo.com/p`.)

For example, if you were considering trading Apple, Inc. (AAPL), you could first look at a chart of the sector to which Apple belongs, which is consumer goods. The market's feelings about that sector can have an influence on every stock within that sector.

Then you could look at a stock of the industry of electronic equipment, which is the industry that Apple is in. Again, how market participants feel about that industry as a whole can have a strong influence on the performance of the stocks in that industry, including Apple.

I explore more examples of sectors and industries in the following sections and explain how you can create your own list for your trading needs.

Sector consensus

Sectors are parts of the economy that share related products or services. Following are some sectors that are often cited:

- Basic materials
- Conglomerates
- Consumer discretionary
- Consumer staples
- Energy
- Financials
- Healthcare
- Industrials
- Technology
- Utilities

Watching the movement of the sectors can provide a good broad market view of what to expect with regard to the overall trend of the market. If most sectors are bullish for the day, then you'd expect an uptrend, especially if you're trading a stock in one of those sectors.

Industry consensus

Each sector is broken down into *industries,* which further differentiate themselves within the broader sector to which they belong. For example, the sector of utilities could be broken down into the following industries:

- Diversified
- Electric
- Foreign
- Gas
- Water

Watching the movement of the industries can provide an even more detailed view of the broad market trend. If most industries are bullish for the day, then you'd expect an uptrend, especially if you're trading a stock in one of those industries.

Creating and analyzing your own list of sectors and industries

Each source of information you consult (broker, website, or newspaper) may have a slightly different list of sectors and industries. The important thing is to create a list of a wide variety of sectors and/or industries and put them into a quote screen, such as the one in Figure 7-4.

Set the (percent) *Change* column on the quote screen to auto-sort so the industries that are positive for the day (that is, have a positive change from the previous day's close) rise to the top, and the industries that are negative for the day move to the bottom. You may also be able to color code them green (for positive) and red (for negative) if your software allows it.

Market Analyzer	
Instrument	Change
^TELECOMM	0.28%
^RETAIL	0.15%
^UTILITIES	0.09%
^HEALTHCARE	0.00%
^CONSUMER	−0.02%
^METALS	−0.04%
^TECHNOLOGY	−0.07%
^FINANCE	−0.11%

Figure 7-4: A quote screen listing various sectors of the market.

When analyzing your sectors and industries, you're looking for two things:

✔ **How many of the sectors are above 0 change and how many are below 0 change from the previous day's close:** The more that are positive, the more bullish the broad market is. If there's a close balance between the two, then it's considered a neutral market.

✔ **The percentage change from the previous day's close:** If the move up or down from 0 is only a few percentage points, then it isn't significant. However, if many of the sectors or industries are approaching or over 1 percent change from the previous day's close, then it's considered a strongly bullish or bearish day.

Getting a "Feel" for the Market: Market Sentiment Indicators

Market sentiment indicators measure the feelings of the market participants regarding how positive or negative they regard the market. Primarily, they're used to provide information of the mass psychology of average traders (not professional traders) as to how bullish or bearish they are about the market in general. Traders and investors alike use this information as another type of broad market indicator in the ways I describe in the following sections.

Mood swings don't always result in market swings

Market sentiment indicators are generally *contrarian indicators,* meaning that when most people are bearish, it may be a good time to buy, and when most people are bullish, it may be a good time to sell. Such sentiment indicators are most useful when they're at extremes and not fairly neutral (which they are most of the time). Swings in sentiment from mildly bullish to mildly bearish haven't proven to be of much significance. Instead, the dramatic emotional swings of people's feeling about the market most often create the highs and lows most pronounced on the charts.

Such recent experiences as the real estate bubble and, before that, the tech bubble both popped at the top of the most enthusiasm on behalf of the masses.

On the other side of the market, I remember my father buying into the market immediately after the 9/11 attacks on New York. The DOW dove down close to 8,000 but then quickly popped back up to over 10,000 in just a few months. He was trading contrarian to the extremely negative sentiment at the time.

Sentiment indicators as contrarian indicators

One of the most commonly used sentiment indicators is the *put/call ratio,* which is simply the ratio of the number of put options to call options. A bullish sentiment occurs when the number of call options traded is greater than the number of put options traded. However, as mentioned in the previous section, only the extreme sentiments provide meaningful signals.

Because sentiment indicators are contrarian indicators, it makes sense to use such indicators that measure the feelings of amateur — that is, losing — traders. The put/call ratio may seem ideal for this because retail options buyers are notorious for losing money. However, keep in mind that options were originally created to manage risk by hedging positions. Therefore, professional traders participate in the buying of options as well and diminish the contrarian effect of using the put/call ratio as a sentiment indicator.

To address this issue, you may want to consult the *equity-only put/call ratio,* which doesn't include the index put buying statistics of the professional traders who are hedging their positions.

You can find the equity put/call ratio on CBOE.com in the CBOE Daily Market Statistics section in the left sidebar.

You can also consult many other sentiment indicators. Here are some good ones you may want to consider:

- ✔ Investors Intelligence published by Chartcraft
- ✔ American Association of Individual Investors Sentiment Survey
- ✔ Barron's Investor Sentiment Readings
- ✔ Money.CNN Fear and Greed Index

VIX: Watching for the Volatility Outliers

VIX is a symbol for the CBOE volatility index. It measures *implied volatility,* which is the expectation of volatility for the S&P 500 over the next 30 days. VIX is a sentiment indicator and has been nicknamed the "fear index."

A high VIX reading indicates that investors expect large moves in the market in the near term, resulting in fear or uncertainty among investors. High readings are traditionally seen as those above a value of 30.

A low VIX reading indicates that investors don't expect large moves in the market in the near term and, therefore, have a lethargic attitude. Low readings are traditionally seen as those below a value of 20.

What happens when you don't watch market indicators?

A common mistake among new traders is that for some unknown reason, they want to fade the market. Something triggers people when the market is going down to want to buy it and when the market is going up, to short it.

One of my mentors called this "kamikaze trading," and it truly is suicide. The way to make the big money in trading is to trade with the trend, not against it.

I have to admit that I suffered from this same problem. It became a habit. I'd look at the market making higher highs over and over and over for hours and figure, "It just can't go any higher!" So I would short the market, and it would go down just enough to execute my trade and then turn around and go back up, taking out my stop.

The one thing that cured me of this bad habit was when one of my trading buddies showed me the up/down volume index. He said when that index is moving clearly up or down and he traded in the same direction, his winning percentage improved dramatically.

I decided to give it a try and have never looked back since. Now, I love to trade the trend in the direction of the up/down volume index. In fact, the only time I feel truly comfortable taking a position against the trend of the market I'm trading is when that trend is against the direction of the up/down volume index.

Chapter 8

Knowing What Time
You Want to Trade

*O*ne of the most important decisions you'll make as a trend trader is choosing a *time horizon* you want to trade in. The time horizon refers to the length of time you expect to hold onto your trades. Do you want to be a short-term trader (a day trader), an intermediate-term trader (a swing trader), or a long-term trader (an investor)?

In this chapter, I share with you the advantages and disadvantages of trading each time horizon and help you decide which may be most suitable for you.

Trading Is All Relative to Time

Students at my seminars sometimes ask, "What is the trend of the market right now?"

That question is impossible to answer because the trend is relative to *the time interval* of the chart. You must decide your chosen time horizon before you can evaluate your trading signals or even something as simple as determining whether the trend is up or down.

In the following sections, I begin with the basics by explaining exactly how to determine various time intervals for your charts.

Understanding time intervals

Depending on the time horizon you choose for your trading style, you need to choose an appropriate time interval to use on your charts for trading. The *time interval* of the market primarily refers to the length of time it takes for each bar to form on a chart. You can set up your chart so each bar lasts for one day, one week, or one month if you plan on holding a position for a long period of time.

The time interval is basically the chosen scale at which you're viewing the market. It's like looking at the moon through a telescope, using three different levels of magnification, depending on whether you want to see the big overall shape of the moon or zoom in on the smaller details.

If you're a day trader, you're more likely to choose a very short length of time for each bar, such as 2 minutes, 3 minutes, or 5 minutes. Figure 8-1 illustrates how each bar on the chart displays four points of data during its length of time:

- ✔ **Open:** The price at which the market started during that time interval

- ✔ **High:** The highest price the market reached during that time interval

- ✔ **Low:** The lowest price the market reached during that time interval

- ✔ **Close:** The last price at which the market traded during that time interval

Figure 8-2 shows an example of looking at a market on different scales, where each bar plots market movement over a very different length of time. Figure 8-2a shows a daily chart, in which each bar displays one day of market activity. Figure 8-2b, on the other hand, shows a 2-minute chart, in which each bar displays 2 minutes of market activity. Look at the bottom of the chart for the time reference (minutes, days, weeks, or months).

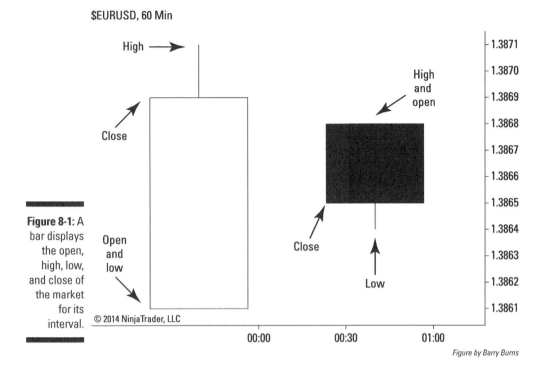

$EURUSD, 60 Min

Figure 8-1: A bar displays the open, high, low, and close of the market for its interval.

Figure by Barry Burns

Discovering the importance of time when trading

Timing is everything because you can't determine trend, or anything else about a market, until you put it in the context of a time frame, or scale. On a 2-minute chart (where each bar displays one day of trading activity), the trend may be up (see Figure 8-3).

However, if you look at the same market (stock, forex pair, or commodity) on a daily chart, the trend may be down (see Figure 8-4).

When you compare the two charts, you may find that the uptrend on the 2-minute chart is simply a brief retrace against the trend taking place on the daily chart.

(a) WMT, Daily

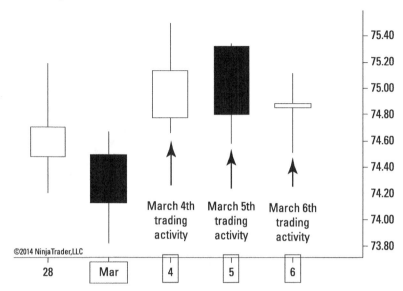

(b) CL 06-14, 2 Min

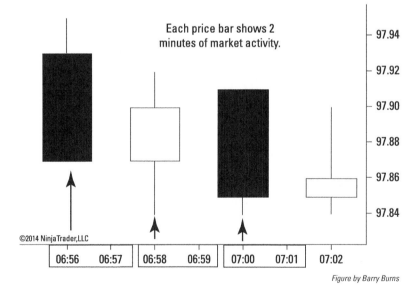

Figure 8-2:
Different
scales of
time can
result in
very differ-
ent trends.

Figure by Barry Burns

IBM, 2 Min

Figure 8-3:
The
2-minute
chart shows
an uptrend.

©2014 NinjaTrader,LLC

Figure by Barry Burns

IBM, Daily

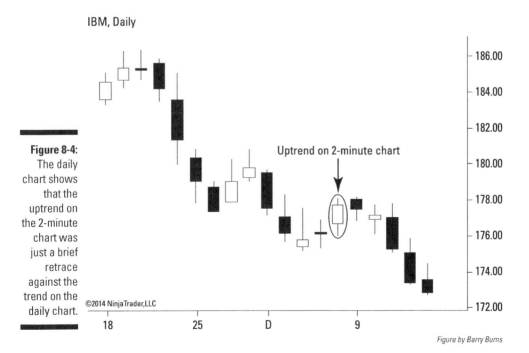

Figure 8-4:
The daily
chart shows
that the
uptrend on
the 2-minute
chart was
just a brief
retrace
against the
trend on the
daily chart.

©2014 NinjaTrader,LLC

Figure by Barry Burns

Day Trading: Taking It One Day at a Time

Day trading is simply defined as entering and exiting the same trade within the same trading day. It can be fun and profitable, but it's certainly not easy and poses as many challenges as benefits.

In this section, I highlight the advantages and disadvantages of day trading to help you determine whether it's right for you. Ultimately, it depends on your schedule and your own personal disposition.

Advantages of day trading

I personally enjoy day trading tremendously. Placing trade after trade throughout the day, actively monitoring every movement of the market, and making fast money are all exciting aspects of day trading. I'm often in and out of a trade within a matter of 5 to 15 minutes. When successful, seeing that you made hundreds of dollars in a matter of minutes can provide an adrenaline rush like no other.

Day trading may also provide you with better leverage than holding positions over night (as in swing trading; see the later section for more on swing trading). At the time of this writing, day trading stocks can provide you with 4:1 leverage as long as you meet certain criteria. (For more on leverage, see Chapter 16.)

Day trading also provides you with another type of leverage, which is that because you're trading so frequently, you can use the same capital in your account to make many trades in a short period of time.

One of the best benefits of day trading is that you avoid *overnight risk.* Overnight risk refers to the fact that when you hold a position over night, your money is exposed to major unexpected moves while the market is closed and you're sleeping. Such unexpected dramatic moves may be caused by surprise economic, political, or military news in your country or another.

These dramatic moves overnight may be caused by truly bad news, or simply rumors, or a change of sentiment about a stock, sector, or industry. These moves show up as *gaps* — significantly different opening prices than where the markets closed the day before — on your chart and can *jump your stops,* providing a huge loss for you when you wake up the next morning. (A *stop* is an order you place to be filled at a certain price if the market turns against your trade; *jumping your stops* occurs when the market gaps to a price that's beyond where you placed your stop order.)

A *stop* is often called a *protective stop* because it's used as a protective measure with the intention of setting the level at which you want to exit a trade that's not going your way. In this manner, you're attempting to limit your risk in the trade.

Disadvantages of day trading

My personal opinion is that day trading requires the most trading proficiency and skill of any type of trading simply because it's so fast paced, and therefore you must analyze the market and make decisions quickly. Day trading is definitely not for everyone; it's difficult, and most day traders lose money. Also, for those who have a job during market hours (which is most people), day trading is impossible simply because their schedule doesn't allow it.

Following are some additional disadvantages (or at least challenges) of day trading:

- **Day trading requires split-second timing.** It doesn't accommodate itself well to people who are slow in making decisions and commitments. To be a successful day trader, you must be able to analyze the market quickly, and when a high-probability trade presents itself, you must execute your trade with speed and confidence.

  You must also be able to manage your trade, maintain impeccable discipline, and manage risk and reward quickly.

- **Day trading can be more emotional than other types of trading.** When you see your profit and loss statement moving up or down quickly, and you have the pressure of the time limitations, it can be very nerve wracking.

- **Day trading can be very boring!** Sure, when the market is moving fast, you have the challenge of making quick decisions and dealing with the emotions of fear and greed. The best day traders I know, however, don't trade as frequently as most people assume. Most of their time is spent sitting and just watching the market doing nothing meaningful. By that, I mean that the majority of the time, the market will move randomly without providing a high-probability trading scenario for you.

  The biggest problem with this is that the boredom makes it hard to concentrate for long periods of time. That leads to distraction in which traders start checking their e-mails, making phone calls, paying bills, and so forth so that when the high-probability trade finally arrives, they miss it because they weren't paying attention.

Swing Trading: Holding On a Little Longer

The term *swing trading* originally referred to holding a position for just a few days. However, the term has expanded in popular usage and now often refers to holding a position overnight (at least two days to distinguish it from day trading), but not as a long-term investment of a year or more.

Check out the following sections for some advantages and disadvantages of this method of trading.

Advantages of swing trading

Swing trading is a lot like day trading, but its differences bring some unique advantages. Swing trading provides benefits for people who have restrictive work schedules and also for those who need more time to make trading decisions.

> ✓ Swing trading can be a good trading style for people who work during market hours but still want to be active, relatively short-term traders.
>
> I day trade and swing trade at the same time. During market hours, I want to focus on my day trading and not be distracted by my swing trading positions. To facilitate this, I place my swing trades the night before the market opens (or premarket). I simply evaluate the price at which I want to enter a trade and place a buy stop at that price. If my trade is filled, I immediately place my protective stop (some trading software will allow you to place multiple orders based on if/then scenarios, or you can do it manually).
>
> ✓ Although overnight risk can be a disadvantage of swing trading, the gaps that sometimes occur overnight can also work in your favor if they gap in the direction of your trade. This allows you to make quick, big, overnight money not available with day trading.
>
> ✓ Swing trading allows you to take more time to analyze the market you're trading and make trading decisions in a more relaxed manner without the time pressure of day trading.
>
> Many swing traders are people who have tried day trading but found that they didn't like "staring at a monitor all day," finding it tedious and boring.

Disadvantages of swing trading

Although swing trading has its benefits, those benefits come with trade-offs. Consider the following disadvantages and challenges of swing trading:

✔ Markets can make dramatic moves overnight while you're sleeping and the market is closed. If such a move is against your trade, it can be a rude awakening when you check your position the next morning. Even placing stops doesn't always protect you from that.

I recommend you discover how to use options to hedge your positions against overnight risk. They can provide better protection against major gaps than protective stops. *Trading Options For Dummies,* by George Fontanills (Wiley), is a great resource. I've personally taken courses from George and found them extremely valuable.

✔ When trading stocks, swing trading normally doesn't provide you with the same amount of leverage as day trading.

✔ You tie up your capital longer with swing trading than with day trading.

Investing: Staying in for the Long Term

I define *investing* as holding a position more than a year. In this section, I provide a quick overview of the pros and cons of this long-term strategy.

Note: Because this book is about trend trading and investing isn't actually trading (I define trading as a short-term activity), this section is brief. If you want more info on investing, check out the latest edition of *Investing For Dummies,* by Eric Tyson (Wiley).

Advantages of investing

The investing time frame is the most popular. Because it's less active, I don't use the term *trading* for investing. Following are some of the advantages of investing, particularly compared to trading:

✔ Investing is the least "active" approach to participating in the markets. It can be good for those who have an interest in the markets but don't have enough interest in it to make it a part of their daily or weekly schedule.

✔ Some people have extreme difficulty doing short-term trading. Some, in fact, believe it's impossible to determine short-term moves with consistent accuracy. For such people, investing may be a good choice.

✔ Holding a position for more than a year potentially allows you to tap into the long-term capital gains tax, which is generally a lower tax rate than short-term capital gains tax. (*Note:* This is not meant to be tax advice. Please consult a competent and qualified tax professional for details about taxes as they apply to the time you're reading this book and to your individual situation.)

Disadvantages of investing

Investing also has some disadvantages that should be considered and weighed against the advantages. Ultimately, it's up to you to decide whether the advantages outweigh the disadvantages for you and your lifestyle. Remember also that you don't need to be an investor to the exclusion of being a trader.

Here are some of the disadvantages of investing over against trading:

✔ Of the three time horizons, investing can be the slowest way to make money, assuming that you could be an excellent swing trader or day trader.

✔ Because investing reuses the same capital very infrequently, the annual returns are generally not as good as a successful professional trader.

Earning an average 10 percent return annually may be considered acceptable for an investor. However, some day traders have made 10 percent returns in a week! That's certainly not meant to be an income claim, nor is that normal, but, yes, it does happen.

✔ Investors notoriously have a very difficult time *outperforming the market* — making investing decisions that result in a better return than if you simply invested that same money into an equity index fund, such as the S&P 500, and didn't touch it. Even many professional fund managers aren't able to do that for their clients after costs.

Triple threat: Multiply your income by using all three trading horizons

Each trading time horizon — day trading, swing trading, and investing — has its advantages and disadvantages. It's up to you to decide which fits you best.

I participate in all three time horizons concurrently. I enjoy day trading during market hours. In addition to the satisfaction of making money, I find day trading fun and exhilarating. After the market closes, I look for swing trading opportunities. I analyze various markets that often become uncorrelated, looking for an exceptional opportunity. I look at various sectors and industries, countries, bonds, commodities (such as gold and oil), and currencies.

When I see a good opportunity, I place a buy stop at the price I want to enter the market the next day. If the market fills my order, I immediately place my protective stop and my option hedging order to protect against a major gap against my position.

I also employ investing in my retirement accounts. My approach to investing is to look at various uncorrelated markets, but because I'm investing for the long term, I'm looking for long cycles to time my entries. What I'm looking for in those long-term cycles is where I can buy a market that's been going down and buy it at a discount (value investing). I'm often looking for four-year cycles and use weekly and monthly charts for my analysis.

Chapter 9

How to Make Money When the Market Goes Up or Down

In This Chapter

▷ Shorting the market and selling before you buy

▷ Going long with the market and buying before you sell

*T*he most common perception of participating in the markets is to buy into them and hope that they go up.

In your everyday life, you typically buy things before you sell them. Whether you're buying a car, a house, or any other item, you generally buy it first and then sell it later when you want a new car or home.

Investing works a little differently. In this case, you're dealing with stocks, mutual funds, and so on. The financial markets allow you to make money whether they're going up or down because you can buy first and sell later, or you can sell first and buy back later.

In this chapter, I show you how you can make money by trading uptrends or downtrends.

Trend Trading to the Short Side

If you have reasons to believe that a market is going to go down, you can make money by *short selling* that market. Short selling (also known as *going short* or *shorting the market*) means that you're selling the market first and then attempting to buy it later at a lower price. It's exactly the same principle of "buy low, sell high," just in the reverse order — you sell high and then buy low. See Figure 9-1 for an illustration of this concept.

GS, Daily

1. Sell short at a high price. ———————➤

2. Buy back at a low price. ———————➤

© 2014 NinjaTrader, LLC

180.00
175.00
170.00
165.00
160.00
155.00

Oct   Nov   Dec   14   Feb

Figure by Barry Burns

Figure 9-1: Shorting the market by selling at a high price and then buying back at a low price.

You may be wondering, how can you sell a stock before you buy it? It's actually not as difficult as it seems. To sell a stock that you don't own, for example, you must first borrow it. Your broker facilitates this process and may let you borrow a stock owned by another trader or, less frequently, owned by the broker himself.

When you're ready to exit your short position, you *cover the position* by buying back the stock you had shorted. In other words, selling before you buy really means you're borrowing the stock before you short sell it.

In this section, I look at the pros and cons of short trading so you can consider whether it's something you're interested in trying.

This discussion is meant to be a simple introduction, not an exhaustive education to fully prepare you for shorting the market. Before shorting the market, talk to your broker about the risks and rules of short selling and educate yourself on all the details. Also be aware that the rules for shorting stocks may be different for shorting futures, spot forex, or other markets. Talk to your broker for details.

Discovering what makes short trading so exciting

Selling first and then buying later (hopefully at a lower price) has several advantages, including the following:

- **Markets tend to go down faster than they go up.** This is because fear is a stronger emotion than greed. When people feel fear, they tend to exit their long positions quickly and massively. Markets can go into a free fall, and therefore it's generally possible to make money faster by short selling than by buying, at least for brief periods of time.

- **By being flexible enough to short sell, you open up your ability to make money in various market conditions.** When you're comfortable going short, you provide yourself more opportunities to make money.

- **Shorting options can provide a hedge against your long positions.**

  - *Options* are contracts that give the owner the right, but not the obligation, to buy or sell a stock at a given price before a certain time. They're much less expensive than buying the stock itself and, therefore, can act as a type of insurance policy against a stock position. Taking a short position on a stock with an option would actually involve buying a put option. That can seem a bit confusing because you have short exposure to the stock as the value of the put option increases as the stock price moves lower. The benefit is that you pay a small premium, which can be thought of as a deposit that allows you to sell the stock at a higher price if the stock moves down.

  - *Hedging* is like buying insurance. It's taking a trade that helps to offset losses you may take on a primary position.

Understanding the challenges of shorting the market

Like most things in the market, and in life, there are two sides to a coin. If you decide to incorporate short selling into your personal trading, it's important to be fully educated about all the implications.

Short selling also has several disadvantages you should seriously consider:

- ✔ **It may feel unnatural, and you may struggle wrapping your head around the concept.** It may be psychologically challenging and feel uncomfortable to you.

- ✔ **Going short is more expensive than going long.** When you short a stock, you're borrowing the stock and have to pay a fee, though nominal, for doing so.

- ✔ **Theoretically, short selling has unlimited risk.** If the market goes against you (by going up), there's no ceiling to how high the price can go.

- ✔ **It may feel unpatriotic to take a position against a business and/or the economy succeeding.** My own father, though a successful trader and investor, refused to short stocks for this very reason. He said that his conscience wouldn't allow him to participate in betting against any company or the economy.

- ✔ **Not all stocks are available for shorting, and some of those that are available aren't always available.** This reduces the universe of stocks available for you to trade.

- ✔ **Short selling must be done in a margin account.** It's up to you to decide whether you're comfortable trading with borrowed money.

- ✔ **If you're short a stock when the company pays dividends, you'll owe the dividend and it will be withdrawn from your account.** Remember, when you short a stock, you don't own it. You're borrowing it from your broker who still owns it, so he will want the dividend if you're holding the short position when the company issues dividends.

- ✔ **If a company spins off part of its operations, creating two companies, you could find yourself with a short position in both companies.** That could be a problem if you're not bearish on both companies.

Trend Trading to the Long Side

Trading to the long side or going long simply refers to buying the market first and then selling your market position later. The idea is to buy at a low price (relatively inexpensive price) and sell at a higher price to make a profit. In other words, "buy low, sell high." Most businesses trade to the long side. A business buys its products at wholesale, sells them to their customers at retail, and makes a profit on the spread. Figure 9-2 illustrates this concept.

GS, Daily

2. Sell at a high price. ──────────►

1. Buy at a low price.

© 2014 NinjaTrader, LLC

Figure 9-2: "Going long" means buying the market and selling later.

Figure by Barry Burns

The terms *buy* and *going long* aren't quite synonymous. *Going long* refers to taking a position where you take ownership of the stock because you're buying first and selling later. *Buying* a stock and *going long* are interchangeable if you buy the stock first. However, the term *buy* is a broader term than *going long* because it can also refer to buying a position that you've first shorted (see earlier section on shorting the market).

In this section, I talk about the benefits of trading to the long side as well as some risks associated with this practice.

Exploring the advantages of going long

Trading to the long side (buying an uptrend) is congruent with how most people think of trading and investing. Buying first and then selling later (hopefully at a higher price) has several advantages:

✓ **It's the order of most commerce and therefore is comfortable.** You don't have to overcome any psychological struggle with this concept.

✔ **Going long is less expensive than going short.** When you short a stock, you're borrowing the stock and have to pay a fee for doing so.

✔ **Buying has limited risk.** The farthest the market you buy can go down is to zero. Be aware that trading with leverage can increase that risk. (For more on leverage, see Chapter 16.)

✔ **Buying into the market, especially stocks, provides support for the company to thrive.** This is purely a matter of conscience that may or may not apply to you. Some people, like my dad, didn't feel right betting against the economy or any business.

✔ **Your profits theoretically have no limit because there's no price restriction on how high the market can go up.** This is in direct contradiction to short selling where your losses have no theoretical limit because there's no restriction to how high the market can go.

✔ **The trend of the stock market over its history has been to the upside.** Therefore, buying the market puts the long-term trend of the stock market on your side.

Being aware of the disadvantages of trading to the long side

Although trading to the long side has many advantages and is the way most companies do business, it also has some disadvantages, such as the following:

✔ **Markets tend to go up slower than they go down, so trading long is a slower way to make money.** Although the markets can definitely make dramatic moves to the upside at times, in general, markets fall faster than they rise.

✔ **If you trade only to the long side, you severely limit your ability to make money as a trader.** You won't be able to take advantage of downtrends and will have long periods when you won't be making money, which is opportunity lost.

Part III

Becoming a Top Trader with the Five-Energy Method

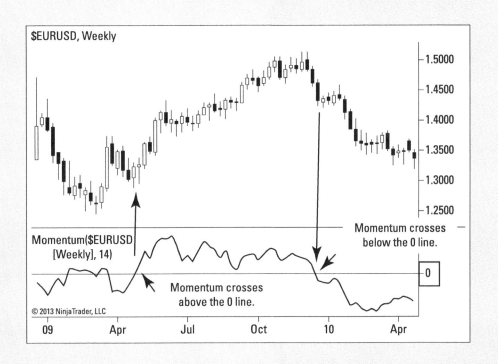

$EURUSD, Weekly

Momentum($EURUSD [Weekly], 14)

© 2013 NinjaTrader, LLC

Momentum crosses below the 0 line.

Momentum crosses above the 0 line.

0

09   Apr   Jul   Oct   10   Apr

In addition to following the strategies covered in this part, head to www.dummies.com/extras/trendtrading for a free article that provides tips for beating out other traders.

In this part . . .

- ✔ Enter a trend at just the right time with cycle timing tools.

- ✔ Enter a trend at just the right price with support and resistance indicators.

- ✔ Determine how strong a trend is by measuring its momentum.

- ✔ Increase your trade's profitability by measuring the scale of the trend.

- ✔ Combine the forces of each tool and strategy to become a top trader.

- ✔ See the five energies in action with real-life trading scenarios so you can apply them yourself profitably.

Chapter 10

Cycle Timing Tools: Finding the Best Time to Enter a Trend

In This Chapter:

▷ Navigating the "wiggle" of the trend

▷ Using the best cycle timing tool

▷ Looking for the final low or the final high

*I*n my work training traders, I find that one of their most common problems is timing the market. In fact, most traders I encounter don't have a solid education about how to time their entries and exits. When I look at their charts, I often see so many indicators that their charts are cluttered and confusing. However, even with all the various indicators they employ, they have no timing indicators or tools at all.

To be successful at trading, you have to create a methodology that establishes a probability scenario that favors you, which is what makes trading different than gambling. But a chart is a two-dimensional object. The right axis measures price, and the bottom axis measures time.

Traders who don't incorporate the element of time into their trading are neglecting fully 50 percent of the information on a chart. You can't develop a probability scenario when you ignore fully 50 percent of the vital information. (And what's more, many traders argue that time is actually even more important than price!)

The topic of time in trading is measured by market cycles, which is a major topic of study both in the markets and in other disciplines. In this chapter, I share how cycles can be used in trading to time your entries and exits in trending markets.

Trading the "Wiggle" of the Trend

Market movement becomes less mysterious and more understandable when you realize one simple fact: People move the markets. Therefore, the nature of the markets is the nature of people, or human nature. The markets don't move based on some magical, unknown principles, nor do they move randomly without any rhyme or reason.

The markets are an enormous auction place, and people's actions — their buying and selling — moves the markets. These actions are based on research but also on their feelings, beliefs, fears, and greed.

While studying in Chicago with one of my trading mentors, I was introduced to a concept that dramatically changed my trading forever. He told me, "Barry, retailers are often right but at the wrong time." Most people with even a small amount of trading experience can look at a chart and determine whether the market plotted on that chart is generally moving up or down. The problem is that stocks, futures, commodities, and currencies don't move in a straight line up or down. They wiggle up or wiggle down (see Figure 10-1).

Again, this reflects the nature of people who get excited then cautious, optimistic then fearful. It also mirrors the human experience of "three steps forward and two steps back."

AAPL, Daily

© 2013 NinjaTrader, LLC

Figure 10-1: Markets wiggle during their uptrends and downtrends.

Figure by Barry Burns

One of the problems with this wiggling is that it can create confusion as to the best time to enter the market. For example, if you buy a retrace in an uptrend and put your stop-loss order below that low of the retrace, you risk being stopped out as the market wiggles against you, making a temporary lower low before the market resumes its move in the direction of the uptrend.

Conversely, if you short a retrace in an uptrend and put your stop-loss order below the high of the retrace, you risk being stopped out if the market makes a higher high before continuing its downtrend, as illustrated in Figure 10-2.

ES 03-14, 3 Min

Figure 10-2: Knowing when to enter a trend is the difference between a winning trade and a losing trade.

© 2013 NinjaTrader, LLC

Figure by Barry Burns

Exploring the Stochastic Indicator as Your Cycle Timing Tool

To find the best time to enter a trade in the direction of the trend, you need an objective instrument that helps you measure cycles accurately.

Before I go any further, let me be very clear about my use of the term *best*. It certainly doesn't mean that you expect to develop a timing tool that's always right. No one can predict the future, and the famous market adage, "The market can do anything at any time," applies to cycles and timing as much as it does to any other aspect of trading. The best you can realistically hope for is to develop a tool that puts the odds on your side. It won't give you perfect certainty, but it can give you a probability scenario that favors you.

Over the years, I've tried many cycle indicators. Some of them are mathematically complex and impressive. Some of them are proprietary and expensive, to the tune of thousands of dollars. After much trial and error, I finally settled on a timing tool that's worked for me better than anything else. The irony is that it's not a cycle indicator at all! I use the *stochastic indicator,* created by Dr. George Lane.

In this section, I introduce you to this valuable indicator and explain how and why I use it as a cycle timing tool.

Realizing the best timing tool isn't a timing tool

The stochastic indicator is an oscillator that's actually designed to measure momentum, not cycles. More specifically, it measures the current closing price in relation to its price range over a defined period of time in the past. The most common period of defined past time is 14 bars.

The indicator assumes that markets with upward momentum tend to close near the highs and that markets with downward momentum tend to close near their lows. The indicator is a *bounded* indicator in that the mathematic formula of the indicator allows it to reach a maximum value of 100 and a minimum value of 0. In other words, the indicator never goes above a reading of 100 or below a reading of 0, no matter how much the market it's measuring moves up or down.

The stochastic indicator is comprised of two lines, identified in Figure 10-3:

- ✔ The %K line measures the value of the stochastic calculation. In Figure 10-3, %K is the thin line that moves faster.

- ✔ The %D line is a three-period exponential moving average of %K. In Figure 10-3, %D is the slower, thick line.

The indicator also has two horizontal lines that are usually placed at the values of 20 and 80, indicating oversold and overbought areas, respectively.

ES 03-14, 5 Min

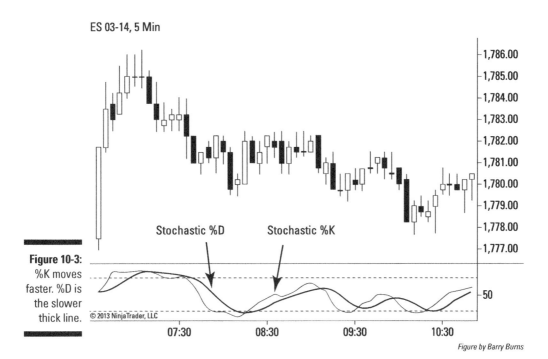

Figure 10-3:
%K moves
faster. %D is
the slower
thick line.

Figure by Barry Burns

You can get a sense of the cycles in the market by looking at the highs and lows of the oscillations of the indicator in Figure 10-3. The crossing of %K above and below %D also helps to visually identify the cycle highs and lows. However, if you study a large sample of market data and look at the indicator in relation to price movement, you'll notice that it's often a bit late. Also, in strongly trending markets, it doesn't locate as many cycle highs and lows as you may like.

Figure 10-4 provides an example of how the traditional settings of the stochastic indicator can produce few cycle high and low signals when the market is trending.

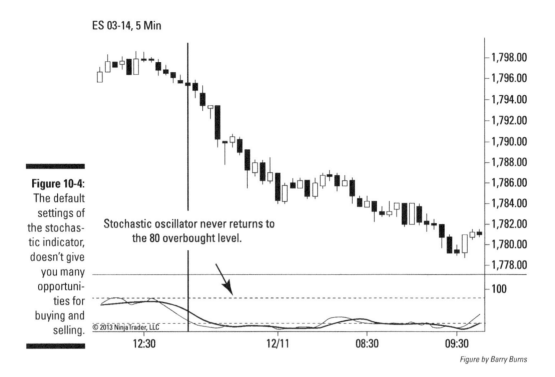

ES 03-14, 5 Min

Stochastic oscillator never returns to
the 80 overbought level.

© 2013 NinjaTrader, LLC

Figure 10-4:
The default
settings of
the stochas-
tic indicator,
doesn't give
you many
opportuni-
ties for
buying and
selling.

Figure by Barry Burns

Optimizing the timing tool for optimal entries

The solution to turning the stochastic oscillator into a cycle indicator that
gives you more opportunities to buy and sell is to simply shorten the time it
measures by changing the inputs of the indicator. The default settings you have
on your charting software may vary. Here are the settings I personally use:

- ✔ Period D (%D): 3
- ✔ Period K (%K): 5
- ✔ Smoothing (Average): 2

As Figure 10-5 demonstrates, the result of these changes is to simply create
more highs and lows on the indicator so that instead of measuring long-term
momentum, the indicator measures short-term oscillations in the market.

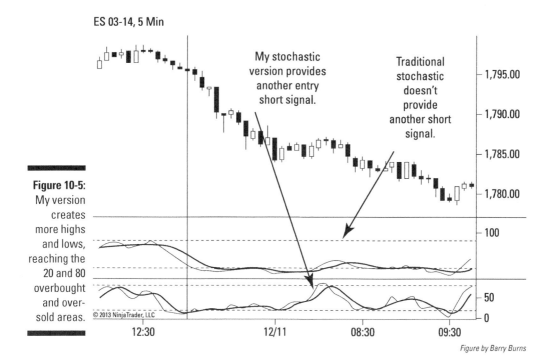

Figure 10-5: My version creates more highs and lows, reaching the 20 and 80 overbought and over-sold areas.

Figure by Barry Burns

Shortening the parameters of the indicator clearly creates more instances where the indicator reaches overbought and oversold levels, thus potentially providing more buy and sell signals.

Finding the Final Low or the Final High for the Best Entry

Why use the stochastic indicator to measure cycles when its formula was designed to measure momentum? Ah, now for the genius of why this momentum indicator works so much better than the indicators I've tried that were designed to measure cycles!

Even people with no knowledge of trading or investing have likely heard the phrase *buy low, sell high.* The key to timing the market profitably is to buy a cycle low in an uptrend or short a cycle high in a downtrend. The problem is how to determine, with high probability, that you're entering on the final cycle high or the final cycle low so that the market doesn't turn around and stop you out.

Although nothing can truly predict the future of the market, before the market turns off of highs and lows, the market often slows down before actually turning. This is called *momentum shift.* In this way, momentum often leads price. You can see this in momentum indicators turning down, while price is still moving up, or conversely, momentum indicators turning up while price is still moving down.

In this way, the stochastic indicator can often help you find the final high or low with extreme high probability.

✓ **Final low:** When attempting to trade an uptrend, you want to buy a cycle low, but you want to get the lowest low before the market continues its move up, after a retrace (wiggle) against the trend. To do this with high probability, look for a momentum shift on the stochastic indicator — a divergence between price and %K. As shown in the example in Figure 10-6, you see a lower low on price but a higher low on %K.

USB, Daily

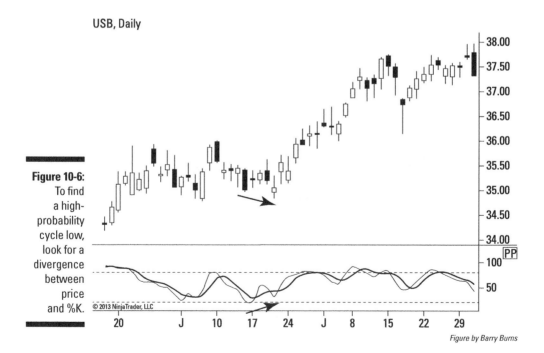

Figure 10-6: To find a high-probability cycle low, look for a divergence between price and %K.

© 2013 NinjaTrader, LLC

Figure by Barry Burns

✔ **Final high:** When attempting to trade a downtrend, you want to short a cycle high, but you want to get the highest high before the market continues its down move, after a retrace (wiggle) against the trend. To do this with high probability, look for a momentum shift on the stochastic indicator. You see a higher high on price but a lower high on %K, as illustrated in Figure 10-7.

GS, Weekly

Figure 10-7:
To find
a high-
probability
cycle high,
look for a
divergence
between
price
and %K.

© 2013 NinjaTrader, LLC

Figure by Barry Burns

Not every cycle low or high has such a divergence pattern on the stochastic indicator, but when you do see them, know that they're high-probability signals.

This alone doesn't make a great trade. Cycles give you information only about timing. They don't give you information about direction (trend does that of course) or how far you expect a move to follow through after you get in (more on that in Chapter 12).

My father's last lesson: The secret of timing

My father was an avid trader. It was his passion in life. He was my first teacher, and trading was a passion we shared our entire lives together.

He was a wonderful father and, fortunately, was strong in mind and body until close to the end of his life. I had the honor of being at his side during his final days, holding his hand, telling him how much I loved him, and thanking him for all he had done for me.

While I was there by my dad's side, I watched the heart monitor for signs of strengthening or weakening. As I watched, I noticed it making the same type of oscillations as in cycle indicators. The heart monitor was measuring something more important than market cycles, though. It was measuring the cycles created by the beating of my dad's heart leading to the circulation of the blood through his body. At times, it was irregular, and just as I thought it would go from a high to a low, it would stay high. But over time, I noticed that there was nearly always a sign that it was ready to head back down — a cycle pattern similar to the divergence on the stochastic indicator.

Even though my dad couldn't talk to me those last few days, he still taught me a valuable lesson about cycles. His last market lesson to me. Thanks, Dad.

Chapter 11

Support and Resistance: Figuring Out the Best Price to Enter a Trend

In This Chapter

▶ Seeing the significance of support and resistance levels

▶ Monitoring previous major highs and lows

▶ Fulfilling prophecy with Fibonacci levels

▶ Mastering floor trader pivots

▶ Watching the waves

▶ Responding to big round numbers

Support and resistance levels are like floors and ceilings in the market. They are price levels at which market participants feel the market will have a difficult time rising above or going below.

For these reasons, support and resistance levels are good price zones to consider entering the market or taking profits.

In this chapter, I share with you some of the most common support and resistance levels used by the trading community.

Grasping the Importance of Support and Resistance Levels in Trading

Support and resistance levels are simply prices at which the people trading the market feel that the market likely won't pass through easily. *Support levels* are prices that traders feel the market is unlikely to go below. *Resistance levels* are prices that traders feel the market is unlikely to go above.

What makes these levels work? The answer to that is quite simple. The market is an auction place, and price moves based on the mass beliefs that the people trading the market put into action.

Traders learn about and therefore watch several types of support and resistance levels. Mass psychology comes into play, and the majority of people watch the market approaching a well-known support or resistance level. En mass, they look to either exit their current position into that level or enter a new position as the market bounces off that level.

Traders use these levels in the following ways:

- ✓ **Support:**
  - Buy at a support level.
  - Take profits at a support level if you've been short.
- ✓ **Resistance:**
  - Short at a resistance level.
  - Take profits at a resistance level if you've been long.

These levels are drawn as lines on your chart. However, every advanced trader knows that those lines aren't really lines — they're zones! Don't expect the market to go up or down and stop exactly at a support or resistance line and bounce off of it. The market isn't that neat and tidy. In fact, the market is pretty darn messy. So be realistic and understand that the price bars won't normally make a high or low precisely at the support or resistance line. Most of the time, the bars go a little beyond them or stop a little before them.

Closely Watching Previous Major Highs and Lows

Previous major highs and lows are one of the most common and reliable support/resistance levels. They work because they're visible without traders having to use any particular indicator. They're obvious to everyone looking at a price chart. Support/resistance levels work because the masses of people trading the market respond to them.

A *major* previous price high or low is simply one that stands out so prominently on a chart that almost anyone looking at it sees it as a significant high or low (see Figure 11-1). There's no objective method for identifying it.

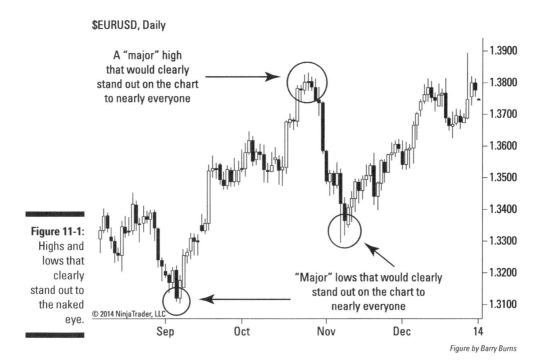

$EURUSD, Daily

A "major" high that would clearly stand out on the chart to nearly everyone

Figure 11-1: Highs and lows that clearly stand out to the naked eye.

© 2014 NinjaTrader, LLC

"Major" lows that would clearly stand out on the chart to nearly everyone

Figure by Barry Burns

The fact that the masses of traders see the major highs and lows makes them significant. When the market approaches those price levels, traders see that the market wasn't able to go higher or lower than that level and are concerned that such levels represent prices that are too high/low for other traders to be interested.

Figure 11-2 illustrates how the market can approach a clearly visible previous high and find resistance. Traders will often sell at such a level because they realize the market participants previously felt that price level was too high and, therefore, may again be unsustainable. The previous high may provide long-term or short-term resistance.

For day traders, another pair of major support/resistance levels is the previous day's high and low. You should always have those levels drawn on your charts because the vast majority of other traders watch them and therefore often buy or sell at those levels.

$EURUSD, Daily

Figure 11-2: The market finds resistance at a clearly visible previous high.

© 2014 NinjaTrader, LLC

Figure by Barry Burns

Mastering Mathematical Wizardry: Fibonacci Levels

Fibonacci numbers are commonly used in trading for support/resistance levels. Some traders believe that these levels work in trading because they're part of the very fabric of nature. Others believe they work because so many traders use them that they function as a "self-fulfilling prophecy."

Fibonacci levels are extremely popular among traders. Whether you believe in their "mystical powers," the fact that traders commonly use them means that they have at the very least a self-fulfilling function. And the markets respond to them, so you should incorporate them into your trading, too.

Defining Fibonacci levels

Fibonacci numbers are named after Leonardo of Pisa who was known as "Fibonacci" (meaning "son of Bonaccio"). He introduced these numbers to the West in 1202; however, they were used in India long before that.

Fibonacci numbers are a sequence of numbers beginning with 1, and then each subsequent number is the sum of the previous two. For example:

$$1 + 1 = 2$$
$$1 + 2 = 3$$
$$2 + 3 = 5$$
$$3 + 5 = 8$$
$$5 + 8 = 13$$
$$8 + 13 = 21$$
$$13 + 21 = 34$$

The sum of each equation is a Fibonacci number in the sequence: 1, 2, 3, 5, 8, 13, and so on.

In trading, Fibonacci ratios are most commonly used, and the most important of these is the *golden ratio,* which is derived by noticing that each number in the Fibonacci sequence is approximately 1.618 times greater than the preceding number. For example:

$$8/5 = 1.6$$
$$13/8 = 1.625$$
$$21/13 = 1.615$$
$$34/21 = 1.619$$

You can find this golden ratio in the structure of many items of nature, from the branches in trees, to veins in leaves, to pedals on flowers, to the formation of the nautilus shell.

Discovering how Fibonacci levels work

For centuries, Fibonacci levels have been used significantly in mathematics, music, and architecture. Some traders are absolutely convinced that Fibonacci numbers have an almost magical power to them. The golden ratio is the primary but not the only ratio used in trading. The other common ratios used are

0

23.6

38.2

50 (not actually a Fibonacci ratio but commonly used by traders)

61.8

76.4 (some traders use 78.6 instead)

100

Traders use these ratios as percentages that the market retraces against the trend, generally as levels at which they consider entering a trade in the direction of the trend. To use your Fibonacci retracements tools in your charting software, start with a significant high, and then drag the tool to a significant low (or vice versa if the market has recently made a large move up). See Figure 11-3.

Figure 11-3: Use significant highs and lows for the drawing of your Fibonacci retracements.

© 2014 NinjaTrader, LLC

Figure by Barry Burns

The tool plots the Fibonacci retracement ratios. The Fibonacci retracement ratios are common price levels at which the market stops retracing against the trend and continues back in the direction of the trend. The tool draws horizontal lines across the chart, indicating the price levels where the market will have retraced 23.6 percent, 38.2 percent, 50 percent, 61.8 percent, 76.4 percent, or 100 percent of the price move from the high to the low you used for your Fibonacci tool. You can see these ratios in Figure 11-4.

STI, Daily

© 2014 NinjaTrader, LLC

Figure 11-4: Fibonacci retracement ratios.

Figure by Barry Burns

The exact method of using the Fibonacci retracements tool varies depending on the charting software you're using. Refer to your software's manual, help files, or support desk for details on how to use the tool on your charts.

Using Floor Trader Pivots Like the Pros

Floor trader pivots are support/resistance levels that floor traders have used in the pits of the exchanges for many years. They define an equilibrium point (considered a neutral market) called the *pivot point* or *central pivot.*

> ✔ The market is considered bullish when it's *above* the central pivot.
>
> ✔ The market is considered bearish when it's *below* the central pivot.

Because the floor traders use these levels, they've become popular among people who trade off the floor, attempting to follow the same techniques used by the professionals trading on the floors of the exchanges.

Calculating floor trader pivots

The most popular method for calculating floor trader pivots is the original formula. The formula uses the previous day's high, low, and close to calculate the central pivot (neutral area for the market):

> Central pivot = (High + Low + Close)/3

Three levels of resistance are plotted above the central pivot with the notations of R1, R2, and R3. And three levels of support are plotted below the central pivot with the notations of S1, S2, and S3.

You then calculate these support/resistance levels based on the following formulas:

> R1 = 2(Central pivot) – Yesterday's low
>
> R2 = Central pivot + (Yesterday's high – Yesterday's low)
>
> R3 = Central Pivot + 2(Yesterday's high – Yesterday's low)
>
> S1 = 2(Central pivot) – Yesterday's high
>
> S2 = Central pivot – (Yesterday's high – Yesterday's low)
>
> S3 = Central pivot – 2(Yesterday's high – Yesterday's low)

Don't worry if you have trouble understanding how to calculate the floor trader pivots. You'll never have to do the calculations manually. You can find plenty of websites that have floor trader pivot calculators to do the math for you; simply type "floor trader pivot point calculator" into your favorite Internet search engine. In addition, many charting software programs have floor trader pivot indicators that automatically draw the levels when applied to your charts.

Other formulas for calculating pivots exist. Some of them have been created by reputable traders and may be useful. However, using the traditional calculation is best simply because it's the one used by most traders. Market movements are often caused in response to what the masses see.

Understanding how and why floor trader pivots work

In Figure 11-5, you can get a feel for how the central pivot is the neutral point, the pivot levels above it (R1, R2, R3) provide resistance, and the pivot levels below it (S1, S2, S3) provide support.

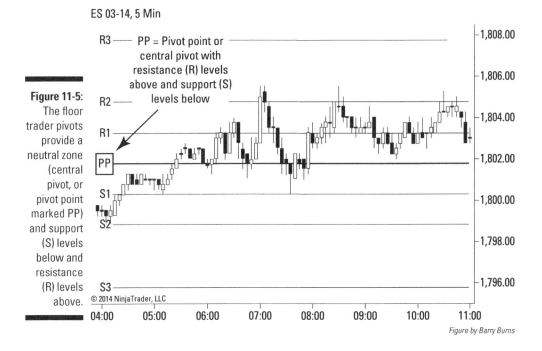

ES 03-14, 5 Min

Figure 11-5: The floor trader pivots provide a neutral zone (central pivot, or pivot point marked PP) and support (S) levels below and resistance (R) levels above.

© 2014 NinjaTrader, LLC

Figure by Barry Burns

This example is fairly typical. Some days, the market stays between S1 and R1. Such days are considered neutral and directionless. They're also characterized by low volatility and don't provide great opportunities for large profits because the range of the market is limited.

When the market gets above/below one of the floor trader pivots, the next floor trader pivot is often used as the next profit target.

Markets rarely break above R2 or below S2. When they do, the market is considered to be in an extremely bullish or bearish mode, respectively.

Riding Wave and Cycle Highs and Lows

You find wave and cycle highs and lows with the cycle indicator (which I describe in detail in Chapter 10). The cycle indicator defines the highs and lows and shows that they're significant; they draw a line in the sand as to whether the market is progressing up or down as the market wiggles within its trend. Figure 11-6 is an example of how the cycle indicator helps locate cycle highs and lows in price bar formations.

Figure 11-6:
Find cycle highs and lows with the objective help of the cycle indicator instead of depending on discretionary visual observation.

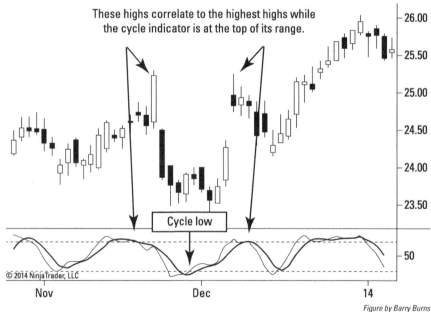

INTC, Daily

These highs correlate to the highest highs while the cycle indicator is at the top of its range.

Cycle low

© 2014 NinjaTrader, LLC

Nov   Dec   14

Figure by Barry Burns

In an ideal uptrend, each cycle high is higher than the previous cycle high. In an ideal downtrend, each cycle low is lower than the previous cycle low.

Unfortunately, markets aren't this neat and tidy. Even though not every cycle high/low follows this pattern, a good uptrend follows this pattern with most cycle highs/lows.

Every uptrend is a series of broken resistance levels. Every downtrend is a series of broken support levels. This leads to the concept of waves. Waves in an uptrend are cycle highs that make a higher high than the previous wave high (see Figure 11-7). A wave low in an uptrend is simply the lowest cycle low between the two wave highs. Waves in a downtrend are cycle lows that make lower lows than the previous wave low (see Figure 11-8). Wave highs in a downtrend are simply the highest cycle high between two wave lows.

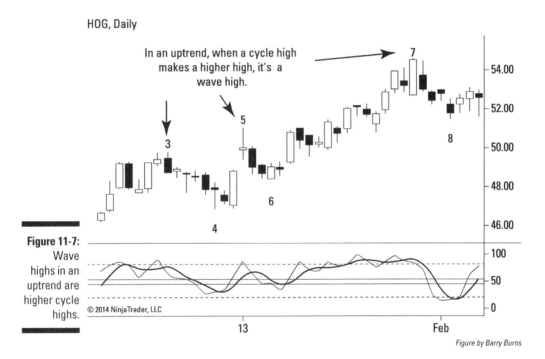

HOG, Daily

In an uptrend, when a cycle high makes a higher high, it's a wave high.

Figure 11-7:
Wave highs in an uptrend are higher cycle highs.

© 2014 NinjaTrader, LLC

Figure by Barry Burns

Cycle highs and lows produce visible highs and lows in the fluctuation of the market wiggling up and down. Other traders can see these highs and lows and may respond to them as support/resistance levels (see Figure 11-9). The more traders see them, the more likely those levels are to provide support and resistance as traders either buy/sell off of them or take profits into them.

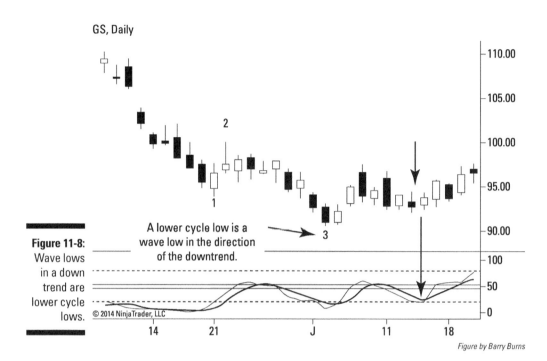

GS, Daily

A lower cycle low is a wave low in the direction of the downtrend.

Figure 11-8:
Wave lows in a down trend are lower cycle lows.

© 2014 NinjaTrader, LLC

Figure by Barry Burns

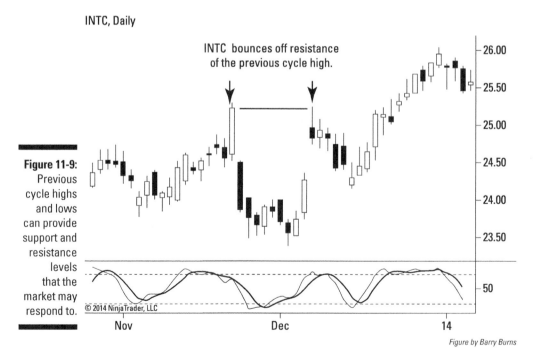

INTC, Daily

INTC bounces off resistance of the previous cycle high.

Figure 11-9:
Previous cycle highs and lows can provide support and resistance levels that the market may respond to.

© 2014 NinjaTrader, LLC

Figure by Barry Burns

This is similar to the major highs and lows described in the section "Closely Watching Previous Major Highs and Lows," earlier in this chapter. The difference is now you have an objective tool for identifying significant highs and lows instead of just using your visual discretion to find the highs and lows that stand out on a chart. The following rules then become evident:

- ✔ Waves are more likely to provide support/resistance because they're more visually prominent on the charts.

- ✔ Waves and cycles on longer-term time frames are more likely to provide support/resistance because those who trade long-term and short-term charts alike will see them.

Wave and cycle support/resistance work equally well for any market you may be trading. They're also applicable to day trading, swing trading, and investing time frames.

Remembering that People Like Big, Round Numbers (And Why You Should, Too)

People are attracted to round numbers. Nothing is innately significant about them for support/resistance in trading; their significance lies only in the fact that the masses of traders respond to them. For this reason, you should be aware that whatever market you're trading will likely respond to big round numbers as at least temporary support or resistance. Figure 11-10 shows an example of AAPL, and Figure 11-11 shows an example of GOOG finding resistance at big, round numbers.

Don't expect the market to respect the exact line you draw as support and resistance levels. The markets aren't as neat, tidy, or generous as that. Support and resistance levels are price zones, or areas. It is perfectly normal, in fact typical, for price bars to go a bit above or below any support or resistance level.

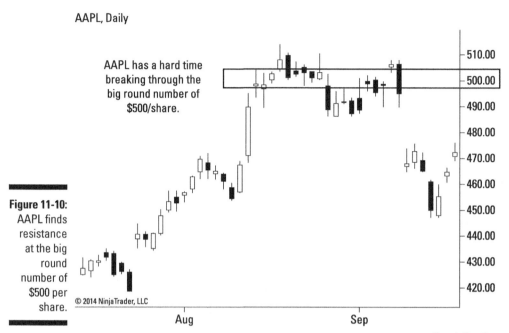

AAPL, Daily

AAPL has a hard time breaking through the big round number of $500/share.

Figure 11-10: AAPL finds resistance at the big round number of $500 per share.

© 2014 NinjaTrader, LLC

Aug   Sep

Figure by Barry Burns

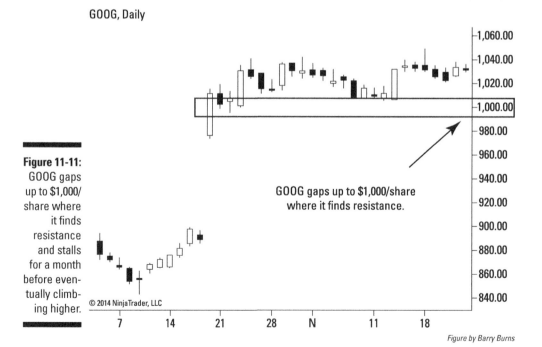

GOOG, Daily

Figure 11-11: GOOG gaps up to $1,000/share where it finds resistance and stalls for a month before eventually climbing higher.

GOOG gaps up to $1,000/share where it finds resistance.

© 2014 NinjaTrader, LLC

7   14   21   28   N   11   18

Figure by Barry Burns

Knowing That 52-Week Highs Are On Everyone's Radar

The highest and lowest prices that a market has traded in the previous 52 weeks are extremely popular support/resistance levels watched by traders and investors. These price levels are viewed as significant because they represent new territory that the market hasn't seen for an entire year.

Most investors and traders consider it a bullish signal if a stock breaks its 52-week high, and this is the most common strategy using these support/resistance levels.

Like most things in trading, there are always the contrarians. These traders look to trade a failure of the more traditional signal that breaking a 52-week high is a bullish signal.

Another approach is to buy off the 52-week low. This is a value trader's approach based on the idea that the stock hasn't been so inexpensive for a year and must, therefore, be a good deal. The problem is that stocks are often priced low because the companies behind the stocks are having significant problems.

Both strategies — buying the breakout of the support/resistance levels or fading the breakout — can be successful. The simple fact that the stock reaches a 52-week high or low doesn't provide enough information to determine whether the stock will break those levels or bounce off them.

Be sure to do additional research, especially with regard to the momentum of the move at the 52-week high/low and also the fundamentals of the company. It is wise, though, to market those levels on your charts because the majority of market participants watch them, and you can expect significant reaction at those levels in one direction or the other.

Do support and resistance levels really work?

Anyone who has traded for even a short time, utilizing support and resistance levels, knows that sometimes the market responds to them, and sometimes it doesn't. Looking at support/ resistance levels alone on a chart doesn't give any indication of which levels stop the market from moving and which levels the market will simply ignore.

One of the questions I receive most often from traders is, "How do I know which support/ resistance levels the market will bounce off and which ones the market will slice right through?" The answer is, "By just looking at support/resistance levels, you don't know which ones the market will bounce off and which ones it will ignore."

You'll notice in the following figure that AUD/ JPY bounces off some support/resistance levels and slices right through others.

To help determine which support/resistance levels the market will bounce off, you look for the confluence of a cycle high or low at a support/resistance level. In fact, you use all five energies together to determine which support/ resistance levels the market will respect. (You can find out more about that in Chapter 14.)

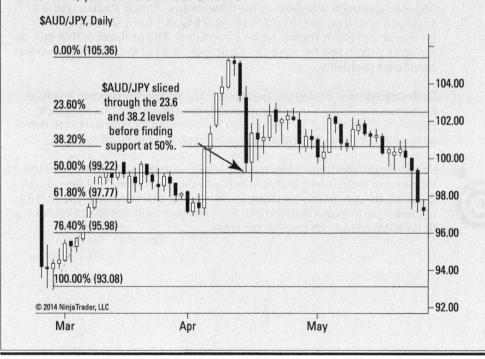

$AUD/JPY, Daily

$AUD/JPY sliced through the 23.6 and 38.2 levels before finding support at 50%.

0.00% (105.36)
23.60%
38.20%
50.00% (99.22)
61.80% (97.77)
76.40% (95.98)
100.00% (93.08)

© 2014 NinjaTrader, LLC

Chapter 12

Using Momentum Indicators to Test the Strength of a Trend

A trend in the market isn't a short-term move but rather an intermediate or long-term move up or down. A trend is easy to determine on a historical chart after the fact, but in the moment-by-moment activity of trading, you have to evaluate at the time you're entering a trade whether you expect the market to continue to move in the direction it's been trending.

This, of course, raises the question, "How can you determine whether the market will continue in the direction of the trend after you enter, or if it will change direction right after you get in?" One answer to that question is to look at momentum. Generally, in trading, the term *momentum* means price acceleration. Investopedia.com defines *momentum* as "the rate of acceleration of a security's price or volume."

Think of momentum as the strength of the trend. When you trade in the direction of the trend, you want to know whether it's a strong trend (in which case you'd expect the market to continue in the direction of the trend) or a weak trend (in which case you'd expect the trend to soon falter). Momentum helps determine whether the trend is strong or weak. You want to trade only strong trends and not weak trends. Therefore, it's always a good idea to evaluate the momentum of the market before taking a trade.

Many tools (often called *indicators*) measure the momentum of a market. In this chapter, I explore three popular indicators of momentum: the momentum indicator, the relative strength index (RSI), and the moving average convergence-divergence (MACD) indicator.

Another way to think about momentum

Imagine a futuristic TV game show where you're sitting at home in front of your TV, watching a bus driving down the city streets. The bus is packed with people yelling at the driver trying to tell him which way to go next. Your job is to predict where the bus is going and type your predictions into a computer one block before the bus gets there.

Is it an impossible task? Almost! But some things could make it easier. Some events could put the odds on your side — even if just for a moment.

For example, if the driver stopped at a traffic light in the right lane and had his right-turn signal blinking, that would be a reasonable indicator that the bus is about to turn right. You could type into your computer that the bus will turn right here and go on at least to the next cross street.

Of course, the bus driver could go straight anyway (ever been behind a driver who's had his turn signal on for blocks without turning?), but the odds are that when people activate their turn signal, they turn in the direction of that signal.

If the driver is crossing an intersection and you can see up ahead that the traffic light at the next intersection is yellow and about to turn red, you could type into your computer that the bus will stop at the next light. Will you be correct? The driver could speed right through the red light without stopping, and that does happen occasionally, but the odds are that the bus will stop at the next light. Even a police car with sirens blaring will slow down at red lights.

If the bus is speeding north (the direction or *trend* of the car) on the street at 65 miles per hour (the speed or *momentum* of the car), the odds are against it being able to stop on a dime at the next intersection. It's pretty safe to say that it would be an exception to the rule and not the driver's intention to stop that soon.

This example illustrates how strong momentum puts the odds on your side that the trend will continue. In trading, if you get into a trend that has strong momentum behind it, you have a high-probability trade that the trend will continue after you enter your position instead of coming to an end immediately after you place your trade.

The Traditional Momentum Indicator

The most obvious indicator for measuring momentum for many traders is the aptly named *momentum indicator*. It simply measures the amount that a market's price has changed (often referred to as *rate of change*) over a given period of time, which you designate (14 bars is a common time period). Another way to express the momentum indicator is that it measures the current bar's closing price to a specific number of previous closing prices (such as the closing prices of the last 14 bars) and gives a reading as to how fast price is moving in a direction.

Because momentum measures the speed (or strength) of a market's movement, the price bars on a chart can continue to move up (indicating an uptrend), while the momentum indicator can move down if the speed (momentum) decreases. This shows that although the trend is still up, it's weakening and may soon be coming to an end.

Following are three common ways of using the momentum indicator to confirm a strong trend for entry and also to determine when a trend is weakening to exit a trade:

✓ Stay with an uptrend as long as the momentum indicator remains above 0, and exit the trade when the indicator drops back below 0. Figure 12-1 shows what the chart looks like when the momentum crosses 0.

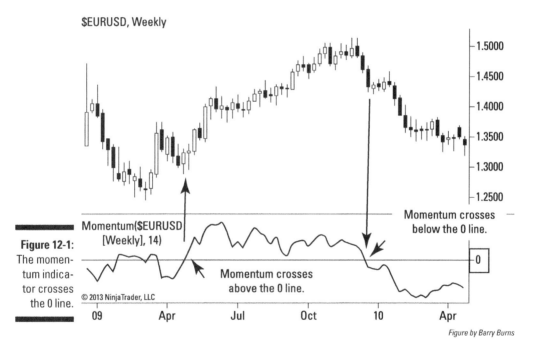

Figure 12-1: The momentum indicator crosses the 0 line.

Figure by Barry Burns

✓ Draw a trend line on the momentum indicator line, and exit your trade when the trend line on the indicator is broken. See Figure 12-2 for an example.

✓ Exit your trend trade when you see a divergence between price and the momentum indicator line, as in Figure 12-3.There's a higher high on price and a lower high on the indicator.

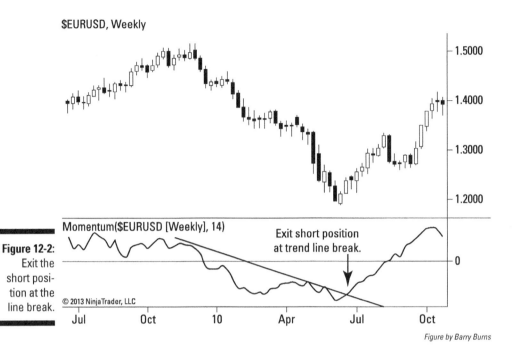

$EURUSD, Weekly

Momentum($EURUSD [Weekly], 14)

Exit short position
at trend line break.

© 2013 NinjaTrader, LLC

Figure 12-2:
Exit the
short posi-
tion at the
line break.

Jul   Oct   10   Apr   Jul   Oct

Figure by Barry Burns

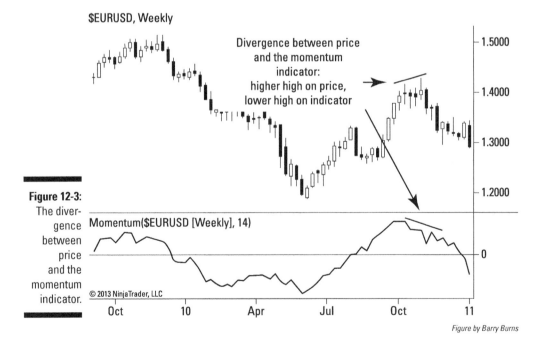

$EURUSD, Weekly

Divergence between price
and the momentum
indicator:
higher high on price,
lower high on indicator

Momentum($EURUSD [Weekly], 14)

© 2013 NinjaTrader, LLC

Figure 12-3:
The diver-
gence
between
price
and the
momentum
indicator.

Oct   10   Apr   Jul   Oct   11

Figure by Barry Burns

The Relative Strength Index (RSI)

The *relative strength index* (RSI) is an indicator that compares upward and downward movements in closing price over a period of time of your choice (commonly 14 bars). As with any indicator, traders use the RSI in many ways. One of the most typical ways is to go long when RSI moves below a value of 40 and then rises above it, as shown in Figure 12-4.

ES 12-13, 5 Min

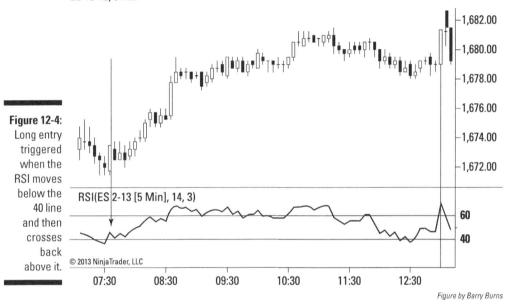

Figure 12-4: Long entry triggered when the RSI moves below the 40 line and then crosses back above it.

© 2013 NinjaTrader, LLC

Figure by Barry Burns

In a downtrend, a short signal is when RSI moves above 60 and then moves back below it, as shown in Figure 12-5.

J. Welles Wilder Jr. developed the RSI and explains it in his book *New Concepts in Technical Trading Systems* (Trend Research). It's a *wild* read, and if you're interested in trends, I suggest you give it a look.

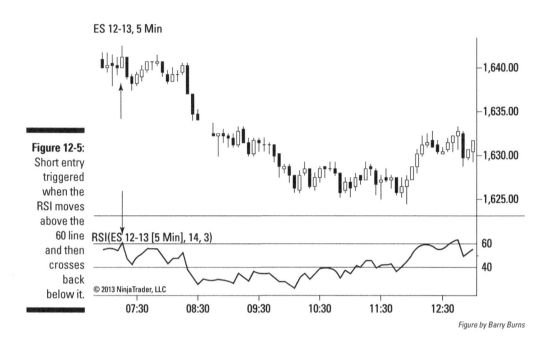

Figure 12-5: Short entry triggered when the RSI moves above the 60 line and then crosses back below it.

Figure by Barry Burns

The Moving Average Convergence-Divergence (MACD) Indicator

The MACD indicator, created by George Appel, is aptly named the *moving average convergence-divergence indicator* because it measures how much two moving averages are moving apart from or toward each other.

The traditional MACD indicator has three plots, which you can see in Figure 12-6:

✓ **The MACD line:** This line simply measures the difference between two moving averages. It's traditionally calculated by subtracting the 26-period exponential moving average (EMA) from the 12-period EMA.

   Note: I mostly look at the MACD line because I relate it to both the cycles of the market and the waves of price action.

✔ **The signal line:** The signal line is a nine-period moving average of the MACD line.

✔ **The histogram:** This measures the distance between the MACD line and the signal line.

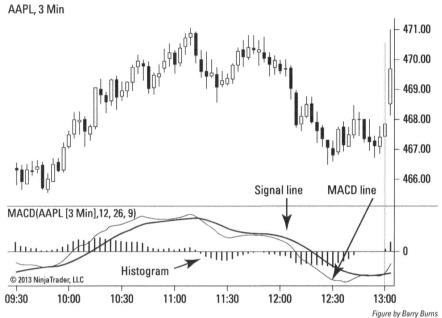

AAPL, 3 Min

MACD(AAPL [3 Min],12, 26, 9)

Signal line   MACD line

Histogram

© 2013 NinjaTrader, LLC

Figure 12-6:
The three components of the MACD indicator are the MACD line, the signal line, and the histogram.

Figure by Barry Burns

When the two moving averages are moving farther apart from each other and down, the MACD line moves down (away from 0). This movement indicates momentum to the downside. When the two moving averages are moving farther apart from each other and up, the MACD line moves up (away from 0). This movement indicates momentum to the upside. Figure 12-7 shows both the downside and upside momentums.

When the two moving averages are moving toward each other and down, the MACD line moves down toward 0. This movement indicates that momentum is slowing or reversing because the spread between the two moving averages is narrowing. When the two moving averages are moving toward each other and up, the MACD line moves up toward 0. This movement indicates that momentum is slowing or reversing because the spread between the two moving averages is narrowing. You can see the slowing or reversing of momentum in Figure 12-8.

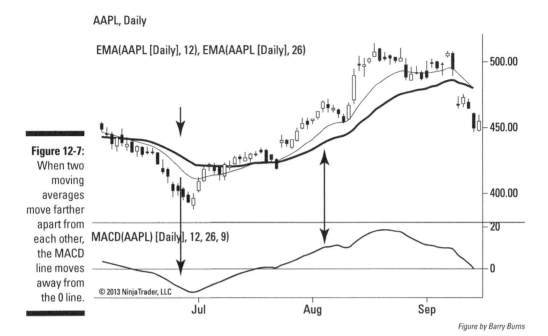

Figure 12-7: When two moving averages move farther apart from each other, the MACD line moves away from the 0 line.

Figure by Barry Burns

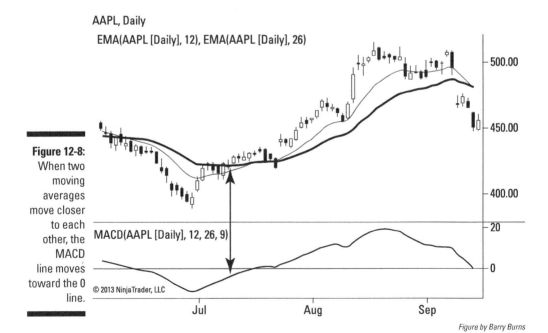

Figure 12-8: When two moving averages move closer to each other, the MACD line moves toward the 0 line.

Figure by Barry Burns

When the two moving averages cross, the MACD line is at a value of 0 because there's no distance between the two moving averages. You can see the two moving averages crossing (and the MACD line going to a value of 0 at the same time) in Figure 12-9.

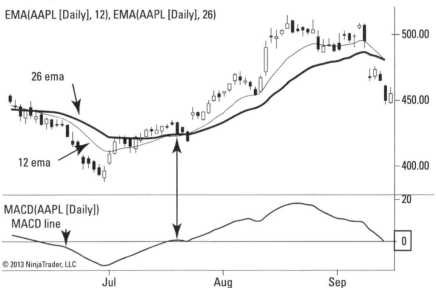

AAPL, Daily

EMA(AAPL [Daily], 12), EMA(AAPL [Daily], 26)

26 ema

12 ema

MACD(AAPL [Daily])
MACD line

© 2013 NinjaTrader, LLC

Figure 12-9: When the two moving averages cross, the MACD line goes to 0.

Figure by Barry Burns

So how do you use the MACD indicator in your trading?

✔ When the trend is up:

  • If the MACD line holds above the 0 line on the retrace in the trend (see Figure 12-10), consider the trend to be strong.

  • If the MACD line returns to the 0 line or below on the retrace in the trend (see Figure 12-11), consider the trend to be weak.

✔ When the trend is down:

  • If the MACD line holds below the 0 line on the retrace in the trend (see Figure 12-12), consider the trend to be strong.

  • If the MACD line returns to the 0 line or above on the retrace in the trend (see Figure 12-13), consider the trend to be weak.

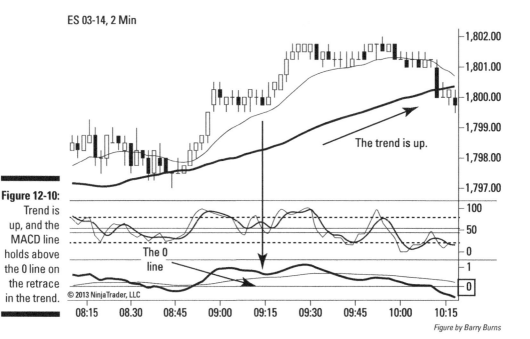

ES 03-14, 2 Min

Figure 12-10:
Trend is
up, and the
MACD line
holds above
the 0 line on
the retrace
in the trend.

The 0
line

© 2013 NinjaTrader, LLC

The trend is up.

Figure by Barry Burns

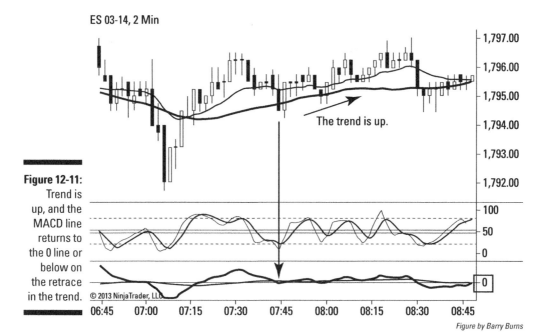

ES 03-14, 2 Min

Figure 12-11:
Trend is
up, and the
MACD line
returns to
the 0 line or
below on
the retrace
in the trend.

© 2013 NinjaTrader, LLC

The trend is up.

Figure by Barry Burns

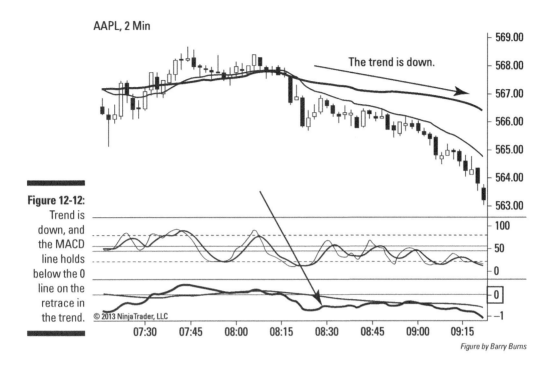

AAPL, 2 Min

The trend is down.

Figure 12-12:
Trend is
down, and
the MACD
line holds
below the 0
line on the
retrace in
the trend.

© 2013 NinjaTrader, LLC

Figure by Barry Burns

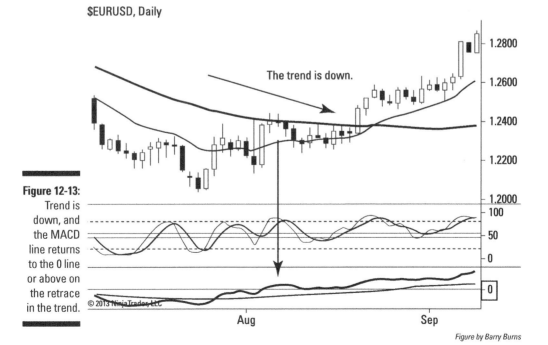

$EURUSD, Daily

The trend is down.

Figure 12-13:
Trend is
down, and
the MACD
line returns
to the 0 line
or above on
the retrace
in the trend.

© 2013 NinjaTrader, LLC

Figure by Barry Burns

Should you ever take a trade that doesn't have strong momentum? The short answer is "yes." If at least four of the five energies support the trade (see Chapter 14 for more on supporting the trade), the energy of momentum isn't always required. You also don't need momentum to support a trend when the market makes an *ABC complex retrace* against the trend.

A complex retrace consists of several cycle highs and lows that don't make higher highs in an uptrend or lower lows in a downtrend. Because a complex retrace against the trend lasts longer than a simple retrace, momentum commonly subsides during the retrace. However, the ABC complex retrace is a common and popular pattern among professional traders. Therefore, even though momentum isn't maintained in the direction of the trend, such chart patterns often resolve into a continuation in the direction of the trend, as you can see in Figure 12-14.

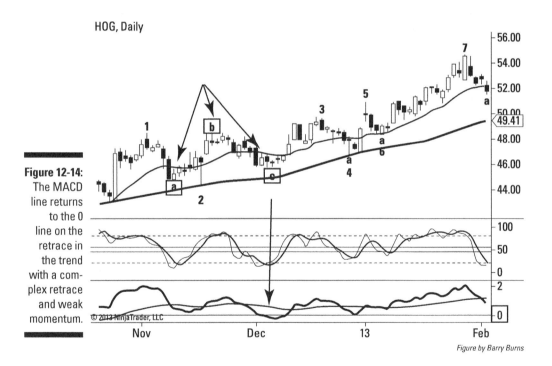

Figure 12-14: The MACD line returns to the 0 line on the retrace in the trend with a complex retrace and weak momentum.

Figure by Barry Burns

Chapter 13

Scale: Confirming the Trade on a Longer Time Interval

*T*he concept of looking at the same thing on different scales has revealed many secrets. The world of science has opened dramatically with the invention and continued improvement of the telescope, which has revealed worlds we never knew existed. Likewise, looking at stocks, futures, and forex on different scales can help reveal things in those markets that would otherwise remain unknown.

Trading multiple time frames of the same market is a very common practice among traders. For example, traders often base their trading on a daily chart (where each bar represents the movement of the market during one trading day) and then also look at a weekly chart of the same market. Trading multiple time frames is also a common practice among day traders. For example, day traders commonly base their trading on a 5-minute chart and also look at a 15-minute chart.

In this chapter, I show you how to use charts of more than one time interval in your trading to increase the probability of success. I cover a traditional approach and then share with you an approach that I use to provide even better confirmation for your trade signals.

Understanding How to Use Multiple Scales in Trading

Consulting various time intervals of the same market provides you with a different perspective in a similar way that you can look at an object with your naked eye or with a microscope. The magnification you use in looking at that object allows you to see things you wouldn't see with the naked eye.

Each time interval chart looks different and provides different signals. Figure 13-1 shows a chart demonstrating that Google's stock on the daily chart is heading down. On this "scale" (where each bar represents one day of trading activity), the trend is down.

GOOG, Daily

© 2014 NinjaTrader, LLC

Figure 13-1:
GOOG is trending down on the daily.

Figure by Barry Burns

If you look at that same period of time for Google's stock but magnify the chart five times and use weekly bars instead (where each bar represents a week of trading activity), you see a very different picture. Figure 13-2 reveals that the downtrend on the daily chart is merely a temporary retrace in a major uptrend on the weekly chart.

GOOG, Weekly

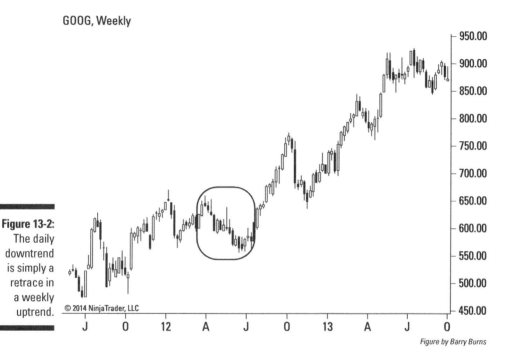

Figure 13-2: The daily downtrend is simply a retrace in a weekly uptrend.

© 2014 NinjaTrader, LLC

Figure by Barry Burns

Seeing contrary trends of the same market on different time intervals can create confusion for traders. The question arises, "Which is the 'real' trend?" The answer is that there's no such thing as a "real trend." The trend is relative to the time interval. So in the case cited in Figures 13-1 and 13-2, the market is in a downtrend on the daily chart but in an uptrend on the weekly chart.

You apply this relativity in trading by simply choosing which time interval chart to base your trading on. You use the trend of that time interval for your analysis of the market and your decision as to whether to trade and in what direction to trade.

Trading with the Bigger Scale Trend: The Common Approach

The most common approach to utilizing multiple time intervals is to use two charts:

- ✔ You use a *setup chart* to look for your trading setups. Common setups may include the head and shoulders pattern, the double top, and retrace in a trend.

- ✔ You use a *long-term chart* to get a bigger picture of the market you're trading.

You can use various ratios between the short-term (setup chart) and the long-term chart (also called the *confirmation chart*). For day trading, I like to use a 1-to-3 ratio between the two charts. For example, if I'm trading a 5-minute chart (the setup chart), I use a 15-minute chart as the long-term chart.

The orthodox approach to using these two time intervals together is to take a trade based on the short-term chart setup only if that trade will be in the direction (long or short) of the trend of the long-term confirmation chart. In other words, if the long-term chart isn't trending in the direction you want to trade, then you'd pass on an otherwise good setup on the setup chart.

The long-term chart acts as a filter to confirm whether the trade setup would cause you to enter in the direction of the long-term's trend. This approach has some degree of logic to it. The long-term chart is considered by some to be the more dominant chart because it shows the bigger picture of the market. It seems logical to trade in the direction ("trend") of that dominant chart.

Unfortunately, that logic has holes in it.

Following are a couple of reasons the orthodox approach of trading only in the direction of the longer-term trend is unwise:

- ✔ **A trend may not exist on the long-term chart.** However, that doesn't mean that the short-term chart won't have one. Markets can make substantial moves on a smaller scale that don't look like much of anything when viewed on the larger scale.

> ✔ **The energy of trend is a lagging indicator.** Therefore, to use the trend on the longer-term chart as your confirmation indicator, you use a lagging indicator on a much slower chart. This results in a very loose correlation between the two charts. The timing between the two charts isn't tight enough to provide timely signals.

Using the Superior Approach and Trading with the Bigger Scale Momentum

Instead of using the trend of the long-term chart to confirm the trade, I prefer to use the energy of momentum (see Chapter 12 for more on this energy). The energy of trend on the long-term chart is so loosely correlated with the short-term chart that I don't even consult it. I take a trade based on the short-term chart whether or not the trend on the long-term chart is in the direction of my trade.

Momentum, however, is so critically important that I won't execute a trade based on a setup on the short-term chart unless I'm taking that trade in the direction of momentum on the long-term chart. It's a filter that keeps me out of an otherwise seemingly good trade.

Because of this type of "veto" power the bigger scale has on trading, I consider the energy of scale, used this way, to be the most important of the five energies (for an overview of the five energies of trading, see Chapter 14).

Now that you understand the concept of confirming the shorter-term chart with the longer-term chart, I get more specific by showing you the exact techniques I use to confirm my trades using the longer-term chart.

Understanding why the bigger scale momentum is superior to the bigger scale trend

The reason I prefer to confirm trades with the energy of momentum rather than the trend on the long-term chart is very simple: Trend is a lagging indicator, and momentum is a potentially leading indicator (see Chapters 4 and 12 for details).

✔ **Lagging indicators** generally give their signals *after* price action has already made its move. Why then would you even be interested in lagging indicators? Because they require more information before they provide their signal (thus not signaling later than other indicators), they tend to be more accurate than leading indicators.

✔ **Leading indicators** generally provide their signals *before* price action makes its move. This is very attractive to traders because leading indicators seem to have predictive powers. However, this early indication comes with a price: Sometimes leading indicators give false signals and, therefore, aren't as accurate as other indicators.

So momentum helps bring the timing of the short-term and long-term charts closer together so they're more in sync. It's really that simple.

Here's a "real world" illustration: I bought my first car when I was 16 years old. I didn't have much money, so the car I could afford had quite a few miles on it. The wear and tear over the years had created a lot of "play" in the steering wheel. I could turn the steering wheel a few degrees to the right or left and it didn't result in the car turning right or left. There was that "play" between turning the steering wheel and it not directly turning the front tires of the car.

In a similar way, you don't want a lot of "play" between the short-term and the long-term charts. You want movement on the short-term chart to result in movement on the long-term chart. For this reason, it's best to use a leading indicator on the long-term chart. Refer to Chapter 12 for a more in-depth discussion, with examples, of how momentum can be a leading indicator.

Trading the bigger scale momentum

Confirming the trade setup on the short-term chart, with the momentum indicator on the long-term chart, is simple and easy. Simply look to see whether the momentum on the long-term chart is moving in the direction you want to trade. If it is, then take the trade; if it isn't, then don't take the trade.

Personally, I like to use the *MACD* (moving average convergence-divergence) indicator (discussed in Chapter 12) for measuring momentum. When using that indicator on the long-term chart, I simply need to have the MACD line (which measures the difference between two moving averages) angling up or down in the direction I'm going to trade. As illustrated in Figure 13-3, I take a trade only when momentum, as measured by the MACD line, is moving in the same direction I'm going to trade.

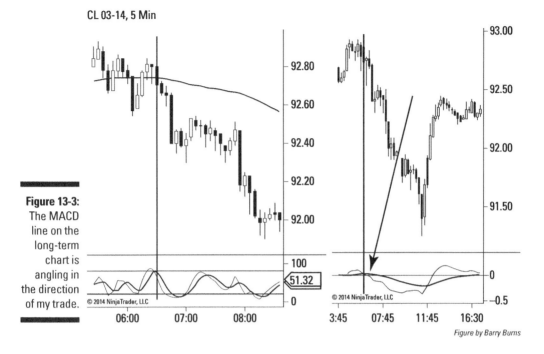

Figure 13-3:
The MACD
line on the
long-term
chart is
angling in
the direction
of my trade.

Figure by Barry Burns

I use momentum as my primary confirmation indicator. I recommend you don't take a trade without momentum on your *fractal chart* (the long-term chart) moving in the direction of your trade. However, you can increase the probability of success for your trades by adding a second confirmation indicator, the cycle indicator.

I measure cycles with the stochastic indicator (see Chapter 10 for details). The stochastic indicator is comprised of two lines:

- ✔ %K, which is the value of the stochastic calculation

- ✔ %D, which is a three-period exponential moving average of %K

    An *exponential moving average* places more weight on the more recent closing prices instead of placing equal value to every closing price over the entire period of the moving average being calculated.

I like to trade in the direction of the cycle on the long-term chart because it adds a second confirmation for my trade. For example:

- ✔ If I'm going short, I want the cycle on the long-term chart to be going down.

- ✔ If I'm going long, I want the cycle on the long-term chart to be going up.

On the long-term chart, this means that I want %K of the stochastic indicator to be angling in the direction of my trade. I like it if %D is also angling in the direction of the trade, but because it's a moving average of %K, it lags behind %K, and therefore it's most important that %K is confirming my trade.

As illustrated in Figure 13-4, when the cycle indicator on the longer-term chart is moving in the direction I'm trading, I have more confidence in the success of my trade.

CL 03-14, 5 Min

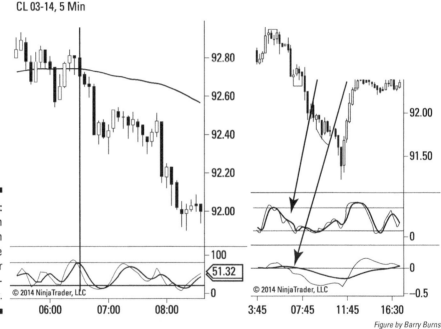

Figure 13-4: Trading in the direction of the cycle indicator on the long-term chart.

© 2014 NinjaTrader, LLC

© 2014 NinjaTrader, LLC

Figure by Barry Burns

Two times that I completely ignore the cycle indicator as a confirmation for my trade on the long-term chart are

- ✔ When I'm buying the market, and %K is at the level of 80 or higher on the long-term chart.
- ✔ When I'm shorting the market, and %K is at the level of 20 or lower on the long-term chart.

I don't use the cycle indicator on the long-term chart if it's more than 80 for long trades or less than 20 for short trades because the stochastic indicator that I use for measuring cycles is a *bounded indicator*. It's "bounded" in the sense that the mathematics of the formula don't allow it to go higher than a value of 100 or lower than a value of 0. Thus, when the market continues moving up after the stochastic indicator is already at the top of the range (near 100), the indicator can't go any higher. It just bounces along the top of the range of the indicator's window, and therefore its readings become meaningless.

The same is true when the market continues moving down after the stochastic indicator is already at the bottom of the range (near 0). Because the indicator can't go any lower, it simply bounces along the lower of the range of the indicator's window, providing meaningless readings.

Figure 13-5 provides a visual example of the bounded nature of the stochastic indicator where price continues to make lower lows, but the stochastic indicator just continues to bounce along the bottom of its range, not providing meaningful signals.

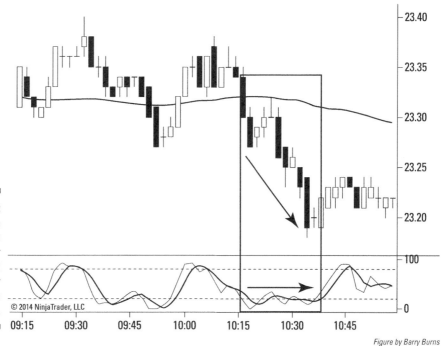

Figure 13-5: The stochastic indicator isn't allowed to go lower than a value of 0.

NEM, 2 Min

© 2014 NinjaTrader, LLC

Figure by Barry Burns

Two time intervals are better than one

The saying that "two heads are better than one" applies to trading, but instead of two "heads," you use two charts that represent different time intervals. One reason for this is that different traders trade the various time interval charts and base their trades on those various time intervals.

Because the markets are essentially auction houses, and price action is based on people's buying and selling in relation to their perceived value of what they see, watching more than one time interval is helpful. Why? Because if more than one time interval shows a buy or sell signal concurrently, more traders are joining that party. And the more traders there are putting their money in the direction of the trade, the more likely it is to follow through.

Chapter 14

Putting It All Together: The Five-Energy Trading Methodology

In This Chapter

▷ Putting all five energies together in one strong force

▷ Trading with the five-energy method

Chapters 10 through 13 cover each of the five energies individually. In this chapter, I share with you how to combine all five energies together to create a high-probability trading methodology.

This chapter is where you take all the information about the five energies and put it together to operate as a well-oiled trading machine designed to make you money!

Combining Forces with the Five-Energy Trading Method

All successful traders do essentially the same thing. They have a method that puts the odds, or probabilities, on their side. You can accomplish this in many ways, which is why many trading methods are available.

Some great traders have taught me their methods, and I've witnessed them make money with them. Through all of my experience and study, I've taken all I've learned and reduced it to a simple five-step process that I refer to as the *five-energy methodology*.

With this method, you simply look at five variables (what I refer to as *energies*) and wait for them to align, giving a buy or sell signal at the same time. Those five energies are

- ✔ Trend
- ✔ Momentum
- ✔ Cycle
- ✔ Support/Resistance
- ✔ Scale

When these five energies all give a buy or sell signal, that's an indication that the odds are on your side, and you have a high-probability trade.

Putting the odds on your side

Having any five chart indicators give a buy or sell signal at the same time isn't enough to create a high-probability trade. If you put five trend indicators on your chart and all five give a buy signal, that isn't significant. Because all five of the indicators are related by measuring the same energy or trend, they're redundant.

For example, say that a person is on trial, and five witnesses testify that he's innocent. Upon further investigation, you find that the five witnesses are the defendant's mother, girlfriend, brother, cousin, and best friend. Knowing that all five of the witnesses are related to the defendant diminishes the trustworthiness of their testimony. However, if five witnesses were all to say that they were eye-witnesses that the defendant did the crime, and none of the witnesses knew the defendant or each other, then their testimony would be more credible.

In a similar way, using five indicators that are all related to each other isn't a credible way to build a case for a profitable trade. The five energies I discuss in Chapters 10 through 13 are uncorrelated to each other. For example, when price (energy 1) is trending up, sometimes momentum (energy 2) is also going up (see Figure 14-1). Other times, when price trend is going up, momentum is flat (as in Figure 14-2). Still, other times, when price trend is going up, momentum is actually going down (see Figure 14-3).

I like to use the 50-period simple moving average (SMA) to measure trend (as I describe in Chapter 6); therefore, I use that indicator to determine trend direction in Figures 14-1 through 14-3 (the line drawn below the price bars).

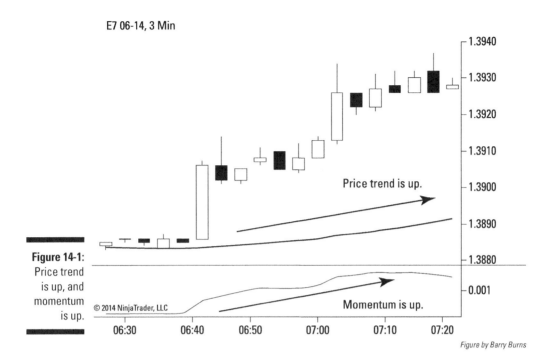

Figure 14-1:
Price trend
is up, and
momentum
is up.

Figure by Barry Burns

Unleashing the power of forces combined

A successful trading methodology doesn't rely on any singular technique, indicator, or price pattern. An often repeated phrase in the trading community is, "There's no Holy Grail in trading."

Profitable trading is similar to profitable poker playing. Just as the professional poker player has no certainty ahead of time of the outcome of any one hand, neither does the professional trader have any advanced certainty of any one trade. Like the professional poker player, however, a professional trader looks at all the variables and is able to calculate the odds, or probability, of success. As a trader, the key is to prepare yourself through study and education to know and understand those variables ahead of time.

When the professional trader, or poker player, has a situation where the variables create a probability of profitability, he puts money on the line. But knowing that no certainty of success exists in this one instance, the pro risks only a small portion of his money on each situation.

What makes trading more like poker and less like gambling at the slot machines is that slot machines are programmed to put the odds in the favor of the "house." If you have a successful trading methodology, the odds (over a large sample of trades) are in your favor.

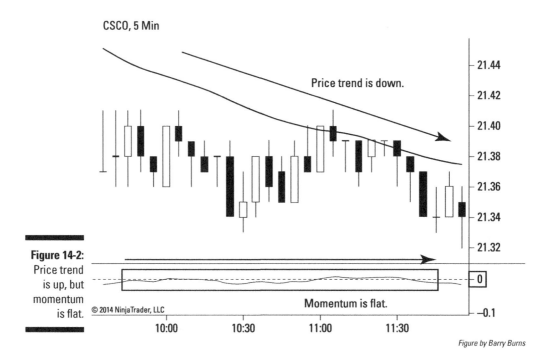

CSCO, 5 Min

Price trend is down.

21.44
21.42
21.40
21.38
21.36
21.34
21.32

Figure 14-2:
Price trend
is up, but
momentum
is flat.

© 2014 NinjaTrader, LLC

Momentum is flat.

0

−0.1

10:00   10:30   11:00   11:30

Figure by Barry Burns

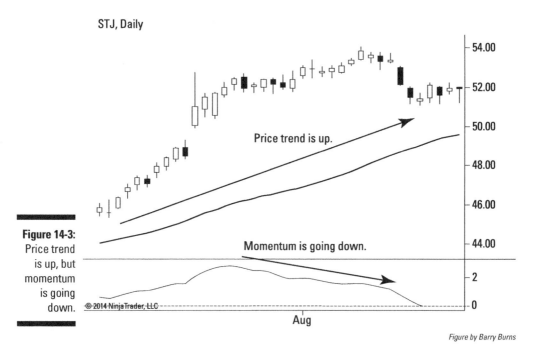

STJ, Daily

54.00
52.00

Price trend is up.

50.00

48.00

46.00

Figure 14-3:
Price trend
is up, but
momentum
is going
down.

Momentum is going down.

44.00

2

© 2014 NinjaTrader, LLC

0

Aug

Figure by Barry Burns

These two energies can go in the same or different directions because they're unrelated to each other.

Each one of these five energies is uncorrelated to the other four, and that's exactly what makes it significant when all five energies give a buy or sell signal concurrently.

Looking for the preponderance of the evidence

Continuing with my legal analogy from the previous section, I build a case for or against a trade by looking at the evidence. One of the biggest challenges in trading is that there's so much evidence you can consider.

Traders commonly feel overwhelmed due to the avalanche of financial information available in the form of news, fundamental analysis, technical analysis, gossip, rumors, expert recommendations, analysts' commentary, economics, and so on. Some people spend endless hours scouring through mounds of information before, during, and after the market closes each day, gathering evidence to trade or not trade any given market or security. I admire their work ethic. In fact, I've been pulled into the bottomless pit of endless information gathering myself.

Watching the results of that type of endless research led me to believe that it didn't help me make more money. And that's what trading is really about: It's a business to make money.

A well-known saying among traders is, "the market can do anything at any time." Taking that into consideration, I realized the following key points when it comes to making money in trading:

- ✔ **Markets are traded by people, and people often make emotional decisions, not rational decisions.** Therefore, building a case for a trade on the foundation of what traders "should do" or what "makes sense" is exactly the wrong way to make money trading!

- ✔ **Markets are very fickle and can change on a dime.** What happened in the Asia session the night before may have some impact on the U.S. market, but unless there was dramatic news, most traders are more interested in what's happening right now, not what occurred several hours ago.

> ✔ **Even if there was dramatic news before the U.S. open, and the market reacted dramatically to it, that still doesn't necessarily predict how people will trade the U.S. market when it opens.** People often have a dramatic knee-jerk reaction to news and then soon calm down and even change their mind about how important it was.

Based on these observations, I trade in the present, on what's actually happening right now in the markets, literally bar by bar. I use technical analysis exclusively for my trading. Reading the charts tells me what traders are actually doing. For this reason, I believe that technical analysis is the math of mass psychology.

Charts don't plot traders' opinions, ideas, beliefs, or thoughts. They plot only traders' buy and sell activity — in other words, their commitments. Charts reveal when people have actually put their money where their mouth is.

Understanding how to read a chart is critical to figuring out what traders are actually doing, how much buying and selling is occurring, whether it's likely to continue or stop suddenly, and when the best time is to join the fun. I read a chart to look for a "preponderance of the evidence," to put the odds on my side by giving me a probability scenario for success. You can do this, too, by looking for an alignment of the five energies.

Why five energies?

Why use five energies? There's no magic to the number five, but I like it for the following reasons:

✔ Einstein is attributed with saying "Everything should be made as simple as possible, but not simpler." Although he wasn't a trader (at least not that I know of), that concept is applicable to trading.

✔ Using five energies gives you enough variables to establish a probability scenario but still keeps the amount of information you process manageable so you don't suffer from information overload, which can lead to confusion and hesitancy.

Discovering How to Trade the Five-Energy Methodology

The five-energy method is fundamentally quite simple. Ideally, you want all five energies to give a buy or sell signal at the exact same moment. However, the markets, like most things in life, aren't so neat, tidy, and generous as to give you all five energies aligning at the same time. So you can allow yourself to take a trade if a *minimum* of four of the five energies align.

Three out of five energies aligning isn't enough. Although you may think it would still put the odds on your side, because more than 50 percent of the energies are aligned, that slight edge is offset by the expenses of trading, such as the following:

- **Slippage:** The difference between the price you intended to enter the market and the price at which you were actually filled.

- **Commissions:** The price your brokerage firm charges for transacting your trade.

- **Exchange fee:** The price the exchange charges for processing your order.

- **The bid/ask spread:** The difference between the price you can buy that market and the price you can sell it.

- **Fixed expenses:** Your charting software, computers, Internet connection, and so on.

In the following sections, I put the five-energy method together for you in one coherent methodical approach. When I look at charts, I always look at them in the same way and follow these steps:

1. **Identify the trend.**

2. **Determine whether it's a strong trend or a weak trend.**

3. **Figure out when to enter.**

4. **Bounce off resistance/support.**

5. **Filter trades with the energy of scale.**

Identifying the trend

The first decision you make with the five-energy method is whether you're going to go long, go short, or stay out.

I measure trend with the objective instrument (indicator) of the 50-period simple moving average (SMA). If it's angling up, I consider the trend to be up (as shown in Figure 14-4). If it's angling down, I consider the trend to be down. If it's unclear whether the 50 SMA is angling up or down, then I consider it to be flat, meaning there's no trend.

Trend simply refers to the direction of the market — up, down, or sideways.

Figure 14-4:
The 50 SMA is angling up, so the market is trending up.

© 2014 NinjaTrader, LLC

Figure by Barry Burns

I like to trade in the direction of the trend when I can get early into a new trend. I consider *early* to mean the first two *retraces* (wave lows in an uptrend or wave highs in a downtrend). A retrace in a trend is a small (in price range) and short-term (in time duration) price move against the direction of the trend. Buying a retrace of price down against the trend potentially allows you to enter at a lower price, as opposed to buying as price is moving up, thus allowing you to adhere to the adage "buy low, sell high."

Figure 14-5 illustrates a first retrace in the trend as evidenced by %D of the stochastic indicator (which I use as my cycle indicator) getting below the value of 55 for the first time after the 50 SMA turned up.

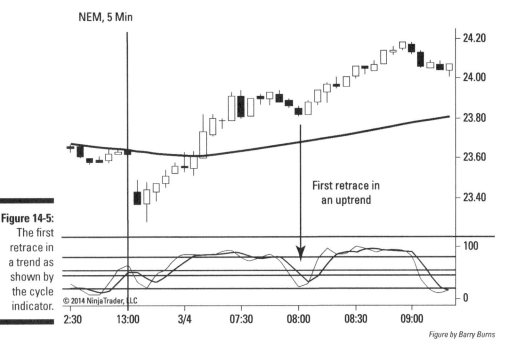

Figure 14-5:
The first retrace in a trend as shown by the cycle indicator.

NEM, 5 Min

First retrace in an uptrend

© 2014 NinjaTrader, LLC

Figure by Barry Burns

Determining whether the trend is strong or weak

After determining the direction I want to trade, I then look at the momentum indicator to see whether momentum (strength) is behind the trend. The trend, as shown by the 50 SMA, tells you only the direction of the market at this snapshot in time. It doesn't tell you whether the trend is strong or weak.

If you execute a trade in the direction of a weak trend, that trend will likely end right after you enter.

The energy of momentum helps determine whether the trend is strong or weak, and you want to trade only in the direction of a strong trend.

Figure 14-6 illustrates how to determine whether a trend is strong. When entering a cycle low on an uptrend, make sure that the momentum indicator (the MACD line) is above the 0 line at the cycle low. When you see that on your chart, you can consider that a strong trend, which will likely follow through and make a higher high after you enter.

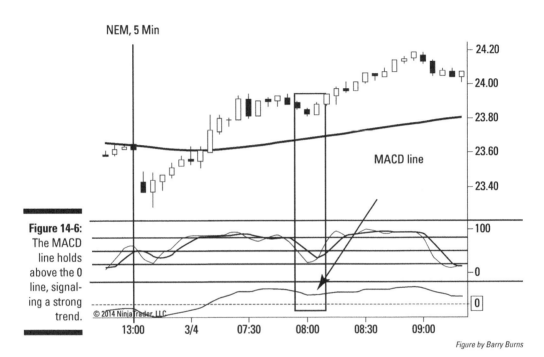

Figure 14-6:
The MACD line holds above the 0 line, signaling a strong trend.

Figure by Barry Burns

Figuring out when to enter

Timing entries is something many traders struggle with. In Chapter 10, I discuss how I time my entries with extremely high probability and avoid getting stopped out frequently.

Figure 14-7 illustrates an example of how the chart looks when the trend is up, momentum is strong, and a mini-divergence pattern shows on the stochastic indicator (price makes a lower low, and %K on the stochastic indicator makes a higher low) on an early retrace in the trend.

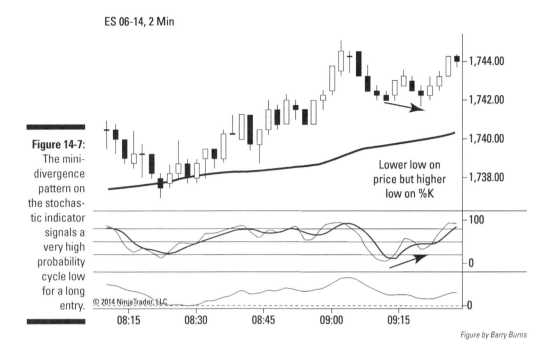

ES 06-14, 2 Min

Lower low on
price but higher
low on %K

© 2014 NinjaTrader, LLC

Figure 14-7:
The mini-
divergence
pattern on
the stochas-
tic indicator
signals a
very high
probability
cycle low
for a long
entry.

Figure by Barry Burns

Bouncing off support/resistance

I prefer to buy and sell retraces in the trend. Some traders prefer to enter trades on *breakouts* — entering the market after price breaks above a previous high (or below a previous low if trading short).

Entering on retraces or breakouts are both valid trading techniques. I have friends who trade breakouts and are successful with it. The concept of trading a breakout is to wait for the market to make a commitment to the upside by moving above a previous high.

Personally, I prefer trading retracements because I enter at a lower price (I tease my breakout trading friends that I'm in before them and they're helping to move the market in my direction). I also prefer trading retracements because my initial risk on the trade is smaller than the initial risk breakout traders generally have.

Breakout traders often criticize retracement traders by saying that we're trading while the market is going against the trend, and therefore it's more risky than their approach. They contest that no one knows how low the retracement will go before, or even if, the market continues in the direction of the trend. Therefore, they believe that trading only when the market has proven it will continue in the direction of an uptrend, making a higher high, is more conservative and reliable.

That argument has some merit. My response is two-fold:

✔ The fact that the market makes a higher high doesn't guarantee that it will continue to move up after you enter the trade. Anyone who has traded for a long period of time can tell you many, many sad stories of false breakouts.

✔ I have greatly diminished the uncertainty of how far a market will retrace by using the mini-divergence pattern on the stochastic indicator. I also increase my odds of finding the final cycle low of the retrace by making sure that the market I'm trading retraces to, and bounces off, a support level (or in the case of trading short, a resistance level). The primary support/resistance levels I use are

- Previous cycle highs/lows

- Previous wave highs/lows

- Floor trader pivots

- Fibonacci levels

I discuss these levels in detail in Chapter 11, but Figure 14-8 illustrates a retrace to a Fibonacci level after which the market moves back up in the direction of the trend.

$AUDJPY, Daily

Figure 14-8:
The market retraces to a Fibonacci support level before continuing with the uptrend.

© 2014 NinjaTrader, LLC

Figure by Barry Burns

Filtering your trades with the energy of scale

In the earlier section "Discovering How to Trade the Five-Energy Methodology," I mention that you can trade when only four of the five energies align, giving you a buy or sell signal. That is true, with this one caveat: The energy of scale must always support your trade. This is the one energy that can't be left out.

This energy acts as either a filter to keep you out of an otherwise valid trade setup on the short-term chart or as confirmation to take the trade. In this way, the energy of scale is the most important of the five energies because you can't take any trade without its permission!

Look for setups on the setup chart, which is the short-term chart, where you analyze the first four energies and make sure they align:

- ✔ Is the trend up, and is it early in the trend?
- ✔ Is the trend strong as indicated by the MACD line being above 0?
- ✔ Is there a retrace against the trend and a mini-divergence pattern on the stochastic indicator?
- ✔ Is the retrace in price bouncing up off a support level?

After you find those four energies aligning in that manner on the short-term chart, look for confirmation of the energy of scale on the long-term chart.

The only signal you need to confirm the trade is that the MACD line on the long-term chart is angling in the direction of the trade. It doesn't matter whether the MACD line is above or below the 0 line. Only its angle is important to confirm the trade.

Figure 14-9 provides an example of how simple it is to read that confirmation of the energy of scale. A fairly steep angle is preferable, but as long as the angle of the line is clearly in the direction of the trade, you can consider it confirmed. If you aren't sure whether the MACD line is angling up or it looks flat, refer to one of my basic rules of trading: "If it's not clear, pass on the trade."

ES 06-14, 2 Min   ES 06-14, 6 Min

Figure 14-9:
Confirmation
of the
energy of
scale on the
long-term
chart.

© 2014 NinjaTrader, LLC   © 2014 NinjaTrader, LLC

Figure by Barry Burns

The market can do anything at any time

The markets are deceivingly difficult to trade. Looking at historical charts from the past can put you in a position of hallucinating that you'd be able to easily make money. This type of imaginary reverse engineering doesn't work in real time.

The markets aren't like a tame, domesticated purse puppy. They're more like a wild tiger. Even when managed by trained, knowledgeable, and loving handlers, a wild animal can turn at any moment.

After trading for several decades, I've seen the markets behave nicely for a period of time and then release their wild fury, leaving a path of swift financial destruction upon those who love it and thought they had it figured out. I've seen the market plummet on good news and jump skyward on horrible news.

I've turned on my computer in the morning to find that over the course of one night, while I was sleeping, I lost a year's worth of hard-earned profits. I've watched fat-finger trades create crazy dramatic moves in a split second. I've witnessed well-respected brokerage firms mishandle clients' money. I've been caught in "limit down" moves.

The bottom line is this: Just when you think you've figured out the market, remember this word of caution: You haven't! The markets are always risky and unpredictable. Therefore, risk management, including stops, hedging, and sound money management, is of utmost importance.

Chapter 15

Seeing the Five Energies in Action

*R*eading about the five-energy methodology is a good place to begin to understand the principles of the trading approach. To take your understanding to the next level, you need to look at examples of the methodology in action.

Technical analysis is a visual approach to trading, so going beyond the words and demonstrating the principles on charts is critical to understanding the method.

In working with students one-on-one, I've learned that they like to see examples using the specific market(s) they're trading. For this reason, this entire chapter is dedicated to example charts of the five-energy method in action, using stocks, forex, futures, and commodities so you can see it applied to the type of market and in the time horizon you trade. I also provide illustrations applied to day trading, swing trading, and investing.

What Real World Examples Can Teach You About Trend Trading

Some trading methods are designed for one type of market or time interval, but you can apply the five-energy methodology to many types of markets and time frames. You simply attach instruments (indicators) to the charts that measure the energies on those charts. Whatever market or time interval you put on the chart, the instruments measure the energy for that market and that time interval.

I don't recommend trading penny stocks or low-volume markets with this or any other method. In addition, make sure your chart has the type of rhythmic sine-wave movement you're looking for. You probably don't want to trade markets that have a lot of gaps between bars because that means your trade executions have a lot of *slippage* — the difference between the price you intended to get filled on your trade and the actual price at which you were executed.

Scoping Out Stocks

My dear ol' dad was a stock trader and my first trading teacher, so my trading career began with trading stocks. In his honor, I begin with showing examples of stock setups using the five-energy methodology.

Day trading stocks

In Figure 15-1, the Charles Schwab Corporation (SCHW) makes a first retrace in the trend (marked by the vertical line) on the 2-minute chart (on the left), which I use as the *setup chart* in this example. The setup chart is the time interval I look at for my technical analysis trade setups, which are the reasons for the trade. When trend trading, I look at the trend on the setup chart.

On this chart, five energies align, supporting a long trade:

- ✔ The *trend* is up, as indicated by the 50-period SMA (simple moving average), which is the thick black line below the price bars.
- ✔ *Momentum* is up, as indicated by the indicator at the very bottom of the chart.
- ✔ The market is creating a *cycle* low, as indicated by the stochastic indicator (in the middle panel of the chart) moving down and then angling back up.
- ✔ The stock is bouncing off the *support* level of the 15 EMA (exponential moving average), which is the thin black line immediately below the price bars.
- ✔ The energy of *scale* (the 6-minute chart to the right of the 2-minute setup chart) is bullish, as indicated by the MACD line (the thin line in the bottom panel that measures momentum) angling up.

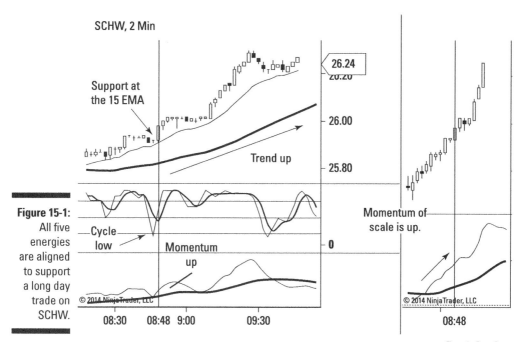

SCHW, 2 Min

Support at
the 15 EMA

26.24

26.00

Trend up

25.80

Figure 15-1:
All five
energies
are aligned
to support
a long day
trade on
SCHW.

Cycle
low

Momentum
up

Momentum of
scale is up.

0

© 2014 NinjaTrader, LLC

© 2014 NinjaTrader, LLC

08:30   08:48 9:00   09:30

08:48

Figure by Barry Burns

Swing trading stocks

The term *swing trading* has many meanings. In the broadest sense of the term, it's a time interval between day trading and investing, but it always refers to the intention of holding a position at least more than one day. You can employ swing trading by using long-term intraday charts or daily charts (in which each bar represents the market movement of one day).

Figure 15-2 provides an example of using a 60-minute chart of St. Jude Medical, Inc., (STJ) for the setup chart and a 180-minute chart to measure the energy of scale (to either confirm or filter out the trade on the setup chart). At the vertical line, there's a first retrace cycle high in a new downtrend. Although a valid reason to trade, it's not ideal because momentum on the setup chart (the thin line on the bottom panel) has retraced to the 0 line, indicating that the corrective move against the trend is stronger than is optimal.

Though momentum on the setup chart isn't supporting the short signal, the rules of the five-energy methodology require that only four of the five energies align in the same direction. Therefore, you're still allowed to take the trade if the energy of momentum is down on the long-term scale chart.

Looking at the 180-minute chart at the vertical line (the time of the trade), momentum (the thin line in the bottom panel) is clearly angling down, thus confirming the short trade.

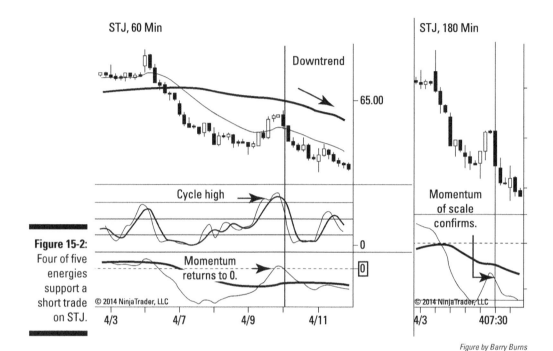

Figure 15-2:
Four of five energies support a short trade on STJ.

Figure by Barry Burns

Investing with stocks

Investing is a bit different from day trading or swing trading in the sense that you're intending to hold for a year or more. This holding period requires that you use much longer-term time intervals for your charts.

Personally, I engage in investing only in my retirement accounts, and it's the one time interval I rely on fundamental analysis as well as technical analysis for my decisions. I intend to hold the stock for a long period of time, so I want to make sure it's a sound company with sound financials and business practices. The factors I consider when choosing my investment vehicles are far beyond the scope of this book on trend trading. However, I always look at the long-term charts of any stock I consider adding to my retirement portfolio.

Because of the long-term nature of the holding period, I use weekly and monthly charts for my investment decisions. The weekly chart (in which each bar represents one week of stock activity) is my setup chart, and the monthly chart is my confirmation chart (measuring momentum on a different scale).

Figure 15-3 provides another example of St. Jude Medical, Inc., (STJ) but this time using the weekly chart as the setup chart and the monthly chart as the confirmation chart to measure the energy of scale. Notice how the setups and patterns of price, the moving averages and the indicators, all look the same regardless of the chart time intervals used. The weekly chart has an early retrace in the direction of a new uptrend. The 15 EMA provides support, the cycle indicator is making a low and angling back up, and the momentum indicator in the bottom panel is holding above the 0 line. At the same time (marked by the vertical line on the chart), the monthly chart on the right shows momentum (in the bottom panel) angling up and thus confirming a long entry.

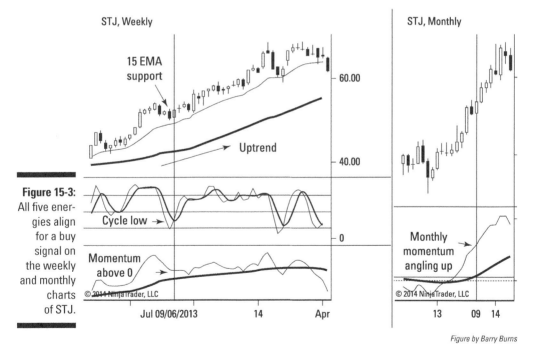

Figure 15-3: All five energies align for a buy signal on the weekly and monthly charts of STJ.

Figure by Barry Burns

Analyzing a sample chart

Here's a chance for you to see how well you can analyze charts with the five-energy methodology. Figure 15-4 provides an example of a potential stock trade setup. Analyze the chart, using the five energies, and determine whether it's a viable trade based on the methodology.

The potential trade setup is where you see the vertical lines intersecting the price bars on both charts. Don't read my analysis of the chart until you've analyzed the chart for yourself and determined the trade's probability of success based on the five energies.

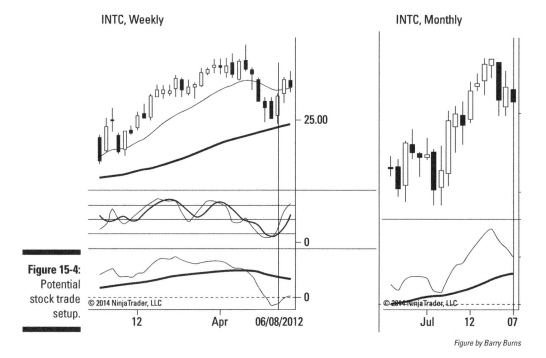

Figure 15-4: Potential stock trade setup.

Figure by Barry Burns

After analyzing the chart for yourself, read the following analysis and compare your answer:

✔ The trend is up, so you're looking for a long trade.

✔ The market has retraced to the 50 SMA, which provides support for the price bars to bounce off and go back up.

✔ The stochastic indicator (in the middle panel) shows a cycle low, meaning that it's time for the market to put in a low and move back up.

✔ Momentum (the thin MACD line in the bottom panel) has gone below 0, indicating a weak trend.

✔ The energy of scale, as measured by the angle of the thin MACD line on the monthly chart, is angling down; therefore, it's not confirming the trade.

In summary, there are two important points:

✔ Only three out of five energies are aligned to support the uptrend to take a long entry. Momentum on both the weekly and monthly charts doesn't support the trade. According to the rules of the five-energy methodology, you need at least four of the five energies to align in the same direction.

✔ Because the energy of scale (the monthly chart in this case) doesn't support the buy signal on the weekly setup chart, the entire trade is disqualified. The energy of scale (the angle of the MACD line on the higher time frame chart) must always support the trade. Even if all four energies aligned on the setup chart, you should never take a trade if the energy of scale doesn't support it.

Finding Out About Forex

The chart patterns and the technical analysis setups for forex are identical to the ones for stocks (see previous section). Although differences regarding pricing, commissions, and order routing exist between stocks and spot forex, the five energies are alive and well in both markets.

Day trading with forex

Figure 15-5 shows an example of a day trade setup, using the Euro/U.S. Dollar spot forex pair. The setup chart is the 5-minute chart on the left, and the energy of scale is measured by the momentum indicator (the MACD line) on the 15-minute chart on the right.

The setup is a first retrace in a new downtrend.

✔ The 50 SMA is angling down, indicating the trend is down. It's early in a new downtrend, so you can look for a short trade.

✔ The 15 EMA provides resistance overhead.

✔ The stochastic cycle indicator reached the level of 80 and is angling back down, indicating a possible cycle high.

✔ Momentum has not quite (though almost) reached the 0 line.

✔ The energy of scale, as measured by the angle of the thin MACD line on the 15-minute chart, is angling down, thereby confirming the short setup.

This trade setup attains a score of five out of five energies aligning for a short signal.

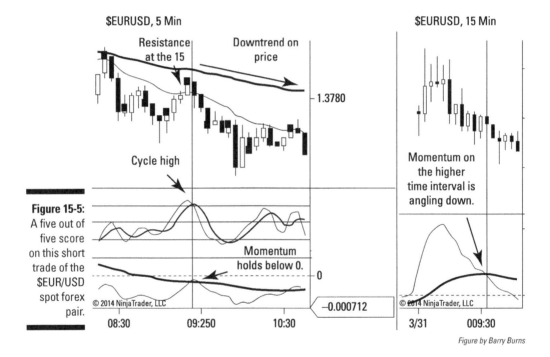

Figure 15-5: A five out of five score on this short trade of the $EUR/USD spot forex pair.

Figure by Barry Burns

Swing trading with forex

A common time interval chart for forex trading is the 60-minute chart. Using the preferred ratio of 1:3 between the setup chart and the higher time interval (the higher scale), I use a 180-minute chart for the confirmation chart.

In Figure 15-6, you see the Australian Dollar/Japanese Yen forex pair making a corrective move against the downtrend. The retrace stops at the 15 EMA, concurrently with the cycle indicator reaching the level of 80 and angling back down. The energy of scale (represented by the energy of momentum on the 180-minute chart) is angling down, thus confirming the trade.

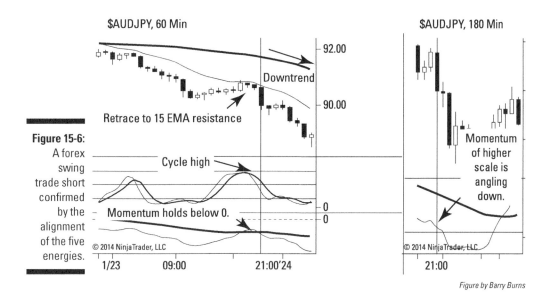

Figure 15-6:
A forex swing trade short confirmed by the alignment of the five energies.

Figure by Barry Burns

Investing with forex

You can trade forex with the spot forex pair, futures, or exchange-traded funds (ETFs). When investing in currencies, I prefer to take a conservative approach and trade ETFs, thus avoiding the high leverage of the spot or futures' currencies.

Figure 15-7 illustrates the CurrencyShares Euro Trust (FXE) Exchange Traded Fund. The weekly chart has a valid short setup; however, the momentum indicator on the monthly chart is angling up, not confirming the trade.

Although you need only four out of the five energies aligning to take a trade, the energy of scale (as measured by the momentum indicator on the higher time frame) must always support the trade.

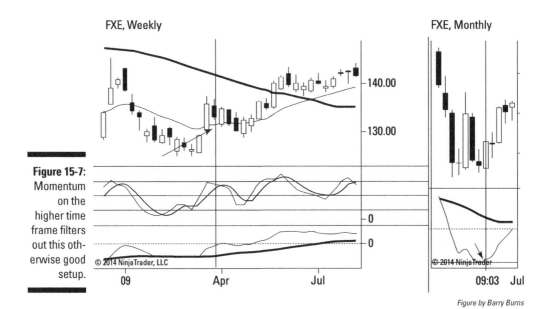

Figure 15-7: Momentum on the higher time frame filters out this otherwise good setup.

Figure by Barry Burns

Analyzing a sample chart

Figure 15-8 provides an example of a potential forex trade setup. Analyze the chart, using the five energies, and determine whether it's a viable trade based on the five-energy methodology.

The potential trade setup is where you see the vertical lines intersecting the price bars on both charts. Don't read my analysis of the chart until you've analyzed the chart for yourself and determined the trade's probability of success based on the five energies.

After analyzing the chart for yourself, read the following analysis and compare your answer:

✔ The trend is down, so you're looking for a short trade.

✔ There's no support to cause a reliable bounce of the market to the upside.

✔ The stochastic indicator (in the middle panel) shows a cycle low, meaning that it's time for the market to put in a low and move back up, but that would be against the direction of the trend.

✔ Momentum (the thin MACD line in the bottom panel) has gone far below 0.

✔ The energy of scale, as measured by the angle of the thin MACD line on the monthly chart is angling down, thus not confirming the buying of a cycle low.

In summary, this trade setup is a mess! There's no confluence of agreement of the energies for a long or short trade.

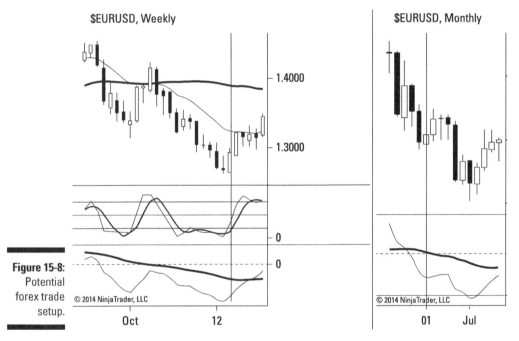

$EURUSD, Weekly

1.4000

1.3000

0

0

© 2014 NinjaTrader, LLC

Oct   12

$EURUSD, Monthly

© 2014 NinjaTrader, LLC

01   Jul

Figure 15-8: Potential forex trade setup.

Figure by Barry Burns

Fiddling with Futures

After my father taught me stock trading, I found another mentor who encouraged me to trade futures. At first, I was a bit reluctant because of the leverage involved. I knew it allowed me to make more money with a smaller account, but it also created the possibility of losing more money, and that scared me.

The leverage provided by futures is a double-edged sword. If you decide to trade futures, don't be afraid of them, because that fear will lead to poor decisions. Instead, make sure you have a healthy respect for the risk that accompanies futures trading.

Futures contracts have expiration dates at which time they stop trading. They normally expire in three months or less. This doesn't make them conducive for long-term investing. For that reason, I show examples only for day trading and swing trading futures in this section.

Day trading with futures

My first experience with day trading was with stocks. They provided thousands of choices, but most of the individual stocks traded in the general direction of the major equity index to which they were associated.

Individual stocks can have dramatic and unexpected heterodox moves based on specific information that comes out about the company behind the stock. To smooth the market action and avoid some of these surprise moves, you can trade the major indexes themselves.

Instead of trading equity indexes of exchange-traded funds, such as the SPY and DOW, I prefer to trade the futures equity indexes because I like the extra leverage involved. The volume of these futures contracts is excellent, and their movements are smoothed because they're comprised of many different stocks.

You can also day trade futures of currencies, commodities, bonds, and other financial markets.

Figure 15-9 offers an example of a setup on the S&P E-minis (ES). This setup is what I call the "first retrace after the cross."

The 50 SMA hasn't started angling down yet, but it's the first cycle high after price has crossed from above to below the 50 SMA. It's a more aggressive trade setup than waiting for the 50 SMA to begin angling down to confirm the downtrend.

The win/loss ratio for this setup is lower than waiting for the 50 SMA to angle in the direction of the trend; however, it generally gets you in the trend earlier and provides a superior reward/risk ratio.

All of the other energies align for a short trade: resistance of the 50 SMA and the 15 EMA, a cycle high, momentum holding below 0, and momentum angling down on the higher scale chart.

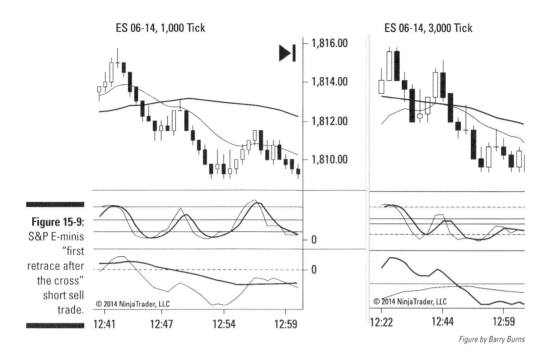

ES 06-14, 1,000 Tick   ES 06-14, 3,000 Tick

Figure 15-9: S&P E-minis "first retrace after the cross" short sell trade.

© 2014 NinjaTrader, LLC   © 2014 NinjaTrader, LLC

12:41   12:47   12:54   12:59   12:22   12:44   12:59

Figure by Barry Burns

Swing trading with futures

Swing trading is different from day trading in one simple way. When you day trade, you're always getting out of your position before the end of the trading day. When swing trading, you're always holding your position overnight, at least from one trading session to another.

The advantage to swing trading is that you may be in a profitable position at the end of the day that you expect to continue moving in your direction the next day. If you're day trading, you must exit your position and sacrifice the rest of the profits potentially available the next day as the market continues to move in your direction. This is the risk of opportunity lost.

The disadvantage of swing trading is that you expose yourself to overnight risk. Futures pits are closed for long hours from one day to the next. Liquidity is low during that time, and surprise news can hit the market overnight that can dramatically change the trend you were trading.

Because of the leverage afforded by futures, I personally choose not to swing trade futures. I only swing trade stocks without the use of leverage. That's where the line of my psychological risk tolerance is and allows me to sleep better. Many traders swing trade futures, so it's a decision you have to make for yourself.

Figure 15-10 illustrates a short signal in a downtrend on the NASDAQ 100 E-mini futures (NQ) on a 30-minute chart. The 50 SMA is down, the 15 EMA provides resistance, the stochastic indicator is up to a value of 80 and angling back down, and the momentum is holding below the 0 line. The 90-minute scale confirmation chart shows momentum angling down to confirm the short entry.

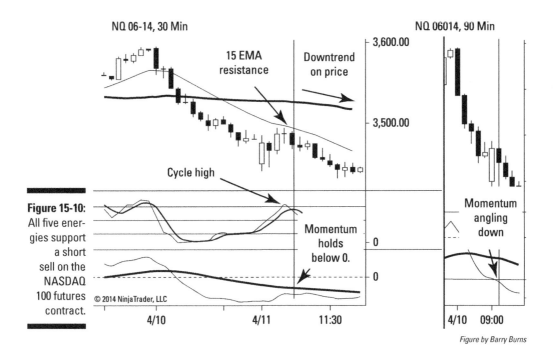

Figure 15-10: All five energies support a short sell on the NASDAQ 100 futures contract.

Figure by Barry Burns

Analyzing a sample chart

Figure 15-11 provides an example of a potential futures trade setup. Analyze the chart, using the five energies, and determine whether it's a viable trade based on the five-energy methodology.

The potential trade setup is where you see the vertical lines intersecting the price bars on both charts. Don't read my analysis of the chart until you've analyzed the chart for yourself and determined the trade's probability of success based on the five energies.

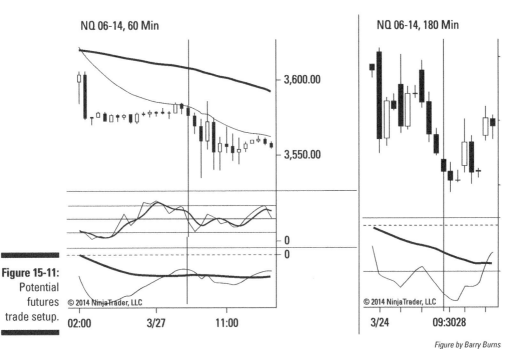

Figure 15-11: Potential futures trade setup.

Figure by Barry Burns

After analyzing the chart for yourself, read the following analysis and compare your answer:

- ✔ The trend is down, so you're looking for a short trade.

- ✔ The market has retraced to the 15 EMA, which provides resistance for the price bars to bounce off and go back down. Also, the fact that the price bars stopped going up at the 15 EMA, instead of retracing higher, shows good relative strength to the downside.

✔ The stochastic indicator (in the middle panel) shows a cycle high, meaning that it's time for the market to put in a high and move back down. In addition, the cycle high is formed by a divergence (see Chapter 10 for details), which makes it an extremely high-probability cycle high.

✔ Momentum (the thin MACD line in the bottom panel) has remained below 0, thus indicating a strong downtrend.

✔ The energy of scale, as measured by the angle of the thin MACD line on the monthly chart is angling down, thus confirming the trade.

In summary, there are two important points: This is a great setup, and all five energies align to confirm a short trade.

Getting Curious About Commodities

Commodities are general resources such as oil, gold, sugar, coffee, soybeans, gas, and electricity. They offer another type of market that can provide trading opportunities generally uncorrelated to equities.

You can trade commodities in spot (cash) or derivatives (such as futures) markets. Numerous exchange-traded funds (ETFs) provide access to various commodity markets as well.

Day trading with commodities

I like to include commodities (especially crude oil and gold) in my day trading because they often move differently than the stock market. So while I love to trade the S&P E-minis, if the stock market isn't moving much on a given day, oil or gold may provide excellent trading opportunities.

Figure 15-12 shows an example of Crude Oil (CL) futures. There's a trend trade setup to go short on the 3-minute setup chart on the left and a confirmation by the momentum indicator angling down on the 9-minute chart on the right.

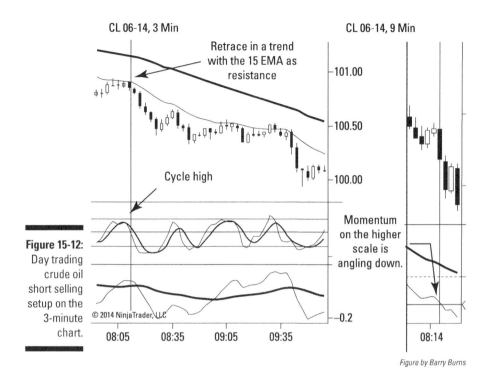

CL 06-14, 3 Min

CL 06-14, 9 Min

Retrace in a trend with the 15 EMA as resistance

101.00

100.50

Cycle high

100.00

Momentum on the higher scale is angling down.

© 2014 NinjaTrader, LLC

−0.2

08:05   08:35   09:05   09:35

08:14

Figure 15-12: Day trading crude oil short selling setup on the 3-minute chart.

Figure by Barry Burns

Swing trading with commodities

I don't like holding highly leveraged instruments like futures overnight, so I use ETFs when swing trading commodities.

Even though ETFs may attempt to replicate the performance of the commodity they track, they're not always identical.

Figure 15-13 shows a setup on GLD, an ETF that has an extremely high correlation to the price of gold bullion (net of expenses).

The 30-minute charts shows a retrace in the trend setup with the 15 EMA as resistance and the stochastic indicator making a cycle high and angling down. Momentum on the setup chart is also angling down, which isn't necessary on the setup chart but does add to the probability of success for the trade. The 90-minute confirmation chart at that same time shows that momentum on that scale is angling down, thus confirming the short trade.

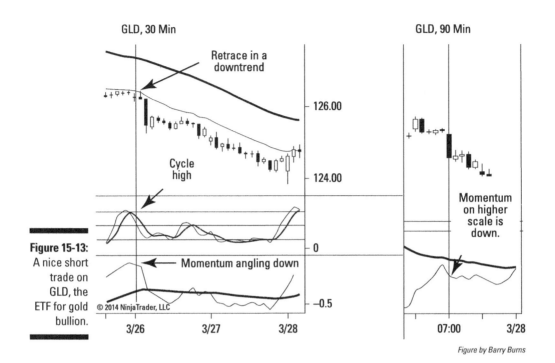

Figure 15-13:
A nice short
trade on
GLD, the
ETF for gold
bullion.

Figure by Barry Burns

Investing with commodities

Figure 15-14 shows an example of a potential investment in the iPath S&P
GSCI Crude Oil Total Return (OIL) exchange-traded note (ETN). (An ETN is
different from an ETF in that ETNs are issued as debt notes, similar to bonds.
An ETF is an asset similar to a stock.)

Check with your tax professional for differences that may exist between how
ETFs and ETNs may be taxed.

On the retrace on the setup chart, the 50 SMA is clearly up, and it's early in
a new uptrend. The 50 SMA provides support, and the market is making a
cycle low.

One potential problem with this setup is that the momentum indicator has gone down to 0. Therefore, the best score you can achieve from this trade is an alignment of four of the five energies.

Looking at the monthly chart to the right, momentum is angling up, thus confirming the trade.

My intention of all trades I take for investment purposes is to hold them for more than a year, but it doesn't always work out that way. I use *trailing stops* — a stop in which you continue to move the price at which you'll exit the market — in case the market turns against me, and if that trailing stop is hit in less than a year, I exit the trade.

As the market continues to move up, I continue to move my stop price up. Doing so allows me to capture more profits instead of allowing the market to make a major move against me and give back all of my unrealized gains. In such a case, what was intended to be an investment turns into a swing trade.

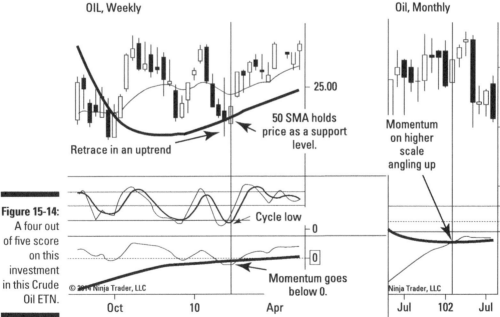

Figure 15-14: A four out of five score on this investment in this Crude Oil ETN.

Figure by Barry Burns

Analyzing a sample chart

Figure 15-15 provides an example of a potential commodities trade setup. Analyze the chart, using the five energies, and determine whether it's a viable trade based on the five-energy methodology.

The potential trade setup is where you see the vertical lines intersecting the price bars on both charts. Don't ready my analysis of the chart until you've analyzed the chart for yourself and determined the trade's probability of success based on the five energies.

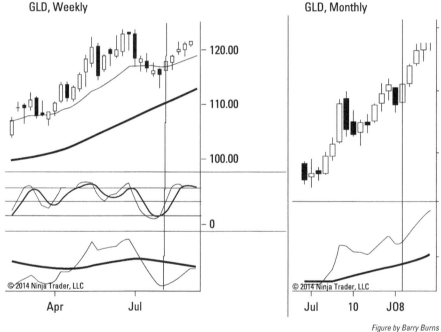

Figure 15-15: Potential commodities trade setup.

Figure by Barry Burns

After analyzing the chart for yourself, read the following analysis and compare your answer:

- ✔ The trend is up, so you're looking for a long trade.

- ✔ The market has retraced to the 15 EMA, which provides support for the price bars to bounce off and go back up. Also, the fact that the price bars stopped going down at the 15 EMA, instead of retracing lower, shows good relative strength to the upside.

✔ The stochastic indicator (in the middle panel) shows a cycle low, meaning that it's time for the market to put in a low and move back down.

✔ Momentum (the thin MACD line in the bottom panel) has remained above 0, thus indicating a strong uptrend.

✔ The energy of scale, as measured by the angle of the thin MACD line on the monthly chart is angling up, thus confirming the trade.

In summary: This is a good setup, and all five energies align to confirm a long trade.

Ogling the Options

Trading options is a specialized area that I don't have the time or space to cover in detail in this book. If you're not familiar with options, you may want to skip this section.

One of the biggest challenges I find options traders wrestling with is that many of them aren't skilled at reading the chart of the underlying instrument upon which they're making an option trade. They may be very familiar with the numerous option strategies — straddles, strangles, butterflies, condors, credit spreads, and so on — and having an intimate knowledge of those option strategies is crucial for trading options, but it isn't enough.

You absolutely *must* understand the energies of the underlying chart of the market you're using for your option strategy before you can make decisions regarding the best strike price, expiration date, and option strategy. Too many option strategies exist to cover them all here, but I present three strategies to illustrate how using the five energies on the underlying chart can assist you in your option trading.

Buying calls or puts in the direction of the trend

Buying puts and calls is the simplest option strategy. It's strategically the same as going long or shorting the market.

The differences include choosing a strike price in or out of the money, deciding on an expiration date (option contracts have an end time after which they're worthless), and dealing with time decay and the other "Greeks." Here's the overall strategy:

1. **Determine the direction of the market, which is energy number 1 (trend).**

2. **Determine the strength of that trend, or momentum, which is energy number 2.**

   This critical element reduces the probability that you'll buy a call in the direction of the trend only to have that trend come to an end immediately after you buy your calls.

3. **Buy a call at the lowest price possible.**

   This requires timing, and that's what cycles (energy number 4) are all about. In some cases, if the market is going down, you may find that calls sell at a discount.

4. **Buy your calls at a support level, energy number 4.**

   Doing so increases the odds that the market may be less likely to continue its correction against the trend and bounce back up.

5. **Buy a call in the direction of momentum on the higher scale chart.**

   This gives you that extra confirmation that the market will go up and that your call purchase will be successful.

Buying puts is similar to shorting the market, so, the same thing applies in using the five energies on the underlying chart to the downside.

Putting in spread strategies in the direction of the trend

Everything comes at a cost in trading. Therefore spread strategies can also limit your reward.

Using the energy of momentum to determine the strength of the market you're trading, along with consulting the wave count of the trend, can provide information as to the price level at which you may be willing to sacrifice reward in exchange for that limited risk.

Place that limited reward level at a price you believe the market is unlikely to reach based on the strength of the market and how far the market has already moved in the direction of the trend.

Selling options against the trend

Instead of investing money to trade in the direction of the trend, some option traders prefer to sell the options to those who buy them, thus collecting a premium for the sale up front. Their hope is that they get to keep the premium when the trader who bought the option is unsuccessful in her trade (perhaps resulting in the option expiring worthless).

To do this successfully, you still need to first analyze the underlying chart with regard to the direction of the market, how strong that direction is, and the timing of the cycle highs and lows. You should evaluate all these factors before making a decision on whether to sell a put or call, at what expiration time, and at what strike price.

You generally don't want to sell a call early in a strong uptrend. Rather, you want to sell a call late in a weak (low momentum) uptrend. You can also sell a call in a downtrend, but not as many traders may be buying calls in such a scenario, and it's also possible that the calls won't be as expensive because there isn't a high demand for them.

When the market looks bullish, people are generally willing to pay more to get in. That means higher premiums for you. The trick is to find a market that looks bullish to most investors and traders, but you're seeing something they don't, such as a trend reversal pattern and/or weakening momentum.

Each situation and each chart is different and must be evaluated individually. This is why it's important to become skilled at reading charts of the underlying market, even if you're trading options.

It's all the same — with a few important differences

The setups I trade using stocks, forex, futures, commodities, or options are all the same with regard to the technical analysis setups on the charts. They're also the same regardless of the holding period I'm trading — day trading, swing trading, or investing.

Here are some practical tips and differences in the various markets:

✔ Consider the risks of using leverage in making all your decisions.

✔ Use risk-aversion and money-management techniques appropriate for the amount of leverage you're employing in your position.

✔ Remember that your margin requirements may change if you hold a position overnight.

✔ With higher priced stocks, you may want to add five or ten cents to your buy/sell stop-limit order.

✔ With spot forex trades, you may need to add the spread to your buy/sell stop-limit order.

✔ Tracking ETFs don't always perfectly correlate to the market they're tracking.

✔ Be aware of overnight risk when swing trading and investing. Consider hedging those positions with options or other instruments.

✔ With forex, it's best to trade during the time of day or night that the currencies in the pair you're trading are most active.

✔ Make sure the market(s) you trade have enough liquidity to allow you to get in and out of your trades quickly and without much slippage.

This list is just a springboard for you to become thoroughly knowledgeable about the ins and outs of any and all markets you trade.

Part IV

Determining Where, When, Why, What, and How to Trade

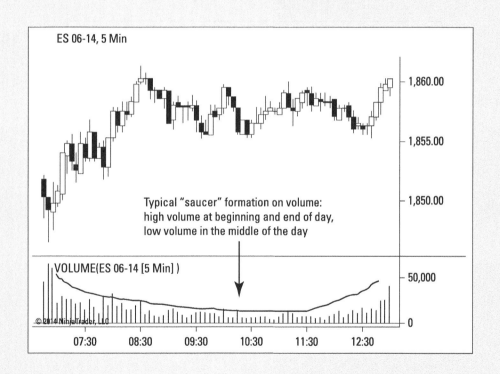

ES 06-14, 5 Min

Typical "saucer" formation on volume: high volume at beginning and end of day, low volume in the middle of the day

VOLUME(ES 06-14 [5 Min])

© 2014 NinjaTrader, LLC

How to Trade

In this part . . .

- ✔ Harness the power of leverage to make more money using less money.

- ✔ Find out when is the best time for you to trade.

- ✔ Spot the best trading opportunities by creating watch lists.

- ✔ Make even more money, using relative strength.

- ✔ Find out how to let your computer do some of the work to scan the markets and find the best trades.

Chapter 16

Understanding Leverage

In This Chapter

▷ Leveraging your way to wealth

▷ Trading options, futures, and money

*T*rading isn't a get-rich-quick business; however, by trading, you can make money faster than normal. One of the techniques people use to get wealthier faster is leverage. And you can use leverage (which I define in this chapter) not only in the financial markets but also in many areas of business.

In this chapter, you find out what leverage is and how to use it in trading to make money faster than usual. You also discover the perils to beware of when using leverage.

Using Leverage for Financial Gain

In mechanical terms, a lever is a bar that rests over a fulcrum, used to move an object at one end by applying force at the other end. It can provide a mechanical advantage by allowing you to move a heavy object with relatively less force than would be required without the lever.

In financial terms, leverage refers to the ability to control a financial asset with a smaller amount of money than the asset is worth. In the following sections, I explore leverage as it relates to using it to make money with a small account and also the risks that accompany it.

Controlling a lot of money with a little money

The use of leverage is paramount to accelerate success in all types of business endeavors. It's commonly used in various ways depending on the nature of the business.

In a traditional business that sells a product or a service, your income is greatly limited if you're operating as a sole proprietor and are the only one operating every aspect of the business. You're limited in many ways, including the following:

- ✔ **The amount of time you can invest in your business:** There are only 24 hours in every day, and you still need to eat, sleep, take care of your family, and lead a balanced life with outside interests. Your business is severely restricted purely by the limitation of man hours.

- ✔ **The skills, knowledge, and talent you possess:** As they say, "two heads are better than one," but as the only worker in your business, you have only one head! This dramatically limits the creativity, knowledge base, experience to access, and skill set available to make your business succeed.

- ✔ **The amount of money you have to invest in your business:** Assuming you don't have unlimited funds in your possession, your financial resources for building the business are limited by the amount of money you personally own or can access based on your individual credit.

To overcome these severe restrictions, businesses often grow by applying leverage in several areas:

- ✔ They hire other people to multiply the man hours that can be applied to working the business.

- ✔ They hire experienced managers who bring with them skills, knowledge, and talent beyond the founder's.

- ✔ They bring in investors and/or partners to help fund the business's growth.

These are all ways of applying the leverage of other people's time, expertise, and money to build a business bigger and faster than would otherwise be possible.

Another very common way that many people use leverage is in buying a home (or for real estate investors, buying many homes, apartments, and commercial property). Few people can afford to buy a home by paying the entire asking price with cash up front. To solve this problem, they approach a bank for a mortgage, which allows them the leverage of buying a home with a down payment relatively inexpensive to the full cost of the house.

This is a perfect example of being able to control an expensive asset with a small amount of money. The use of this type of leverage results in people owning a home that's their largest asset by the time they retire.

The use of leverage is also available for traders in many cases. The amount of leverage made available to an individual depends on several factors, including the type of financial instrument being traded. Generally speaking, stock brokers may provide 4-to-1 leverage to pattern day traders who qualify. Overnight leverage for stocks may be 2-to-1 leverage. Futures are commonly known for offering much more leverage, often in the neighborhood of 10-to-1 or 20-to-1.

Spot forex has a reputation for offering some of the highest leverage available. It varies by country and broker but can be as high as 50-to-1 in the United States at the time of this writing.

The advantage of leverage is clear: You can control more shares, contracts, or lots of a market while committing less of your own money to the position. This allows you to make more money faster than if you put up the entire value of the investment. This dynamic of controlling a lot of money with a little money makes leverage the secret to getting wealthy.

Making a money-management plan

Although leverage helps a successful trader make money faster, it has an equally, or even more dramatically, detrimental effect on unsuccessful traders. Such traders will rack up losses more quickly and in larger amounts when using leverage.

Unfortunately, the use of leverage appeals greatly to traders who don't have much money to open a trading account, because the initial deposit requirements are smaller. These are usually the same traders who aren't in a position to trade successfully. In fact, being "underfunded" is well known as one of the primary reasons for failure among retail traders.

Money-management rules to keep your losses in check

The purpose of money-management rules is to help prevent you from losing all your money (also known as "blowing out your account"). Following are some money-management rules to consider:

✔ **Only risk a small amount of your total account per trade.** You want to keep your risk low, perhaps 0.5 to 1 percent.

✔ **Only risk a small amount of your total account per day.** This is called a *daily stop.* Perhaps set a rule that if you lose 3 or 4 percent of your total account in a given day, you'll stop trading for that day.

✔ **Only risk a small amount of your total account per week.** This is called a *weekly stop.* Perhaps set a rule that if you lose 5 percent of your total account in a given week, you'll stop trading for that week.

✔ **Only risk a small amount of your total account per month.** This is called a *monthly stop.* Perhaps set a rule that if you lose 10 percent of your total account in a given week, you'll stop trading for that month.

✔ **Only risk a small amount of your total account per quarter.** This is called a *quarterly stop.* Perhaps set a rule that if you lose 15 percent of your total account in a given quarter, you'll stop trading for that quarter.

✔ **Only risk a small amount of your total account per year.** This is called a *yearly stop.* Perhaps set a rule that if you lose 25 percent of your total account in a given year, you'll stop trading for that year.

Keep in mind that these are only examples. You'll have to set your own specific numbers. Your numbers should be set at a level where, if hit, you realize that you're doing something wrong and you need to either change your trading methodology, work on your trading psychology, or get more training.

Be sure you have enough money in your account to allow you to survive a series of losses (known as *drawdowns*) without diminishing your account size where your broker will initiate a *margin call*. (A margin call occurs when the amount of money in your account goes below the required minimum of your broker. If you can't replace the money quickly, your broker may liquidate your open positions.)

You need a sound money-management plan to help mitigate such painful losses. (See the nearby sidebar, "Money-management rules to keep your losses in check," for tips on money management.)

Even with the use of leverage, I make it a practice to never risk more than 2 percent of my entire account on any one given trade. Doing so allows me to survive a series of losses (a natural and common occurrence) and still have money to trade when the market starts cooperating with my trading methodology again.

Trading with a Smaller Account

Trading financial instruments that provide more leverage than the stock market allows you to participate in the trading world with a smaller account. Just remember to use sound money-management principles, especially limiting the percentage of your account you devote to any single trade.

In the following sections, I introduce you to three financial markets that allow you to use leverage and, therefore, allow you to trade with less money in your account than you would otherwise need.

Opting for options

Options are contracts that give you the right, but not the obligation, to purchase a stock (or future or currency) at a predetermined price and during a predetermined time period. They don't give you ownership of the market upon which you're taking a contract. Although it can be said that options provide leverage, they do so in a different way than stocks, futures, or forex. The amount of leverage is subject to many variables beyond the scope of this chapter, but for the sake of illustration, you may be able to control a stock position worth $30,000 with only a $1,500 investment in options.

If you decide that options may be for you, make sure you get a thorough education before participating in the options markets. You need to consider many variables when trading options that don't apply to other markets.

Here are just a few factors that make options more complicated trading tools than other financial instruments:

- ✓ **Options have various strike prices.** You choose a price at which you want to buy the stock.

- ✓ **Options expire on a certain date.** If you're holding the option on that date, it'll be worthless, and you'll lose all your money.

✔ **Options experience time decay.** *Time decay* means that the value of an option can reduce simply with the passage of time as it approaches its expiration date.

✔ **The expected (implied) volatility of options is figured into the pricing.** If market participants expect the market to experience a lot of volatility (and thus the possibility to earn a lot of money), the option will be priced higher to account for that extra profit potential.

✔ **Liquidity of options varies dramatically from one contract to another.** The strike price and expiration date of an option you want may be hindered by low liquidity, which can make it hard to get the price you want because only a small pool of buyers or sellers are interested.

On the other hand, you can use options effectively as a type of insurance to hedge against losses of your stock, future, or currency positions. For this reason, I encourage you to become educated about them.

Building a fortune with futures

At the beginning of my trading career, I traded stocks because my first teacher, my dear ol' dad, was a stock trader. So, naturally, when I started day trading, I traded stocks. I did that for many years, but then eventually I was introduced to the *futures* market by one of my mentors.

When you buy a *futures* contract, you're not buying the asset like you would a stock. You're buying a contract that obligates you to buy the market (commodity, financial instrument, currency, and so on) at a predetermined time and price.

A futures contract and an options contract have several differences, but one of the primary differences is that an options contract doesn't obligate you to buy or sell the underlying asset, whereas a futures contract does (if held to the date the contract expires; see the previous section for more on options).

Now, I rarely day trade stocks because the amount of money I have to tie up in my trading account is beyond what I want to commit. Day trading futures, however, allows me to control a large asset with a smaller account, thus allowing me to do other things with the rest of my money.

I put off day trading futures because I was afraid of the high leverage. And that fear isn't a bad thing. You want to listen to your fears and understand that they're warning you of potential danger. Indeed, leverage is a two-edged sword and, therefore, comes with some danger that needs to be taken seriously.

I started slow and over time became more comfortable with the leverage. It was exciting to be able to make money faster than with stocks and with committing less of my own resources.

To help manage my healthy fear of the leverage, I use *hard stops* — working orders you actually place in the market at a price in which you'd no longer want to be in the trade if the market turns against you. I also hedge my positions with options (so if the market goes dramatically against me, I make money on the options contracts to help offset the money I lose on the futures contracts).

Making money by trading money (forex)

Most people are familiar with their ability to trade stocks and commodities, but it's also possible to trade money! Trading money is called *trading currencies* or *forex* (also called FX or currencies and stands for foreign exchange). Trading currencies is trading the current exchange rate between two countries' currencies.

You can trade currencies in two ways. The first is through a *futures exchange*. In that case, they function like other future contracts that are based on the prices at some time in the future. A second way to trade currencies is to trade *spot forex,* sometimes called *cash forex,* because its valuation is based on the prices of the currencies exchange rates in the present.

Unlike stocks and futures, spot forex isn't traded through a central exchange, such as the NYSE, NASDAQ, or the CME Group.

In the past, the retail spot forex market experienced many abuses and even fraud. Since 2010, however, more regulation has been implemented to avoid many of the previous problems.

A couple of the most popular advantages of trading spot forex are

- ✔ Up to 50-to-1 leverage, thereby allowing traders to participate with much smaller account sizes
- ✔ Twenty-four-hour trading, making the market available for short-term trading to those who work during normal stock market trading hours

Start strong in your trading career

In my decades as a trader, I've heard many stories of woe from traders who have "blown out their account" (meaning they lost all the money in their trading account). Don't start your trading career irresponsibly. Blowing out your account is too easy, especially when employing leverage in a small account.

To help yourself start strong when you start trading, follow this process:

1. **Get an excellent education.**

   Begin with free information online to get the basics of terminology and concepts. Read books to deepen your knowledge base. Take an excellent trading course that teaches a specific trading methodology that includes not only trade setups but also money management and the psychology of trading. Hire a mentor to work with you one on one. You may also want to hire a coach to help you with your unique psychological challenges in trading.

2. **Get some practice.**

   When you're ready to start trading, do so on a simulator or a demo account so you can practice entering and exiting trades on an execution software program without risking real money. The design of the simulator should be as close to real money trading as possible.

3. **Go "live" with a small amount of real money.**

   After you've been profitable on the simulator for at least several consecutive months and then when you feel confident, begin trading with a small amount of real money. Take it slow because trading with real money is a completely different psychological experience than trading on a simulator. It's normal for this to adversely affect your trading results. Expect that. Work on your psychological issues to overcome it.

4. **Increase your trades wisely.**

   When you become consistently profitable over a long period of time, you may choose to use your profits to increase the size of your trades. Always stay true to your money-management rules. Be aware of your psychological threshold — that is, how much money you trade starts to create fear in you. Trading with fear is never a good idea! Respect your own limits.

Chapter 17

Choosing a Trading Time That Works for You

. . . .

In This Chapter:
▷ Day trading for immediate gratification
▷ Taking the relaxed approach to trading
▷ Trading the night away

. . . .

*T*hanks to the speed and low cost of technology, the access to worldwide information, and the tighter spreads and lower costs of trading, anyone with capital has the ability to trade the financial markets.

The edge of the professional floor trader, or specialist, over the retailer has diminished significantly. In fact, my last visit to the floor of the Chicago Mercantile Exchange (CME) was quite an eye-opener. The number of people trading on the floor has reduced drastically. The playing field between floor traders and retail traders has been greatly leveled, and you have choices that retail traders before you never dreamed of.

Along with that opportunity has come the ability to trade nearly any time of day or night. In this chapter, you discover the choices you have when it comes to trading times, so you can figure out which option is best for you.

Day Trading During Open Outcry Hours

The exciting advances in technology have made it possible for the average person to have lightning-quick access to market data and execute trades with such blazing speed that you can sit at home and participate in quick, short-term trading and scalping trades that may last only a few minutes. That technology led to the popularization of *day trading* — the practice of entering and exiting trades on the same day, thereby not holding trades overnight when they may be exposed to dramatic moves caused by news while the markets are closed.

Day trading can be exciting because of the speed with which you can make money. Rather than waiting years to make a return (or not) on your investment, day trading offers the potential to make hundreds or even thousands of dollars in a matter of minutes.

Of course, like most things, there are two sides to every coin. Day trading is extremely risky because you can also lose hundreds or thousands of dollars in a few minutes. A lot of marketing hype surrounds day trading, so I caution you that although it's possible to make that type of money, and some people do, the fact is most people lose money day trading. It's much harder than it looks.

One of the most dangerous aspects of day trading is the allure of fast money and the adrenaline rush that can accompany making that fast money. Experienced traders know that the worst thing that can happen to new traders is for them to experience too much success.

Consistent profitability comes only after a long time trading in the trenches. Early success is luck and can create a false sense of confidence that leads newbies to overtrade, break their trading rules, or start trading with too much capital. These behaviors lead to losing a healthy respect for the market, followed by losing money.

Successful day trading is a profession, not a get-rich-quick-scheme in which an e-book or some special software makes you rich overnight. Like any other profession, day trading (or any type of trading for that matter) takes a commitment to long-term education, practice, serious study, and experience. It also requires that you have access to *discretionary money* — funds that you could lose without severely damaging your overall financial health — because trading is a business that takes money to make money. You should trade only with money you don't need for retirement, your emergency fund, your kids' education, your home payment, your monthly expenses, and so on.

Also, day trading usually requires that you're available to trade during normal business hours. Therefore, unless you're retired, work outside of regular business hours, or are independently wealthy, day trading may not fit into your schedule.

During *open outcry hours* (the hours when the floor of the exchange is open for trading), the volume is at its highest and there's the most activity. That is my favorite time to *day trade* futures and stocks. I talk more about the best times to day trade in the following sections.

Trading stocks and futures when you can

With the expanding access of the markets to retail traders, stocks and futures have been made available for electronic trading beyond the open outcry hours of the exchanges. The volume of trading during those times is typically very low, and therefore the markets move very slow. It can take hours for a trade to develop that would have taken minutes during open outcry hours.

Another problem with trading stocks and futures outside of open outcry hours is that the low volume can lead to bad fills — the price at which your order is executed. If not a lot of people are trading at any given time, there may be a large difference between the *bid* (the price traders are willing to buy the market for) and the *offer* (the price that other traders are willing to sell that same market for). That difference is called the *spread*.

Whether you get filled at the price you want may or may not happen depending on what type of order you use.

For example, if you use a *market order* — an order that gets filled at the best price available at the time you place the order — you may have intended to buy shares of a stock at $25.10. However, if you place that order premarket or post-market, there aren't a lot of people trading at that time, and the spreads are large, you may find that you bought the stock for $25.25!

You can help avoid that by placing a *limit order* — an order that assures you get filled at the price you designate or better — but then you risk the chance of not getting your order filled at all.

For example, if you placed a limit order to buy a stock at $25.10, you'd be filled only at the price of $25.10 or lower. But if no one offers to sell you the stock at that price, you won't have your order filled, and you'll suffer the potential of losing an opportunity to participate in the stocks ascent to higher prices.

When I day trade stocks and futures, I trade them during open outcry hours to avoid the potential dangers of slippage. In the United States, the New York Stock Exchange (NYSE) is open from 9:30 a.m. to 4:00 p.m. Eastern Time.

The futures markets vary a bit regarding their most active trading times. Go to the website of the exchange that handles the futures market you want to trade and find the open outcry hours.

If you're like most people and have a job during normal business hours, it may still be possible to trade some futures contracts before work. In California, where I live, active trading of the Euro futures begins around

5:00 to 5:30 a.m. I'm fortunate enough not to have a job, but if I did, I could trade the Euro early in the morning, and even stocks and the E-minis from 6:30 a.m. to perhaps 7:30 a.m. before going to work.

You don't have to trade all day to make money. Many traders, including myself, day trade only a few hours per day.

Trading during the most active and exciting times of day

Trading during the open outcry session provides you with the most liquidity, tightest spreads, and fastest market movement for making money. However, even within the open outcry hours, markets are more active during certain times of the day than others.

First thing in the morning

Generally, the most active time of day is within the first hour of a market's open for the day. For this reason, some traders choose to trade only the first one to three hours of the day.

Trading the open can be very exciting because often a flurry of activity creates big fast moves, potentially resulting in big fast profits. Beware, however, that some of those orders may be *market on open orders* that were placed ahead of time and have little to no significance to the activity of the market at the time of the open. (Market on open orders are placed before the open of the market to be filled as soon as possible when the market opens, at whatever price the market is trading. A market on open order can be used to enter a new trade or exit an existing trade.) Therefore, market on open orders can wreak havoc with technical analysis signals until those market on open orders have been processed.

The "second open" after lunch

The middle of the day is lunch time, and activity (volume) generally slows down significantly. If you're on the floor of the exchange, you'll see many of the professional traders hand over their tasks to lower-ranking members of their firms and leave the building to go to lunch.

The idea that market activity dies down during lunch time is well known, and anything that becomes common knowledge usually stops working. I've noticed that this pattern isn't as consistent as it used to be. Watch for exceptions when the midday doldrums start later than usual, begin earlier than usual, or are skipped altogether.

Sometimes, professional traders stay on the floor through lunch time, or at least part of it. Being able to see that is one of the advantages of trading on the floor rather than trading from your home or office.

After lunch is over, a new surge of volume comes into the market, which I call "the second open." Volatility, volume, and activity picks up dramatically again.

I always watch for a trading opportunity right after lunch to participate in the large move that often follows. This second open is often a safer open to trade than the open at the beginning of the day where you have to contend with less meaningful market on open orders.

Pull up a chart of the markets you normally trade and plot volume at the bottom of the chart. Scroll through about a month of charts, and you'll see the basic meta-pattern of the times of day that market is normally active and the times it's quiet.

Figure 17-1 shows the typical pattern of high activity in the morning and afternoon and low activity midday. That pattern is revealed by the saucer pattern of volume.

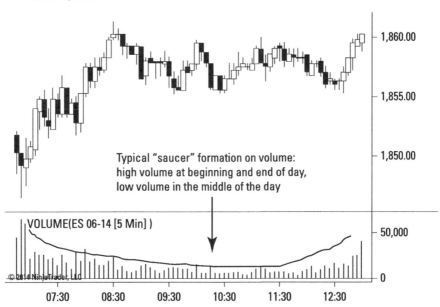

Figure 17-1: High activity in the morning and afternoon with low midday activity.

Figure by Barry Burns

News events that affect the market

Market activity and volume can pick up dramatically when news items are released. These items can occur any time of day, even outside of open outcry hours. Such news may pertain to a company, the economy, politics, war or terror attacks, and significant events around the world.

Not all news is equal when it comes to trading. Only the news that market participants expect will affect market valuations have a dramatic effect on the market. Some news-announcement calendars rate the importance of the news in relation to its market-moving significance.

The significance of the news-to-market valuation doesn't always make big moves in the market. Traders have built into the market's pricing their expectation of the news before it's released. Large price movements are most often caused when the news released is dramatically out of sync with the expectations.

Always be aware of scheduled news announcements and also be mentally prepared should surprise news be released.

Swing Trading for Those Who Have to Work for a Living

Swing trading is short-term trading that involves holding your position overnight from at least one day to another. It's a very popular style of trading among people who aren't able to trade during the day, but day traders also use it as an additional style of trading.

I enjoy swing trading, but I keep my swing trades separate from my day trades. In fact, I use separate brokerage accounts for day trading and swing trading. During market hours, I focus on my day trading and mostly ignore my swing trades. After the market closes, I consult my swing trading positions and make decisions to implement the next day.

In the following sections, I share with you some of the advantages that swing trading has over day trading.

Trading stocks after work

Swing trading is a viable option for people who want to trade frequent short-term positions but aren't available during open outcry hours because they work during normal business hours. The benefit of swing trading is that you can focus on your job while at work and then do your market analysis after you return home.

Consult your charts and search for any high-probability setups that have the potential of triggering the next day. You can then place a buy or sell stop order at the price you want to enter the market. The next day, the market will either move to your trigger price or it won't. If it does, you get automatically filled, and your position is initiated.

You can tie an "if, then" order with your entry that automatically places your stop loss order if your trade is executed. Consult with your broker to determine whether he offers that functionality.

 You may want to place your entry order as a *limit order* so you're filled only at the price you want or very close to it (based on the price range you establish in your order). A limit order is one in which you aren't guaranteed to be filled, but if you are filled, it will be at the price that you designated (or better).

Taking your own sweet time

Swing trading offers a potential advantage over day trading for those who want more time to analyze charts and make trading decisions.

One of the most challenging aspects of day trading is that it's fast moving. When a trade setup occurs, you have to analyze the setup quickly to evaluate exactly how good that setup is and then make a speedy decision to execute your trade.

Time pressure can make day trading very stressful and lead to bad decisions (which may have been obvious given more time to analyze the trade). It also isn't conducive to individuals with personality types who are uncomfortable making quick decisions.

As a swing trader, you have the advantage of analyzing charts after the markets have closed. Without the time pressure of having to make a decision before the opportunity has passed, you can do your analysis in a relaxed manner and with a clear head, which may result in you making better decisions.

Forex Trading Around the Clock

Forex is an abbreviation for "foreign exchange" and refers to the exchange rates between two currencies. You're able to trade those exchange rates because they're in constant flux.

The forex market is enormous in size, trading trillions of dollars per day. Although this size is often touted as an advantage of the forex market over other markets, it's a bit deceiving. The forex market doesn't have a central exchange; therefore, the liquidity for your personal trading is limited by the liquidity of forex trading conducted through your brokerage firm. Even with that, however, forex trading of the most popular pairs has tremendous volume.

In the following sections, I share with you the importance of knowing the best times to trade any given forex pair.

Trading the sun around the clock

A benefit often cited about forex trading is that currencies trade around the clock, 24 hours per day. This schedule allows you to trade any time of day or night you're available. So trading forex can be a valid choice for those who want to trade short-term positions but can't day trade during normal business hours.

Although currencies trade 24 hours per day, futures currencies are generally not as liquid as spot (cash) currencies outside of normal business hours. Even spot currencies don't trade with the same level of volume 24 hours per day. The volume tends to "follow the sun" around the globe.

Knowing which currencies to trade and when

A simple phrase to help you know which currencies to trade and when is "Don't trade where the sun don't shine!" In trading forex, consult a timeline that shows you where it's day time, and trade the currency associated with that country. At that time, that currency will be trading most actively. You can find such timelines on the Internet, and some will even allow you to set the timeline based on your time zone. Here are a few:

✔ forex.timezoneconverter.com

✔ www.forexmarkethours.com

✔ www.worldtimebuddy.com/forex-hours

A second consideration of the best time to trade currencies is when the currencies of two countries are trading at the same time. Trade the currency pair of those two countries, and you take advantage of the volume of both currencies at the same time. You may also want to consider the overall volume of the currencies. Some currencies trade very low volume, even during their most active times of day. Other currencies are very popular and consistently trade in high volumes.

The six "majors" (most frequently traded currencies) are

✔ The euro (EUR)

✔ The U.S. dollar (USD)

✔ The Japanese yen (JPY)

✔ The Great Britain pound sterling (GBP)

✔ The Australian dollar (AUD)

✔ The Swiss franc (CHF)

The most commonly traded currency pairs are

✔ EUR/USD

✔ USD/JPY

✔ GBP/USD

✔ USD/CHF

The way to trade the forex market with the most volume and activity is to trade the four most commonly traded currency pairs during times when one, or preferably both, of the countries associated with those currencies is actively trading during those countries' daylight business hours. Because these countries are scattered across the globe, you can trade currencies whenever it's convenient for you as the sun moves across the planet from Australia/Japan to Great Britain/Europe to United States/North America.

My 13-hour trading day

Back "in the day" when I was a young trader, I was so passionate about trading that I never wanted to stop. My friends thought I was crazy, because while they looked forward to weekends and holidays so they didn't have to go to work, I hated weekends and holidays because the markets weren't open!

I live in California, so my trading day started at midnight and ended at 1:00 p.m. Pacific Time. I would trade the European markets and the Asian markets while they were active. Then when New York opened, I traded the U.S. markets until they closed.

Being youthful and filled with passion about learning as much as I could as quickly as I could, it was fun, and I gained a lot of experience in a short amount of time. The downside was that my schedule was different than everyone else's, so while my friends were awake, I had to sleep so I could get up before midnight to start trading. My social life wasn't much in those days! Also, I don't think staring at my seven monitors for 13 hours over the course of several years did my eyes any favors. I found myself getting headaches and getting moody.

I'm still passionate about trading, but now I trade only one to three hours per day. I find that's enough for me at this stage in my life. It doesn't feel like a chore, I still look forward to trading every day, and I can also enjoy other things in life and lead a wonderful, balanced lifestyle.

Chapter 18

Creating Watch Lists to Find the Best Opportunities

***

In This Chapter

▶ Hunting for bull and bear markets

▶ Creating candidates for day trading

▶ Keeping watch for swing trading and investing

***

A common question I'm asked from traders is, "What market is the best to trade?" After talking to traders who ask that question, I've come to understand that the question behind the question is really this: "With which market will I make the most money?"

No single market always provides you with the best opportunities. The "best market" to trade varies from time to time. In this chapter, I show you how to find good, high-probability markets to trade at any given time.

Finding the Raging Bull and Bear Markets

If you scan the world of financial markets, you'll be able to find a strong bull market somewhere and a strong bear market somewhere. Some traders prefer to simply pick about one to three favorite markets and trade only those markets. They feel that if they focus on a couple markets they follow closely every day, they'll tap into the "personalities" of those markets and develop an intuitive sense of how they move, which will help them trade those markets better than other traders.

Knowing people who do that successfully, I won't argue the validity of that approach. However, the concept of markets having a personality has never made sense to me personally. In addition, that approach limits the number of their high-probability trading opportunities.

On the other hand, there are thousands of stocks in the U.S. alone, and not all of them are prime trading candidates.

In the following sections, I help you filter the universe of stocks to determine the qualities you want in a good candidate for trading and how to find those candidates.

Figuring out where to look

Instead of "getting to know the personality" of a single market, I like to look at a wide variety of markets to uncover the money-making opportunities I can take advantage of right now.

Every market cycles between times of chaotic, random movement (in which no high-probability trading opportunities exist) and structured, orderly movement (in which high-probability trading opportunities abound). By trading only one market, you're committing yourself to long periods of sitting on the sidelines during the chaotic cycle, not making money.

Instead of waiting for a new orderly cycle to begin (and making no money while I'm waiting), I prefer to search the various financial markets to find one that's in an orderly cycle now, so I can make money now. With so many various types of financial markets available, sorting through them all to find one that's providing a favorable probability scenario to trade is a daunting task, so I create a list of just a few based on the following criteria:

- ✔ High average daily trading volume
- ✔ Tight bid/ask spreads
- ✔ Pricing that fits money-management rules for the size of the account
- ✔ Representatives from various financial vehicles that don't always correlate with the others

Creating a watch list

This section covers in more detail the criteria I use to make a watch list. These four criteria will give you a good start, but feel free to add other criteria if you like.

Good average daily trading volume

The point of this criteria is that the market has enough liquidity (active trading) that you're able to get in and out of trades at the price you want, with the size order you want, when you want. That means that the actual average daily trading volume required may vary from one trader to another, based on the number of shares, lots, or contracts each one trades.

For example, if you trade 10,000 shares at a time, you don't want to trade a stock that trades an average of only 100,000 shares per day because you're making 10 percent of that market. A general rule is that you want your position not to be more than one-tenth of 1 percent of the average daily trading volume.

Markets have extraordinary trading volume from time to time, so be sure you don't look at the volume of a market on only one day for this criteria.

Instead look at the average daily trading volume over a period of at least 90 days. You want to make sure that the market has consistently enough volume to provide the liquidity you need on whatever day you decide to make a trade.

Tight bid/ask spreads

When you enter a trade, you want to get filled as close as possible to the price you want to pay.

If the price buyers are willing to pay and the price sellers are willing to receive differs greatly, you may end up paying more than you wanted for the trade. This is called "slippage" and can be seen as an added cost to your trade. Slippage is much more common in lightly traded, low-priced markets than in high-volume, expensive markets.

Pricing that fits money-management rules

One of the money-management rules you should have addresses the percentage of your entire trading account that you're willing to risk on any one trade. My rule is that I won't risk more than 2 percent of my trading account on any one trade. That risk refers to the difference from my entry price to my stop-loss price. The more money you have in your account, the higher priced markets you can trade.

For example, if you have $1,000 in your trading account and you want to trade a stock that's worth $100 per share, the maximum you can afford to buy is ten shares. However, that isn't responsible money management because then you're risking all your money on one stock. On the other hand, if you had $1 million in your account, you could easily afford to trade a $100 stock and not be in danger of risking too large of a percentage on any one trade.

Representatives from various financial vehicles

To find a bull or bear market in one place when other markets are in chaos cycles, you need to look at markets that are uncorrelated to others. If you trade only equity indexes, you won't find as many opportunities because the major equity indexes generally move in concert with each other, just with different relative strengths.

Using Watch Lists for Day Trading

Employing watch lists for day trading is a bit different than using watch lists with other time frames because the opportunities come and go fast on the short-term charts used for day trading. Day trading doesn't allow you to spend a lot of time looking at a large number of markets for trading opportunities. When you find a good trading opportunity, you don't have much time to analyze it and trade it.

In the following sections, I'll share with you exactly how I create my watch lists to find excellent day trading opportunities.

Watching uncorrelated markets

I keep my watch list for day trading short because of the limited time available to analyze and trade. For my personal setup, I have seven monitors and watch five markets: I dedicate one monitor to my execution platform, a second monitor for watching the overall picture of the market that day, and the other five monitors to watch the S&P E-minis, the euro, crude oil, gold, and bonds. Each monitor is dedicated to one market, and each of those five markets have a low correlation to the other four.

Those markets have a relationship, but they're uncorrelated enough that, at any given time, one of them will often be in an orderly cycle when the others aren't. Trading very short-term intraday charts doesn't afford me the luxury of pulling up chart after chart, waiting for them to load, and then analyzing them. I keep the charts of those five markets up at all times so I can be watching them constantly, literally bar by bar.

Sampling some sample lists

You can day trade many markets, depending on your preferences. For example, if you're a stock trader, you may want to trade stocks from various sectors or industries, including any of the following:

- Agriculture
- Clean energy
- Cyclicals
- Oil
- Pharmaceuticals
- REITS
- Retail
- Technology
- Utilities

If you're a commodities trader, you could trade

- Coffee
- Cotton
- Gold
- Natural Gas
- Oil
- Silver
- Soybeans
- Wheat

And if you're a currencies trader, you could trade

- ✔ EUR/USD
- ✔ USD/CHF
- ✔ USD/JPY
- ✔ AUD/JPY

Analyzing Opportunities for Swing Trading and Investing

Swing traders have the luxury of time to analyze trade setups, evaluate them, and execute trades. The slower pace of swing trading also affords you the ability to work with larger watch lists, granting you a larger number of trading candidates from which to find a great opportunity.

In the following sections, I show you specifically how I find the best markets for swing trading at any given time.

Diving into a plethora of opportunities

When looking for my swing trading opportunities each day, I use the *quote screen* offered by my charting software platform. A quote screen is a separate window on your charting software and looks like a table with rows and columns. In the far left column, you enter the symbol of the market you want to monitor. You can create other columns to the right of it that provide various values depending on the functionality of your software.

Typically, you can show the amount (by points or percentage) the market is up or down for the day, the price of the market, and perhaps even the value of some charting indicators. Because swing trading affords you the time to look at more markets than day trading, you can create a long list of markets to watch.

Depending on the functionality of your software, you may be able to link your quote screen to your charts with a button on the top of your chart window and your quote screen window. When you make them the same color, it links the two windows together (as shown in Figure 18-1). The advantage of linking is that you don't have to type in the symbol of each market you want to review. Simply click on the symbol in the quote screen, and it automatically brings up that market on your chart window.

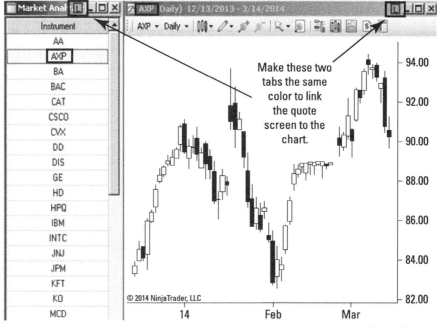

Figure 18-1:
Link the
quote
screen to
your charts
by making
the tabs the
same color.

Figure by Barry Burns

Sampling a sample list

Table 18-1 shows a sample watch list that you can use as a springboard to create your own watch list. The symbols listed here may be different from the symbols from your data provider for the same markets. For that reason, I include a column providing the name of the market so you may consult your data provider for those market symbols.

Table 18-1	Sample Watch List	
Symbol	*Description*	*Average Volume*
	~FUTURES	
ES	E-Mini S&P 500	1,727,262
NQ	E-Mini NASDAQ-100	241,042
TF	Russell 2000 Index Mini Futures	104,094
YM	E-Mini Dow Futures ($5)	141,469

(continued)

Table 18-1 *(continued)*

Symbol	Description	Average Volume
BP	British Pound Sterling	89,572
EC	Euro FX	168,233
JY	Japanese Yen	115,121
GC	Gold	144,897
CL	Crude Oil	244,824
	~SMALL CAP VALUE & DEEP VALUE	
IWN	iShares Russell 2000 Val ETF	949,554
	~LONG INDEXES	
DIA	SPDR DJ Industrial Average ETF	7,209,529
IWM	iShares Russell 2000 ETF	35,555,568
QQQ	PowerShares QQQ Trust Series 1	28,917,373
SPY	S&P Dep Receipts	119,153,143
	~LEVERAGED LONG INDEXES	
DDM	ProShares Trust Ultra Dow 30	282,654
MVV	ProShares Ultra MidCap 400	663,792
QLD	ProShares Ultra QQQ Trust	1,926,696
SSO	ProShares Ultra S&P 500	6,138,892
UWM	ProShares Ultra Russell 2000	532,388
	~TRIPLE LEVERAGED LONG	
ERX	Energy Bull 3x Shares	316,391
FAS	Financial Bull 3x Shares	5,921,918
TNA	Small Cap Bull 3x Shares	10,231,753
	~TRIPLE LEVERAGED SHORT	
ERY	Energy Bear 3x Shares	397,360
FAZ	Financial Bear 3x Shares	7,054,191
TZA	Small Cap Bear 3x Shares	12,168,068
	~SHORT INDEXES	
DOG	ProShares Trust Short Dow30	528,876
PSQ	ProShares Trust Short QQQ	423,531
RWM	ProShares Trust Short Russ2000	1,547,453
SH	ProShares Trust Short S&P 500	4,152,371

Symbol	Description	Average Volume
	~LEVERAGED SHORT INDEXES	
DXD	UltraShort Dow 30 ProShares	901,087
QID	UltraShort QQQ ProShares	3,380,581
SDS	UltraShort S&P 500 ProShares	10,781,778
TWM	ProShares Ultra Short Russel2k	2,522,968
	~OTHER LEVERAGED LONG INDEXES	
AGQ	ProShares Ultra Silver	2,202,009
DGP	DB Gold Double Long ETN	290,367
DIG	Ultra Oil And Gas ProShares	74,284
UCO	ProShares Ultra DJ-AIG Crude	1,164,525
UGL	ProShares Ultra Gold	181,267
URE	Ultra Real EstateProShares	144,381
UYG	Ultra Financials ProShares	166,559
UYM	Ultra Bas Mat ProShrs	71,352
	~OTHER LEVERAGED SHORT INDEXES	
DUG	UltraShort Oil And Gas ProShrs	122,618
EUO	ProShares UltraShort Euro	602,316
GLL	ProShares UltraShort Gold	262,465
SCO	ProShares UltraSh DJ-AIG Crude	1,679,782
SKF	UltraShort Financials ProShare	553,596
SRS	UltraShort Real Estate ProShrs	186,878
YCS	ProShares UltraShort Yen	284,831
ZSL	ProShares UltraShort Silver	474,187
	~ETF CURRENCIES	
FXA	Currency Shares Australian $	170,433
FXE	Currency Shares Euro Trust	308,651
UUP	PowerShars DB US Dollar Bull	1,055,047
	~HEAVILY TRADED SPOT FOREX	
EURUSD	Euro/U.S. Dollar	
GBPUSD	British Pound Sterling/U.S. Dollar	
USDCHF	U.S. Dollar/Swiss Franc	
USDJPY	U.S. Dollar/Japanese Yen	

(continued)

Table 18-1 *(continued)*

Symbol	Description	Average Volume
	~OTHER SPOT FOREX	
AUDJPY	Australian Dollar/Japanese Yen	
AUDUSD	Australian Dollar/U.S. Dollar	
CHFJPY	Swiss Franc/Japanese Yen	
EURAUD	Euro/Australian Dollar	
EURCHF	Euro/Swiss Franc	
EURGBP	Euro/British Pound Sterling	
EURJPY	Euro/Japanese Yen	
GBPCHF	British Pound Sterling/Swiss Franc	
GBPJPY	British Pound Sterling/Japanese Yen	
NZDUSD	New Zealand Dollar /U.S. Dollar	
USDCAD	U.S. Dollar/Canadian Dollar	
	~COUNTRIES	
EPP	iShs MSCI Pacific exJapan ETF	870,768
EWA	iShs MSCI Australia ETF	1,562,545
EWC	iShares MSCI Canada ETF	1,298,862
EWD	iShares MSCI Sweden ETF	145,913
EWG	iShs MSCI Germany ETF	2,768,911
EWH	iShs MSCI Hong Kong ETF	2,932,854
EWI	iShs MSCI Italy Capped ETF	1,446,125
EWJ	iShares MSCI Japan ETF	29,580,123
EWK	iShs MSCI Belgium Capd ETF	72,887
EWL	iShs MSCI Switzerland Cppd ETF	332,367
EWM	iShares MSCI Malaysia ETF	1,792,929
EWN	iShs MSCI Netherlands ETF	289,444
EWO	iShs MSCI Austria Capped ETF	123,413
EWP	iShs MSCI Spain Capped ETF	634,451
EWQ	iShs MSCI France ETF	450,263
EWS	iShs MSCI Singapore ETF	1,506,952
EWT	iShares MSCI Taiwan ETF	6,433,728
EWU	iShares MSCI UK ETF	2,430,598

Symbol	Description	Average Volume
EWW	iShs MSCI Mexico Capped ETF	3,202,868
EWZ	iShares MSCI Brazil Capped ETF	16,976,053
EZA	iShs MSCI So Africa ETF	405,278
ILF	iShares Latin Am 40 ETF	503,120
INP	iPath MSCI India Index ETN	90,605
PGJ	PwrShrs Golden Dragon China	175,396
	~OTHER MARKETS TO WATCH	
BBH	Mkt Vectors Biotech ETF	87,252
DBA	PowerShares DB Agriculture Fd	570,886
DBB	PowerShares DB Base Metals Fd	114,501
DBC	DB Commodity Index Tracking Fd	2,549,793
DVY	iShares Select Dividend ETF	823,720
EEM	iShares MSCI Emerg Mkt ETF	65,332,341
EFA	iShares MSCI EAFE ETF	15,290,590
FXI	iShares China Large-Cap ETF	19,008,708
GLD	SPDR Gold Trust	9,867,697
GOOG	Google Inc Cl A	1,926,084
IAI	iShs US Broker-Dealers ETF	62,136
IGE	iShs GS Natural Resources Fd	295,860
IGV	iShs North Ameri Tch-Software	82,259
IYM	iShares US Basic Mat ETF	356,515
IYR	iShares US R/E ETF	12,663,722
IYZ	iShares US Telecom ETF	309,621
KIE	SPDR S&P Insurance	98,772
OIH	Mkt Vectors Oil Services ETF	3,140,227
OIL	iPath Goldman Sachs Crude ETN	567,675
PBW	PwrShr WilderHill Clean Energy	438,916
PHO	PwrShs Water Resources Prtflio	84,231
RTH	Mkt Vectors Retail ETF	50,172
SLV	iShares Silver Trust	11,204,237
SLX	Market Vectors Steel	62,654
TIP	iShs TIPS Bond ETF	683,675

(continued)

Table 18-1 (continued)

Symbol	Description	Average Volume
TLT	iShs 20+ Yr Treasury Bd ETF	8,894,413
VDC	Vanguard Consum Staples ETF	59,878
VNQ	Vanguard REIT ETF	3,365,648
VTI	Vanguard Total Stock Mrkt ETF	2,468,057
XHB	SPDR S&P Homebuilders	6,438,283
XLB	S&P Sel Materials Spdr Fund	5,561,816
XLE	S&P Sel Energy Spdr Fund	9,341,488
XLF	S&P Sel Financial Spdr Fund	41,504,532
XLV	S&P Sel Health Care Spdr Fund	5,943,735
XLY	S&P Sel Consum Discretion'y Sp	5,881,601
XME	SPDR S&P Metals & Mining	2,715,817

If you trade what's popular, you'll become unpopular

The markets are well known for trading based on a herd mentality. Most people pride themselves as being unique individuals, and certainly in many ways they are. On the other hand, human beings are social in nature, and therefore the herd mentality is engrained into our psyches. This isn't necessarily a bad thing. Working as a team on projects, making an effort to get along with others, and capitalizing on the concept of "strength in numbers" are some of the benefits for being social in nature.

In trading, it can also work both ways. For markets to have strong moves, normally a market needs to have a lot of interest and a lot of money moving it. The approach of investing in growth companies is based on this philosophy — trading or investing in what has a lot of interest and is making big moves now. The approach of value investing is the opposite — looking for opportunities that aren't popular now but will (hopefully) be later when others see what you see.

Both approaches can work. The approach that doesn't work is being too late to the party. It's often said that when you start seeing a company being glorified on the cover of magazines, newspapers, and television, the train has left the station, and it's the worst time to invest.

Consistently, perfect timing is impossible. Entering too early before other people are interested in a stock makes it unlikely the stock will rise in the immediate future. Entering too late, after it's so popular that your great-grandmother is invested, and the deal is probably done. Trend trading provides an ideal compromise between those alternatives: Buy the market as early as possible in a new trend.

Chapter 19

Using Relative Strength to Make More Money

In This Chapter

▶ Looking at what trends are hot and which are not

▶ Watching strength signals to determine your move

▶ Being the first to the party (of the trend)

I explain in Chapter 18 that buying into a market that's overly popular will normally get you in late to the party and often just before the market turns around. However, it doesn't mean that you should ignore such markets. They can still present significant opportunities, just in the opposite way most people would guess.

In this chapter, I show you how to spot trading opportunities, using the concept of *relative strength*, which is the measurement of the strength of one market relative to the strength of another market. (***Note:*** The term *relative strength*, as I use the term in this chapter, has no correlation to the Relative Strength Index [RSI] often included in the list of indicators of charting software platforms.)

Knowing how to use relative strength may enable you to find potentially great trading opportunities early and at a good (low) price.

Finding What's Hot Now

The use of relative strength can help you choose which market is likely to offer the best opportunity in a new trend. In this section, you find out how to measure relative strength and how to a read a relative strength chart in order to spot the hot trends.

Measuring relative strength

As I mention earlier, relative strength is the measurement of the strength of one market relative to the strength of another market. For example, when two markets are moving up, one is moving up with more strength.

The major U.S. stock indexes normally trade in concert with each other. In a sustained uptrend of the stock market, the DOW, S&P 500, NASDAQ, and Russell 2000 all trend up, but one moves up faster than the others.

In Figure 19-1, both the S&P 500 (the thicker line) and the DOW (the thinner line) are moving up. However, at their last value on the right side of the chart, the S&P 500 has more relative strength than the DOW.

^DJIA, Daily

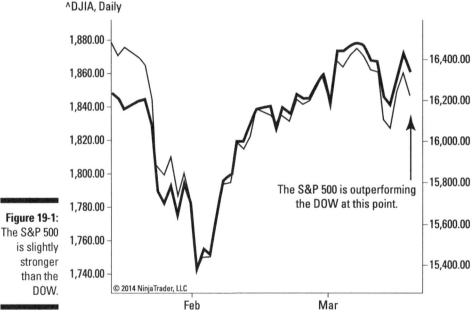

The S&P 500 is outperforming the DOW at this point.

Figure 19-1: The S&P 500 is slightly stronger than the DOW.

© 2014 NinjaTrader, LLC

Figure by Barry Burns

Not all trends are created equal. Some are stronger than others. The strongest trends make you more money, so those are the ones you want to trade.

After you've established the trend of a market, determine which subset of that market you want to trade by measuring relative strength. Here's how:

1. **Plot the two markets you want to compare on a chart.**

   Have them start plotting on some date in the past (on a daily chart, I'll often have them begin plotting 90 days prior to the current date).

2. **Use a percent change chart for both markets.**

Instead of measuring how much the markets move up or down in price, a *percent change chart* measures what percentage the markets move up or down from the starting point you set.

Reading relative strength

You can read the relative strength chart in a crude manner as I demonstrate earlier in Figure 19-1.

At first glance, you may think that whichever market is higher is the one that has the superior relative strength, but that's not necessarily true. More accurately, you need to observe how the two markets are moving toward or apart from each other. If one market is moving farther apart from the other to the upside, then it's gaining in bullish relative strength.

Figure 19-2 shows a time when the company Apple, Inc., (AAPL) was outperforming the S&P 500, as illustrated by the thin line (Apple) pulling away from the thick line (the S&P 500).

After outperforming the S&P 500 for a few weeks, Apple then had a sharp change in its relationship with the S&P 500 and clearly underperformed, as illustrated in Figure 19-3.

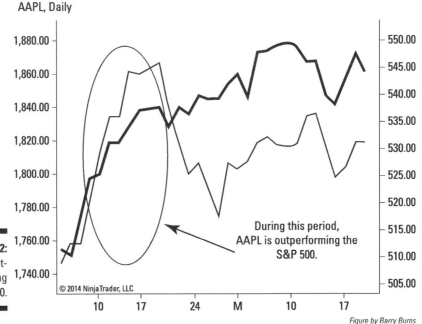

Figure 19-2: Apple is outperforming the S&P 500.

During this period, AAPL is outperforming the S&P 500.

© 2014 NinjaTrader, LLC

Figure by Barry Burns

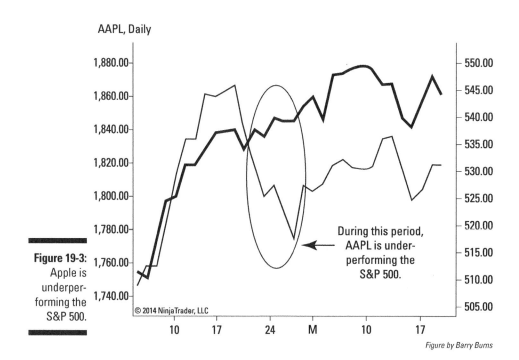

AAPL, Daily

During this period, AAPL is under-performing the S&P 500.

© 2014 NinjaTrader, LLC

Figure 19-3: Apple is underper-forming the S&P 500.

Figure by Barry Burns

Using the terms *outperforming* and *underperforming* are from a bullish per-spective of the market. In other words, you use them when looking to buy the market. However, if you're bearish — that is, you believe the market is going to go down — you can use the terms in the opposite direction.

A market can be moving away from another market to the down side and thereby have a superior bearish relative strength, which could be a good signal if you want to execute a short sale.

One line pulling away from another isn't the only way to read a shift in rela-tive strength. After one line has been moving away from the other and the spread between the two lines diminishes, it also demonstrates a shift in rela-tive strength between the two markets, as illustrated in Figure 19-4. Here, Starbucks Corporation (SBUX) has superior relative strength (and is thus outperforming) to the S&P 500, even though the line representing it (the thin line) is below the thick line of the S&P 500.

The spread between the two lines diminishing doesn't necessarily mean that the two lines are angling toward each other. They both may be moving up, for example, but the distance between them is getting smaller. In this case, the market represented by the market of the bottom line would be gaining in rela-tive strength over the market represented by the top line.

SBUX, Daily

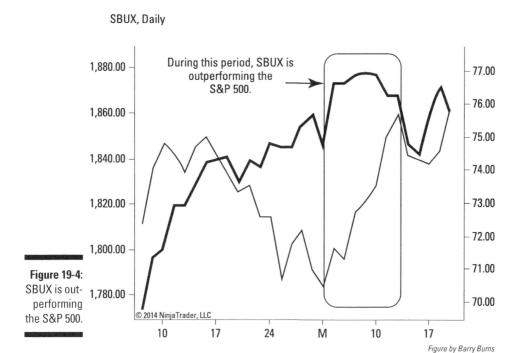

Figure 19-4:
SBUX is out-
performing
the S&P 500.

Figure by Barry Burns

To help read the relative strength between the two markets, I add an indicator that measures the *spread,* or difference, between the two markets. To
do so, you choose one market as your benchmark (I've been using the S&P
500 in the examples in this section) against which to measure other markets. If the line of the spread indicator is trending down, then the market
you're measuring is declining in relative strength against the benchmark
(underperforming).

In Figure 19-5, both the S&P and Halliburton Company (HAL) are moving up,
and it may not be clear whether Halliburton is outperforming or underperforming the S&P 500. However, by looking at the spread indicator, which is
trending down, it becomes clear that Halliburton is actually underperforming
the S&P 500.

If the line of the spread indicator is trending up, then the market you're measuring is increasing in relative strength against the benchmark (outperforming), as illustrated in Figure 19-6.

HAL, Daily

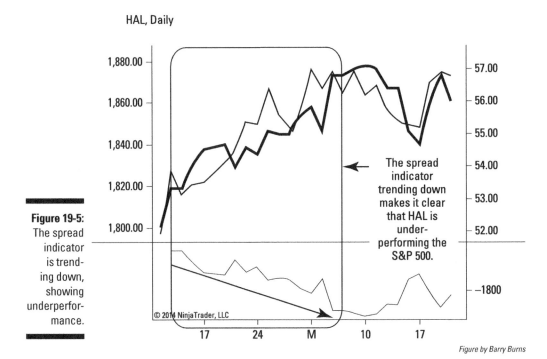

Figure 19-5:
The spread indicator is trending down, showing underperformance.

The spread indicator trending down makes it clear that HAL is underperforming the S&P 500.

© 2014 NinjaTrader, LLC

Figure by Barry Burns

^AERO_DEF, Daily

^AERO_DEF (Daily), ^SP500 (Daily)

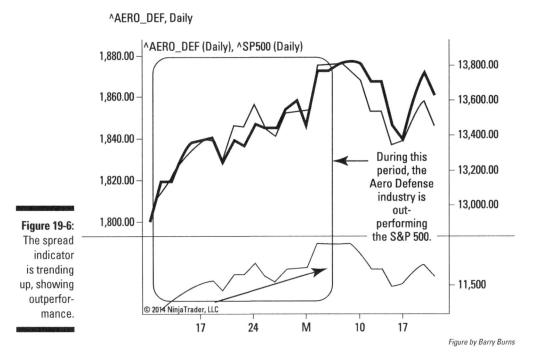

Figure 19-6:
The spread indicator is trending up, showing outperformance.

During this period, the Aero Defense industry is outperforming the S&P 500.

© 2014 NinjaTrader, LLC

Figure by Barry Burns

Getting in Early While the Iron's Hot

As with most things in trading, you want to enter early in a new directional move to make your reward as large as possible. Trading shifts in relative strength is the same. You want to get in early before everyone else does and before the move in your direction is over.

You also want to make sure that you're not too aggressive interpreting relative strength shift signals that may turn out to be false signals.

In the following sections, I show you how to determine when to get into a trade using relative strength signals and how to reduce your chances of taking relative strength signals that will fail.

Knowing when to enter on relative strength signals

Looking at the spread indicator in Figures 19-5 and 19-6, you may notice a lot of wiggles up and down. The spread indicator doesn't just move in a straight line, but, much like bar patterns on price charts, it "wiggles" while it trends up and it "wiggles" while it trends down. Therefore, I draw trend lines on the spread indicator, and the first signal I look for to enter a shift in relative strength is a break of the trend line, as shown in Figure 19-7.

Another signal I look for to enter a shift in relative strength is a new higher high or lower low on the spread indicator, as shown in Figure 19-8.

Protecting yourself against false relative strength signals

Like all other technical analysis indicators, I never rely on the measurement of relative strength alone in making trading decisions. It's just one among many other energies I consider when taking a trade. It provides an opportunity to consider entering a market precisely because using it effectively could help you outperform the S&P 500, which is the benchmark that many fund managers are measured against. Watching the spread indicator is another way of trading the trend. Rather than the trend of a single market, however, it's the trend of one market in relation to another.

As wonderful a tool as the spread indicator is, I can tell you from experience that it gives many false or very short-term signals. The best way to avoid those false signals is to pull up a chart of the market that appears to be starting to outperform the S&P 500 (or whatever benchmark you're using) and analyze that chart on the basis of the five-energy methodology (see Chapter 14).

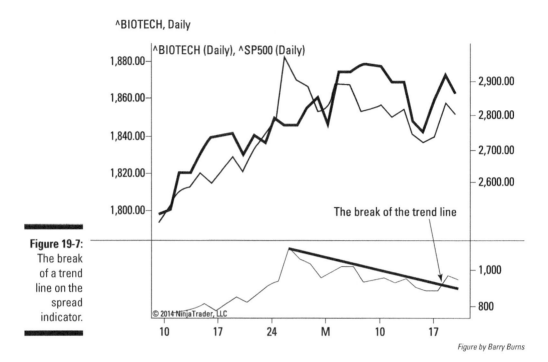

Figure 19-7:
The break of a trend line on the spread indicator.

Figure by Barry Burns

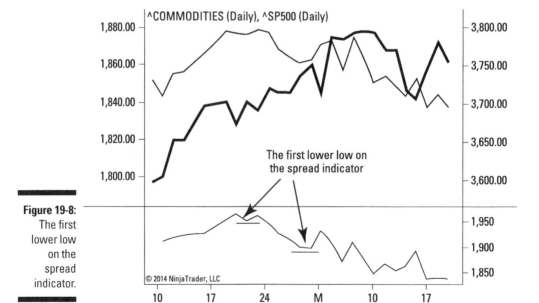

Figure 19-8:
The first lower low on the spread indicator.

Figure by Barry Burns

Only trade a market that's beginning to outperform your benchmark when you get a legitimate setup confirmed by the five energies in the market you want to trade.

Buying What No One Else Wants — Yet

An exciting way to use relative strength analysis is to find *value plays* in which you can buy a stock at a bargain basement price. Instead of trading markets that are outperforming the S&P 500, look for those that are dramatically underperforming.

Trading out-of-favor markets is a contrarian approach that may bring great rewards by getting you in before everyone else, thus helping you catch a major market move.

In the following sections, you examine the advantage and disadvantage of getting into a new directional move early.

Jumping in early on a trend

A famous saying among traders is, "The trend is your friend until the end."

Waiting for too much confirmation of a trend before jumping onboard isn't such a smart move. The longer a trend continues, the closer it's getting toward its end. So you want to enter a trade before the market has moved too far and nearly all those interested have already entered.

Another way to look at that same saying is, the longer a trend continues, the more likely it is to reverse and begin trending in the opposite direction! That gives you the opportunity to jump early into a new trend because the trend is clearly established and seen by everyone else.

This principle is the same one behind trading trend reversals on price patterns, and it's also the idea behind trading relative strength trend reversals.

Risking being first to jump

Trading trend reversals is one of the most risky setups to trade. When it works, and the market begins a trend in the opposite direction, it's the best reward-to-risk ratio trade possible. However, catching the very end of a trend is notoriously difficult to do; therefore, while the reward-to-risk ratio is wonderful, the win/loss ratio is typically very low.

Don't get me wrong: You can trade trend reversals successfully, but it often takes several attempts to truly get in at the end of a trend. The only way to survive multiple failed attempts in the process is by implementing excellent money-management and risk-management techniques.

In addition, even if you manage to catch the very end of a trend, there's no guarantee the market will reverse and trend in the opposite direction. Many trends simply end with the market consolidating or evolving into chaotic movements for long periods of time.

Finally, this type of trading requires tremendous patience, perfect discipline and nerves of steel. It's certainly not for most people.

The correlation between risk/reward ratios and win/loss ratios

Professional traders are extremely disciplined at monitoring their performance and monitoring their numbers. Two of the most important numbers measured are a trade's risk/reward ratio and win/loss ratio. Traders talk a lot about what those ratios hypothetically should be. However, what you really need to know is what those ratios actually are in your own trading.

You may hear the risk/reward ratio defined by the amount you're willing to risk on a trade against the profit target you have for the trade. That's hypothetical, and in the real world of trading, it's critical you work with your own real numbers. You need to know your own risk/reward ratio, which is the average per trade dollar amount of your actual losses against the dollar amount of your actual wins.

The win/loss ratio is simply how many of your trades make money over the number of your trades that lose money.

With both ratios, you should also factor in commissions for a realistic number. I know traders who show a positive value in one of both of the ratios, but it turns negative when commissions are factored in.

There are four possible scenarios for your trades:

- ✔ You have a better than 50/50 win/loss ratio, and you have a better than 1:1 risk/reward ratio. This scenario is ideal, and it's what I constantly strive for.

- ✔ You have a better than 50/50 win/loss ratio, and you have a worse than 1:1 risk/reward ratio. You can be a successful trader with these ratios. This is typical of scalpers.

- ✔ You have a worse than 50/50 win/loss ratio, and you have a better than 1:1 risk/reward ratio. You can be a successful trader with these ratios. This is typical of pure trend traders.

- ✔ You have a worse than 50/50 win/loss ratio, and you have a worse than 1:1 risk/reward ratio. You're in trouble!

Track your ratios continually. Analyze both your winning and losing trades and always be working on finding ways to improve both ratios in your trading.

Chapter 20

Scanning Markets with Technology

. . . .

In This Chapter

▷ Putting your computer to work for you

▷ Mining for day trading gold

▷ Uncovering swing trading opportunities

▷ Digging for investment treasures

. . . .

*O*ne of the most common questions I hear from traders is, "How do I find good stocks, currencies, or futures to trade?"

I address that answer in a couple different ways in the preceding chapters. In Chapter 18, I show you how to create watch lists of uncorrelated markets. In Chapter 19, I discuss how to use relative strength to find which markets are stronger than others as well as how to find markets that may be about to make a major turn in direction.

In this chapter, I walk you through how to use computer programs to do the leg work in finding trading opportunities for you. Scanning for day trading, swing trading, or investing opportunities have their own unique characteristics, and I discuss each of them in this chapter.

Getting Chummy with Your Computer

Trading has come to rely on technology to such an extent that it's important to develop savvy with technology to be an effective and efficient trader.

In this section, you'll become familiar with various aspects of computer technology you need to know in order to take advantage of all the trading tools available.

Reviewing the software you need

Scanning the markets for opportunities involves using software that's specifically designed for that purpose. A good place to start is to find out whether the charting software you currently use has a scanning module built in. If so, you may be able to use what you already have.

With relation to where the software resides, two types of programs exist:

- ✔ **Software that's installed on your computer:** One of the advantages of this type of software is that you may be able to do scans without being connected online. It may also be faster as long as you have the computer power to run the program.

- ✔ **Software you access through the Internet (installed on the providing company's server):** This type of software doesn't take up space on your hard drive and may provide faster searches if your computer isn't very powerful.

In regard to how the software finds opportunities, the two types of programs are

- ✔ **Scanning software:** Scanning programs access a large database of markets looking for the criteria you designate. They're designed to search huge numbers of markets (even 10,000+) and use a large combination of variables for your search. I discuss this type of software throughout this chapter.

- ✔ **Sorting software:** Sorting programs are designed like spreadsheets. You enter market symbols in the far left column and then searchable variables in the other columns. The table then sorts, from top to bottom, the results of the scan that matches your criteria. You can find out more about this type of software in Chapter 17.

Understanding how software can help

You can look for good trading opportunities manually by simply putting a few charts on your screen that you continuously watch. That approach is certainly viable, but it limits the number of market opportunities you'll see.

You can access more opportunities by pulling up charts of many markets, one after another, but that's a very laborious task. It's also slow, so by the time you bring up the chart of a market, you may have missed a great trading opportunity.

Using software to find opportunities makes your job easier and faster. The computer program can continuously search thousands of markets for your criteria and alert you the moment your criteria are met for any market.

A computer program can scan for such things as

- Whether the 50 SMA is angling up or down

- The stochastic indicator bouncing off the bottom of its range

- Significant candlestick patterns

- Fundamental analysis, such as price/earnings ratios

- Fibonacci levels

- Price patterns, such as double tops, head and shoulders, and triangles

- Potentially thousands of other criteria depending on the power of the program

I've tried several scanning programs that claim to be able to find price patterns, such as head and shoulders and triangles, but I haven't found them to be very accurate in identifying these patterns in a way that I find acceptable. Although scanning programs can be perfectly effective at identifying more simple criteria, I haven't found one that precisely identifies the multi-bar formations.

Scanning for Day Trading

Speed is the primary difference in using software to scan for day trading opportunities as opposed to scanning for swing trading and investing ideas (which I discuss later in this chapter). Intraday trading is fast. The bars open and close quickly, and therefore opportunities appear and disappear quickly. Several practical implications of this include the software, how it's programmed, and even how your own brain is wired! In the following sections, I explain the need for speed when it comes to your technology for day trading and your own reflexes.

Acquiring fast technology

In Chapter 2, I discuss the requirements of a fast computer, fast data, fast Internet service, and fast software to engage in day trading. Whew! Because day trading is so fast, you need to also have fast scanning software to sort through the hundreds or thousands of markets you're searching.

In addition to these factors, the speed of the scan varies, depending on the number of markets you're searching and also the number of criteria you have in your scanning formula.

The speed of intraday scanning software varies dramatically. Before you commit to a software vendor, ask for a short trial to see whether its software will scan fast enough for your liking.

Being quick with your reflexes

When your scanning software produces a result that matches your criteria, you need to be quick to pull that market up on a chart and analyze it for yourself before making the final decision whether to take the trade, at what price to enter, and where to place your initial stop loss. The opportunity will pass you by if you're too slow.

You'll also lose time while you select the market that came up with a positive result on your scan, and that market populates on your chart. When one market shows a positive result, it's not uncommon for other markets to show positive results (especially with equities where most stocks trade in a similar manner). You may find yourself wanting to look at more than one of the positive scan results to find the best one, again delaying the time between identifying a candidate and executing the trade.

Because of this time lapse of identifying, uploading the chart, analyzing, and executing the trade, I recommend writing day trading scan formulas slightly differently from swing trading or investing scans.

To give you more time in the process, you can program your scans to show potential setups before they're confirmed. For example, one of the criteria I use in my day trading "buy" scans is to have the stochastic %K indicator go down below the value of 20 and then angle back up on a closed bar. In practice, if everything else matched my rules for the trade, I'd buy 1 tick/penny/pip above the high of the bar that created the hook back up on %K.

On the other hand, in my swing trading and investing scans, I program the software to show only the results if the price bar that created the hook back up on %K has closed. On my day trading scans, I program the software to show the results as soon as %K angles back up intra-bar (while the price bar is still active).

It takes a certain type of mentality to be able to day trade a large number of markets using a scanner. It's certainly not for everyone. You'll know if it's right for you only by trying it in the heat of the action. As with everything new you try in trading, do it on a demo account or a simulator.

Scanning for Swing Trading

Utilizing scanning software for swing trading is much easier than for day trading. You have much more time to analyze the market and to make decisions. This is especially true if, like me, you swing trade using daily charts, giving you the luxury of scanning and making decisions during the calm of after-market hours.

That extra time also means your computer, Internet connection, and scanning software doesn't have to be as fast or powerful. I explore the specifics needed for swing trading in the following sections.

Navigating 10,000 opportunities

When you have more time, your scanning software can search a larger universe of markets. This is especially appreciated if you scan the entire database of thousands and thousands of stocks.

After the market has closed at the end of each trading day, I eat lunch (it's only 1:00 p.m. here in California!), go to the gym, then come back home and do my swing trading scans while the market is closed. This gives me plenty of time to scan a huge number of markets to find a great opportunity.

Because the market is closed, I can relax with a cup of coffee, take my time and enjoy analyzing the results of the scan, and place my orders to be filled the next day after the market opens.

Some swing traders look for swing trading setups intraday rather than waiting until the end of the trading day. Such traders often use long-term intraday charts such as 15-minute, 30-minute, or 60-minute charts.

If you scan for swing trade setups intraday, you won't have quite the luxury of time that comes from scanning when the market is closed. You'll have to use intraday scanning software, which requires more computer power.

Intraday swing traders often choose their style of trading because they don't like to have their eyes glued to the monitors all day, watching every move of the market. For such traders, I recommend you find scanning software that provides audio alerts when your scanning criteria is met. This allows you to give your attention to other things until the software alerts you to a possible setup.

Taking stock of the tools of the trade

A good online scanning program for stock traders is Stock Fetcher. It's inexpensive and scans thousands of stocks with amazing speed. You can check out some of the pre-programmed scans created by other members, or you can create your own.

The pre-programmed scans are based on various moving averages, volume spikes, price breakouts, candlestick patterns, Bollinger Band patterns, gaps, double tops/bottoms, cup and handle patterns, Fibonacci levels, P/E ratios, triangles, and many, many other criteria. You don't have to be a programmer to create the scanning formulas. The language used to create your scanning criteria is simple English, and the syntax of the formulas is easy to understand. (*Note:* At the time of this writing, the site is only for scanning stocks and exchange-traded funds [ETFs].)

Another good program is the hard drive–based Explorer, which comes with MetaStock. (MetaStock was the first computer charting program I ever used, and I still enjoy using it to this day.) It's an excellent program with an amazingly robust ability to scan markets. I especially like that it allows you to scan multiple time frames. Most scanning programs don't allow that, but it's critical to me because I won't take a trade unless it's confirmed by the energy of momentum on the longer-term time frame (the energy of scale detailed in Chapter 13).

Shameless plug and legal disclosure: My company, Top Dog Trading, created a plug-in for MetaStock that plots the five-energy methodology on the charts and also helps you find trading opportunities based on that method, using MetaStock's Explorer function.

Check with your charting software provider to see whether it offers a scanning solution. If not, or if it doesn't provide all the functionality you desire, do a search online to become aware of the current options available to you.

Scanning for Investing

When day trading and swing trading, I scan exclusively for technical analysis signals. I'm purely interested in what the chart says without any interest in the fundamentals behind the market (sales, earnings, book value, and so on). When it comes to scanning for investment opportunities, however, I look at the fundamentals as well.

My dear ol' dad was primarily a fundamental analyst and coupled it with a little technical analysis (mostly moving averages and volume). I take the opposite approach: I'm primarily a technical analyst and couple it with a little fundamental analysis. I explore the scanning options for investing in the following sections.

Approaching investment opportunities

Before I make an investment, I look at a chart of the market I'm looking to invest in and analyze it according to the five-energy methodology (see Chapter 14). Out of the many different approaches to investing, three of the most common approaches are

- ✔ **Income:** Using bonds and equities that produce dividends and other types of monthly, quarterly, or annual payments

- ✔ **Growth:** Looking for markets that are hot right now and jumping onboard (a type of trend trading)

- ✔ **Value:** Looking for markets you believe are worth more than their current price. (Warren Buffett is one of the most famous investors in this category.)

All three approaches are viable, and I personally do all three.

Income investing is often done with stocks and various investments depending on how aggressive you want to be. However, traditionally, income investors tend to be a conservative breed, looking to put their money into solid companies with low volatility and medium-sized dividends. Bonds, utility stocks, REITs (Real Estate Investment Trust), MLPs (Master Limited Partnerships), dividend paying stocks, and preferred shares are market vehicles often used by income investors.

In relation to trend trading, however, when looking for growth opportunities, I look for a market that has begun a new trend. I scan for markets that are making a first retrace in a trend, or at least a first retrace after the cross of the 50 SMA.

When looking for value opportunities, I search for a market that has been in an extended bearish trend, looking to trade a trend reversal to the long side. It's also important to check a company's fundamentals because if its stock has been going down for a long time, it may be due to a major problem that may not be resolved for a long time — or ever.

Trading trend reversals is a low win/loss ratio trade. Catching the final low in a downtrend isn't easy and may take several attempts. In addition, even if the downtrend does end, it doesn't necessarily follow that the market will then begin an uptrend. It may simply consolidate and move sideways for a period of time.

Going back to the fundamentals

An extended bearish downtrend isn't enough to say that the market is undervalued. It must first be qualified as a value market, using fundamental analysis and only after qualifying it as such do I then look at the chart.

Many, if not most, markets are bearish and priced low because they're bad investments. You should avoid these markets completely. They're not value plays; they're priced correctly and are simply bad investments.

The value investing approach stands counter to the efficient market hypothesis that the pricing of a market reflects everything that can be known about that market, and therefore all markets are priced as they should be. To qualify a market as a value play, it must be considered underpriced. In other words, it's a good market that should be priced higher, but for some reason, the market participants aren't appreciating that yet.

You can choose from approaches to determine what constitutes an underpriced, value market, but being successful at value investing hinges on doing so correctly (not an easy task). For stocks, it often involves determining the value of the business itself (looking for strong balance sheets, excellent earnings, and so on), and comparing that with the price of the stock of that business.

To find out more about value investing, you may want to consult the classic book *The Intelligent Investor: The Definitive Book on Value Investing. A Book of Practical Counsel,* by Benjamin Graham (Revised Edition published by Collins Business), and *Security Analysis,* by Benjamin Graham and David Dodd (6th edition published by McGraw-Hill). Warren Buffet references these authors with much admiration.

Everyone's situation is different and needs to be addressed individually. If you want assistance with your investment decision, seek a competent and qualified professional investment advisor.

The perils of overoptimizing

After getting the results from your scans, look at the charts of the markets the scanning software found and analyze those charts yourself before making a trading decision. I emphasize that because some trading software allows you to automate your trades. You can create a trading system and have the computer automatically place the trades for you. Personally, I'm not comfortable doing that.

In today's markets, a huge percentage of trading is computerized, or automated trading. Although this type of trading definitely has a place and can be done with success, keep in mind a few facts before you get swept in:

✔ The professionals aren't using the kind of "robots" you see popping up on websites for you to buy online.

✔ Even the systems the pros use aren't always profitable.

✔ Professional firms have mathematical, financial, and programming geniuses working for them.

✔ Professional firms have trained risk managers monitoring the system at all times.

Some scanning programs allow you to run your scans using historical data and produce a report of how many trade setups based on your criteria occurred in the past and what the results of those setups would have been (wins, losses, and so on). This type of "back testing" is meant to help you determine whether your trading system is viable. It also allows you to continually change various components of your trading system's criteria and run tests on every change, until you find a system that would have been profitable over the historical period you designate.

The shortcoming of this approach is that the computer is simply finding what would have

worked in the past. This is called *curve fitting* and is generally disregarded as a viable way to create a profitable system. To address this concern, most traders who create systems this way, now do out-of-sample testing. They take a system that's been tested profitable over a period of history in the past and test it on another period of history that wasn't used in the original testing. If it's profitable in this out-of-sample testing, then it's considered a viable trading system.

In actual practice, the first, second, tenth, and hundredth tweaks in the system usually don't provide profitability. The trader ends up endlessly making changes to optimize the system to produce the most historical profits. Although this approach certainly presents a more convincing case for a trading system, it can be argued that making all those changes overoptimizes the system to fit the data in the past. To believe that an automated system designed to fit historical data of the past will be a profitable trading method in the future, you have to believe that historical market performance is somehow predictive of future market performance.

Contrary to this, a common disclaimer in relation to investing is that "past results are not indicative of future returns" (or something similar). Part of my career was spent creating these types of systems. It never ceased to amaze me how my systems would work in back testing and in out-of-sample testing but then would be unprofitable when I started trading them in the present market. I'm certainly not going to say that you can't create a consistently successful automated trading system (emphasis on the word *consistently*). Just be warned of some of the false assumptions and the marketing hype surrounding this approach to trading.

Part V

Managing Risk and Following the Keys to Success

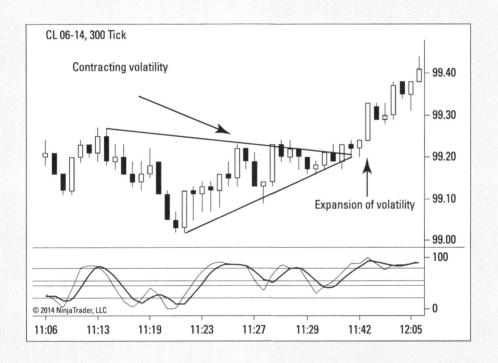

CL 06-14, 300 Tick

Contracting volatility

Expansion of volatility

© 2014 NinjaTrader, LLC

Find out the Holy Grail of trading success by heading to
www.dummies.com/extras/trendtrading.

In this part . . .

✔ Discover how to diversify your trades so that you don't have all your eggs (or dollars) in one trading basket.

✔ Minimize your risk by hedging your trades.

✔ Get a crash course in simple money management as it relates to trading.

✔ Find out ways to keep track of your trades and understand why doing so is so important to success.

✔ Review your documented trades to learn from your successes and your mistakes and improve your trading.

Chapter 21

Practicing Diversification

● ●

In This Chapter

▷ Mixing up your trading markets and methods

▷ Foregoing trend trading for other strategies

● ●

Diversification has long been one of the hallmarks of traditional investing wisdom. The idea is that by diversifying the markets in which you trade or invest, you minimize your risk. It's congruent with the old adage, "Don't put all your apples in one basket."

In this chapter, I show you several methods to diversify your portfolio. You can choose one or more depending on which ones appeal to you.

Trading Various Markets

The most common technique used to diversify portfolios is to invest in a diversified mix of markets. In this section, I show you a couple of ways to do that.

Uncorrelated markets

Diversifying your risk isn't as simple as trading more than one stock. Most stocks tend to move in relatively the same pattern of the stock index to which they belong (S&P 500, DOW, NASDAQ, and so on).

To truly diversify, you need to trade markets that don't normally trade alike. Here are a few examples of markets that often have various degrees of correlation, thus providing risk diversification:

✔ U.S. equities

- Large caps

- Small caps

- Various sectors within the world of equities, such as basic materials, consumer discretionary, consumer staples, energy, financials, healthcare, industrials, technology, telecommunications, and utilities

✔ Real estate

✔ Gold

✔ International stocks

✔ Emerging markets

✔ Frontier stocks

✔ U.S. investment grade bonds

✔ U.S high-yield bonds

✔ International bonds

Value stocks and growth stocks

Another way to diversify your trading or investing portfolio is between value stocks and growth stocks.

Value stocks may not look good at the time you view them because they're by definition stocks that are underpriced based on the value of their underlying businesses. These contrarian plays may be hard for some traders to get excited about, but if their business is sound, they can bring huge financial rewards when the market realizes their true value.

One challenge with value stocks is timing. You may have to wait a long time before the rest of the market participants recognize the worth of your value stocks. They can underperform the rest of the market for a long time.

Growth stocks are stocks that are hot right now. They're defined as stocks that are growing at this moment and, therefore, can provide growth to your portfolio while you're waiting for your value stocks to catch up.

Using Different Trading Methods

When most people think of diversification, they think of investing in various markets as discussed in the previous section. However, another, often overlooked, way to diversify is to employ several trading methods concurrently to cash in on different types of market opportunities, depending on the design of the trading method.

My method (the five-energy method; see Chapter 14) always looks for retraces, or corrections, in the market. However, sometimes the market moves so aggressively that it doesn't make a significant retrace in the trend for me to find an entry based on my rules. In such a market move, my method would leave me on the sidelines with an opportunity lost.

Another method, perhaps based on Bollinger Bands or breakouts of certain levels, could potentially provide entries into such aggressively moving markets and allow you to profit from that market move.

Utilizing several diverse trading methodologies allows you to take advantage of more trading opportunities and thereby potentially increase your profits.

Is the five-energy method the best trading method ever created?

Because I created the five-energy trading method, people often assume I think it's the best method for trading any market at any time. I'm proud of it, and it works better than anything else I've personally tried in my decades of trading. On the other hand, I have many friends who trade other methodologies very successfully. Therefore, I know that other valid approaches to trading exist. Which method works best for you may be a matter of personal taste.

Some methods will feel more natural or make more sense to your way of thinking, your risk tolerance, and your personal psychological profile. You need to be flexible and acknowledge that different approaches work and be open to using more than one of them yourself to diversify your trading even beyond the various markets you trade.

Employing Trading Strategies Other Than Trend Trading

Although trend trading is my favorite way to trade, you may want to consider other viable options to trading, which I explore in this section.

Markets trend only approximately 20 percent of the time, so by limiting yourself to trend trading, you're severely limiting your trading opportunities. By trading not only other trend trading methodologies but also entirely different trading strategies, you can diversify your trading approach to capture more profits.

Momentum trading

In Chapter 12, I discuss the energy of momentum to confirm a trend. The energy of momentum also signals trade setups that aren't reliant on the energy of trend. Some of these trade setups are quick little scalp trades where you look for only a small profit. The risk/reward ratio isn't great, but the huge win/loss ratio makes up for that.

Other times, a momentum trade can trigger before a new trend is started, thus getting you into a trend trade before it's even confirmed. For example, one strategy may be to enter on the first cycle low after the *MACD signal line* (moving average of the MACD line) turns up.

In Figure 21-1, the trend is down, as indicated by the 50 SMA. Looking at the MACD indicator, which I use to measure momentum, the long rectangle identifies the first cycle low after the MACD signal line begins turning up. Also note that the MACD line stays above the MACD signal line at that point.

That cycle low is a place I'd consider going long based purely on a momentum shift in the market.

To take such a trade, I'd need at least three of the other four energies to support the trade by also giving buy signals. (See the chapters in Part III for more about the different energies.)

The probability of success would be even greater if this signal occurred after a downtrend of more than five waves (see Chapter 5). The probability of a trend reversing on a momentum shift signal (or any other signal for that matter) increases if the trend is extended beyond an average trend length.

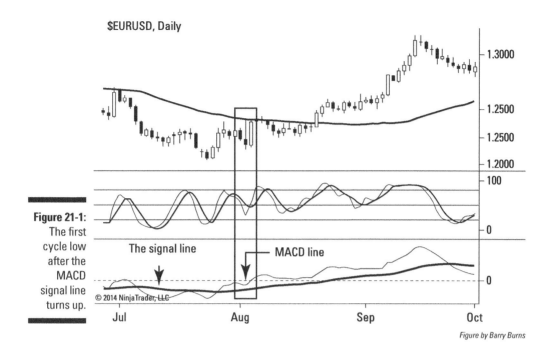

$EURUSD, Daily

1.3000

1.2500

1.2500

1.2000

100

The signal line

MACD line

0

© 2014 NinjaTrader, LLC

0

Jul   Aug   Sep   Oct

Figure 21-1:
The first cycle low after the MACD signal line turns up.

Figure by Barry Burns

Contraction/expansion trading

I was the head moderator of a live trading chat room for about three years. The members of the chat room were there to tap into my live market analysis, but I learned something from them as well. Hearing the chat room members express their thoughts of the market while I watched the charts gave me an insight into the thinking of amateur traders when the markets were doing certain patterns. The repetition over those three years engrained in my thought process the thoughts of amateurs when the market would do certain things, because I would hear the same comments over and over.

For example, when the market was trending up, inevitably the amateur traders in the room would start saying that they were shorting the market, adding such comments as the following:

"This market is way overbought."

"It can't possibly go up any more."

"This is way beyond the average true range."

"It looks like a reversal pattern to me."

"This market looks toppy."

They were almost always wrong. The market would go down just enough to fill their short order and then go back up to make higher highs and stopping them out for a loss. It was uncanny how this would happen day after day. Something in human nature is contrarian to following the trend of the market.

Another example of a pattern of mass psychology with regard to a chart pattern is when the market would get quiet. On the chart, this would be expressed as the range of cycles getting narrow and no clear direction (trend) to the market. This type of market behavior would inevitably produce the same reaction among all the amateur members of the trading room:

"This market sucks today."

"This is a good day to play golf."

"I'm bored. Bye everyone."

"It's a bad day for trading."

"I'm going to play tennis."

Inevitably, soon after the traders making these types of comments left the trading room, the market would start making a big move. The traders who were able to read the signs and be patient were able to profit tremendously.

The reason this happened repeatedly is because there's a cycle in the market between *contraction* (low volatility) and *expansion* (high volatility).

A low-volatility market is indeed normally an unprofitable one to trade, and even if you do, the profits are small because of the small range of price movements. Patient professionals, however, see low-volatility markets as a very exciting opportunity because they know that they're followed by large price movements when a new high-volatility cycle begins.

A good example of this cycle is the *triangle price pattern* — where the cycle highs and lows are converging over time. I love trading triangles and would point them out in the trading room every day. Others in the room granted me the title "The Master of Triangles."

I found it interesting that no matter how many times I'd point out the triangle patterns, most of the traders in the room could never identify them on their own. The triangle patterns all have the following principles in common:

- ✔ A symmetrical triangle has lower highs and higher lows.
- ✔ A descending triangle has lower highs and equal lows.
- ✔ An ascending triangle has equal highs and higher lows.

When trading triangles, I'm aware of the contraction cycle, and I'm looking to trade the breakout of the triangle when a new expansion cycle begins. The easiest way to identify triangles is to simply connect the cycle highs with a straight line (trend line) and then connect the cycle lows with a straight line. When you see a convergence between the line connecting the cycle highs and the line connecting the cycle lows, you have a triangle formation.

Here are three common approaches for entering a triangle trade:

- ✔ Enter as the market breaks out of the trend line connecting the highs or lows of the triangle.
- ✔ Wait until after the market breaks out of the triangle formation and enter on the first retrace.
- ✔ Trade "inside" of the triangle, entering on one of the cycle highs/lows bouncing off the trend lines connecting the cycle highs/lows.

The last approach is the most aggressive but also offers the best potential risk/reward ratio.

Figure 21-2 illustrates a triangle pattern where the market experiences a low volatility cycle (continually narrowing price range movement) while forming the triangle, followed by a high volatility cycle after the breakout of the triangle formation (with price bars covering a wide range in a short period of time).

Figure 21-2: A triangle price pattern.

CL 06-14, 300 Tick

Contracting volatility

Expansion of volatility

© 2014 NinjaTrader, LLC

Figure by Barry Burns

The most common question I'm asked regarding triangles is, "How do you determine whether the market is going to break out of the triangle to the upside or the downside?" Although no one can predict the market's future movement perfectly, I execute triangle trades only in the direction of momentum on the higher time frame. In other words, as with trend trades, I take momentum trades only in the direction of the energy of scale (as I explain in detail in Chapter 13).

Being aware of overdiversifying

Although diversifying is a well-accepted standard practice among investors, it has some potential downsides.

First, there are times when normally uncorrelated markets start trading in a similar manner. Early in my career, I was told that one of the foundations of diversifying was to be invested in both bonds and equities because they normally traded contrary to one another. Although this is often true, it's certainly not always the case. In some periods, bonds and stocks both move up or down at the same time. That's why it's important to learn to read charts for yourself and not just take other people's advice, especially if they aren't experts in the field.

Of course, the argument can rightly be made that bonds provide income while they fluctuate in valuation, but some stocks provide income in the form of dividends as well. The question of diversifying into both stocks and bonds is much more complex than this, and I personally do diversify, using both financial vehicles. I just want you to be aware that at times, you may think you're diversifying by investing in various markets only to find that those markets aren't providing the type of diversification they have in the past.

Another issue to be aware of is overdiversifying. You may invest in a large number of different types of markets that have low correlation to each other. However, by doing so, you may find that your long-term profits are very moderate because you're almost always in a market that's going down while another one is going up.

This makes it tough to outperform the overall market. On the other hand, it's nearly impossible for the average person to outperform the market anyway. Still, if outperforming the market is your goal, you should be aware of this.

Diversification isn't necessarily designed as a tool to outperform the market. One of its primary functions is to help reduce the volatility of your portfolio (minimizing dramatic drawdowns of equity in your account), thus helping you psychologically stick to your strategy.

Chapter 22

Hedging Your Position to Protect You from Losing All Your Money

*E*ven the best traders make mistakes and lose money. In fact, good traders lose money at times even when they don't make mistakes! No certainties exist in trading. It's all about managing probability scenarios. Therefore, even high-probability trades, executed perfectly, will sometimes turn into losers.

You never know ahead of time whether any one given trade will be a winner or a loser. So you need to manage your risk, knowing that any trade can lose money. Traders commonly use *protective stops* (an order placed at a price at which the trader wants to limit losses if a trade turns sour). I personally always use *hard stops,* which are orders placed into my broker's execution platform. However, stops don't always protect you.

Other than using stops (which may or may not be filled where you want them to be), many professional traders *hedge* their positions. This involves taking a position that offsets the risk of your primary position. I introduce the idea of hedging positions in this chapter.

Protecting Your Hard-Earned Money with Options

One of the most common ways to hedge a primary position (a stock, forex, futures, or commodity trade) is through *options*. An option is a contract that provides you the right (but not the obligation) to buy or sell a stock, currency, commodity, or other market asset at a given price.

In the following sections, I give you the lowdown on options and buying puts, selling covered calls, and taming your trades when you choose to do both.

Getting to know your options

When you buy an option, you're not buying the market itself. You're buying only the right to buy or sell the market. Why would you do that? The benefit to buying an option is that you can choose the price at which you're willing to buy the market in the future. For example, you can buy it at today's price, and if the market goes up in the future, you'd then be able to buy it at a discount because you'd pay only today's price (which would be lower than the price in the future in this example).

Options have time limits, called expiration dates. The contract is good only until the option expires. You can buy short-term options or long-term options, but you'll pay more for the long-term options.

For this privilege, you must put up a down payment (called a *premium*), which is a fraction of the price of buying the market itself. If you choose not to exercise your right to buy the underlying market of the option before the expiration date, you lose your premium.

In this way, buying an option contract is very much like buying an insurance policy. You pay a small premium (the cost of the option contract) to protect you against your primary market position going against you dramatically.

- ✔ If the market doesn't turn against you, you lose your premium, but it's a price you may be willing to pay to protect against disaster.

- ✔ If the market does gap dramatically against you, the option will kick in at the price you choose and give you the right to sell a position in the stock at the pre-determined price, thus offsetting part of the loss on your primary position.

If you believe the market is going up, you'd buy a *call,* which is similar to buying the market, or going long (see the later section "Getting paid to protect your position: selling covered calls" for more details). If you believe the market is going down, you'd buy a *put,* which is similar to shorting the market (see the next section "Buying insurance against losing money: Buying a put").

You can also sell options, in which case you collect the premium that a person who's buying the option is paying. This approach is appealing to many because you make money up front when you sell the option instead of waiting for the option to expire. Your hope is that the option will expire worthless so that you get to keep the entire premium.

Normally, you need to own the market of the option you're selling. If you don't, it's known as a *naked option.* Your broker may not allow you to sell naked options. They're considered very high risk because if the buyer of the option decides to exercise the right to buy the market at the agreed upon price, you'll need enough money to buy the market and deliver it to the buyer (likely at a lower price than you bought it).

When buying or selling options, you need to be very careful about the contract you buy. Here are some things to look at before buying an option contract at any strike price or expiration date:

- ✔ **Is there a lot of volume and open interest to make sure enough participants are trading that contract to ensure that you get filled at a good price?** Some contracts have such low trade volume that you may not be able to get out of a position when you want to.

- ✔ **Is there a tight bid/ask spread?** The greater the difference between the bid price and the ask price, the more money the option will be costing you for the round trip and the easier you'll generally be able to get in and out of your trade.

- ✔ **Is the price a fair one (or even underpriced) based on a reputable option pricing model (often included in the option chain quotes)?** The Black-Scholes Model is one of the most used option pricing models.

Buying insurance against losing money: Buying a put

Buying a put against your long position in the market is the most basic and easiest to understand option hedging method. Because options are highly leveraged, only requiring a small down payment, you can buy insurance in case your primary position goes down drastically.

Insurance costs money. In the case of buying a put to help offset some of the risk of a long position, the fact that you're buying an option means that the underlying market of your primary trade has to go up more than the price of the option before you're in a net profit position.

When buying a put, you're buying the right to sell a position at a certain price. For example, in stocks, one put option contract allows you the right to sell 100 shares of the stock. This could be very helpful if your primary market position turns against you (assuming your primary position is long the market).

Factors that impact the price of your put option

The price at which you can exercise your put (sell the market asset) is called the *strike price.* The closer your strike price is to the current price, the quicker the protection kicks in should the market turn against you. However, the price of the option contract will also be higher because you're buying more insurance.

Think of the price of the option contract like a deductible with your insurance. The more you're willing to pay out of your own pocket, the cheaper your insurance will be because you're assuming more of the risk yourself.

Another variable that determines the price you pay is the *expiration date* you choose. As I mention earlier, options have an expiration date at which time they expire worthless. If you want more insurance after your option contract expires, you have to buy another option contract. The more time you want the option contract to last, the more you'll pay for the option, again because you're buying more insurance.

A third issue that determines the price you pay for your put option is the *implied volatility* — the expectation of traders as to how volatile they expect the market to be in the future. High volatility means the market has large swings, covering a wide price range in a short period of time. When this occurs, the price of buying a put option for insurance increases because, once again, you're buying insurance for a wide range of prices.

Looking at an example of how buying a put provides a hedge

In this section, I walk through an example of how buying a put could provide you a hedge, or insurance, against your primary position taking a nose dive, causing you to lose a lot of money.

Say that you buy 100 shares of a stock at $90 per share. Your investment at risk would be $9,000 ($90 × 100). For the sake of this example, you can buy a put at the strike price of $80 for $235.

In the price quotes (called an *option chain*), the price of the option is $2.35, but because each option represents 100 shares of stock, you multiply $2.35 by 100 for the actual cost of $235 for the right to sell 100 shares of the stock at $80.

You also have to consider what expiration month you want for your option contract. The longer the contract lasts before it expires, the more you'll pay. For example, assume that you're buying a put that expires in 90 days. Because you bought the stock at $90 but bought the put for a strike price of $80, you're assuming the risk of a $10 drop in the stock (if the stock drops from $90 to $80 because your put won't start providing protection until it goes below the strike price).

The reason you may choose to buy a put at such a lower price and thus give up that amount of protection is to get cheaper insurance. The difference between the $90 and the $80 is similar to a deductible you'd accept on an insurance policy in exchange for paying a lower monthly insurance premium.

So what is your insurance worth? If the stock goes down to $80, your loss on the stock is $10 per share (the $90 price at which you bought the stock minus the $80 price at which the option contract allows you to sell the stock). You bought 100 shares, so your total dollar loss on the position is $1,000. To that, you must add the price of buying the put, which was $235, so your loss is actually $1,235, which is more than it would be if you hadn't bought the put. However, if the stock continues to go down, your put option can come to your rescue. You have the right to sell the stock at $80, even if the stock goes lower than $80, thereby limiting your downside risk. If the stock were to go down to $10, you can still sell it at $80 (thus avoiding an actual loss of $8,000 if you bought 100 shares at $90 and didn't have the put option hedging your position).

REMEMBER

Here are two other important factors to keep in mind as you deal with buying and selling put options:

- ✔ Before expiration, you can sell the put option you bought and thus recover some of the premium you paid so you don't lose that entire amount. When you do this, you also lose your insurance on the position.

- ✔ The value of your put will change over time based on the implied volatility and the amount of time left before expiration (the closer to expiration, the lower the price of the option). Time isn't on the side of an option buyer.

Getting paid to protect your position: Selling covered calls

Selling covered calls is another strategy to protect your position. In this strategy, you buy a position in a market and you sell a call on that same market. You avoid the expense of buying insurance — in fact, you actually get paid to protect your own position!

The main differences between buying a put and buying/selling a covered call are as follows:

- ✔ When you're buying a put, you're spending money up front. Because you're buying a put, you can make money on that option if the market goes down.

- ✔ When you're selling a call, you're receiving money up front. Because you're selling a call, you keep the premium you've received up front if the market goes down.

Making money, rather than spending money, to protect your position is obviously preferable and sounds too good to be true, and there is a little tradeoff. When you buy a put, your protection kicks in at the strike price and continues to cover you as far as the market goes down. On the other hand, when you sell a call, your protection kicks in immediately (because you receive the premium immediately), but you're protected only to the extent of the value of the premium collected. You're therefore unhedged from the point the market goes down more than the amount of premium you received for selling the call.

Looking at an example of how selling a call pays you a hedge

Here's an example of how selling a call can provide protection should the market move down, against your long position.

Say that you buy a stock at $90. To hedge your position, you sell a call option at $105. By selling that call option, you're giving someone else the right to buy the stock away from you for $105 per share. Because the price of the stock is only $90 today, no one is likely to buy the stock from you at $105. However, if the stock goes up to $120, someone would be able to buy the stock from you for $105 rather than $120.

This example illustrates one aspect of the risk of selling a covered call — you're limiting the potential profit on your primary trade. On the positive side, you'll immediately receive the premium the option buyer pays you for selling the call option. In this case, say it's $115 for one contract. You've now made instant money. Instead of buying a hedge, you're being paid for your hedge! So why wouldn't everyone do this instead of paying to buy a put?

Reviewing risks and other points to keep in mind

Like everything in trading, for every upside, there's a downside. In this case, there are at least two drawbacks of selling calls to hedge your asset's position:

- ✔ **You risk opportunity lost because your profit is limited.** If the stock price goes above the strike price, the buyer of your call will most likely buy the stock away from you.

- ✔ **Your protection to the downside is hedged only by the amount you received from selling the option (which isn't much!).** Therefore, you still have the severe risk if the market tumbles dramatically.

Options have expiration dates at which time they become worthless. Choose a strike price of the call you're selling that you consider unlikely for the market to reach before the option expires.

Here are several issues to keep in mind when selling a call:

- ✔ **You want to keep the premium you're paid for selling the option.** Therefore, you want to sell *out-of-the-money calls* — calls with a strike price above the current price of the market. If the market goes above the strike price, you'll likely have to sell the underlying market to the option buyer.

- ✔ **The more out of the money the strike price of the call, the less likely it is that the strike price will be hit.** That lower probability is offset by the fact that you'll receive less premium than you would selling calls with strike prices closer to the current price.

- ✔ **Selling short-term calls (60 days or fewer before expiration) increases the odds that the call will expire worthless and you'll get to keep the premium.** Option prices generally deteriorate at a faster rate the closer they get to their expiration date.

✓ **Selling options with high implied volatility increases the price of the option, which is good when you're selling.** If the implied volatility diminishes, the price of the option often goes lower, even if the price of the underlying market doesn't go down, thus reducing the likelihood of the call you sold being exercised (the buyer exercising the right to buy the market at the strike price).

✓ **Your best-case scenario is if the stock goes up so you make money on your underlying position but doesn't go up enough for the buyer of the option to want to exercise the option.** This allows you to make profit on your underlying position and also make money on selling the call.

An interesting time to implement a covered call is when your analysis indicates that you've reached a cycle high in an uptrend and expects a retrace in the trend to begin. If your analysis is right, you're biding time while the market moves down and thus selling the call at a time when the market isn't likely to be moving up in the direction of the call buyer's direction. Of course, waiting until such a time means that the market you're trading is unhedged until that time. It's your decision to weigh the pros and cons of the strategies and the time you choose to engage them.

Taming your trades: Put a collar on their necks

Putting collars on your trade is a strategy that combines buying a put and selling a call, with a twist. That twist is that you buy and sell them at different strike prices. You can play around with various strike prices for buying the put and selling the call to find which combination provides you the best protection.

Buying the put then selling the call at different expiration dates can lead to very complex variables, which you shouldn't attempt until you're thoroughly educated in options.

When you combine the buying of a put with the selling of a call,

✓ You get the benefit of buying a put in that you enjoy the limited risk to the downside that covered calls don't provide.

✓ You overcome the problem of the high cost of buying a put, in that the money you receive from selling the call you sell helps offset the price of buying the put.

✓ You still have the limited reward that comes with selling the call.

In short, combining these strategies provides you limited risk and limited reward.

For example, say you buy a stock for $90. You buy a put with a strike price of $80 for $235. You can sell a call with a strike price of $105 for $115. In this case, your net cost for protection is $120 (the $235 you paid to buy the put minus the $115 you collected for selling the call).

This would cut your cost of insurance almost in half against simply buying the put. You still get the protection of the limited risk to the downside should your asset plummet. For that lower premium, you willingly sacrifice some profit potential to the upside because the buyer of your call option will likely exercise it and buy the stock away from you if the stock goes higher than $105 before the call option expires.

Diversifying to Protect Yourself

Another approach to hedging your primary trade is to take a position in another financial instrument that's inversely correlated to the primary market you're trading. You can do this by using *defensive stocks.* These types of stocks sell basic necessities that people need regardless of the state of the economy: utilities, food, oil, healthcare, household products, and personal care products. Because regardless of the economic cycle, people need electricity, food, gas, and medicine.

The so-called *sin sector* — that is, stocks that have to do with drinking, smoking, gambling, and so on — can also provide a defense against a bad economy. People still tend to buy cigarettes and alcohol in a bad economy.

This approach isn't to be taken lightly, though. During tough economic times, people may still buy such items, but they'll likely seek out more inexpensive and generic brands.

When one market is going up, the other tends to go down. All hedging comes with a price, and the problem with this approach is that if the two markets are perfectly inverse to each other, you'd never make a net profit! (See Chapter 21 for a more detailed look at this type of diversification.)

Another concern is that even markets that are generally considered uncorrelated may at times move in the same direction. There are always exceptions to the rule. When this occurs, then you're losing money in both markets.

Keep in mind that even if the inverse market you use to hedge a position does move up when your primary market moves down, there are no guarantees that it will move up to the same degree as your primary market.

Hedging doesn't require that you completely eliminate losses. You can hedge to offset some of your losses. Another way of doing this is to buy income-producing stocks, such as those that pay dividends. This way even when the stocks are going, the drop in price is offset somewhat by the income of the dividends you receive.

The benefits and pitfalls of insuring your trades

There's no "best way" to hedge the position of your primary asset. To continue with the analogy of an insurance policy I use throughout this chapter, like any type of insurance, there's always a cost. You have to make your own personal decision as to

✔ How much coverage you want

✔ How much deductible you're willing to cover yourself

✔ The cost of premiums you're willing to pay

✔ How long you want your insurance to last

✔ The tax ramifications

It's up to you to choose the policy that best fits your budget, your risk tolerance, and your time horizon. Before trading options, it's vitally important to become extremely well educated about them. Options are quite complex and risky. Be sure to read the disclosure statement at www.optionsclearing.com/publications/risks/riskstoc.pdf, which explains the characteristics and risks of options:

Options don't always move in direct correlation with their underlying market. I've heard the lament of many traders complaining that their stock went up, but their option contract didn't. That can occur for several reasons, but to impress upon you the complexity of options (and thus motivate you to study them further before you consider trading them), you need to become familiar with the "Greeks:"

✔ Delta: The amount by which an option price is expected to change as its underlying market changes

✔ Gamma: The expected rate of change for an option's Delta for every one point change in the underlying market

✔ Theta: The amount an option's price will decline over time

✔ Vega: The expected change in the price of an option due to a change in the volatility of its underlying market

Sound daunting? Good! Then I've done my job. Don't trade options until you've been thoroughly educated in them.

Chapter 23

Using Stop Signs to Keep You Safe

A popular saying among traders is, "Keep your losses small and let your winners run." Traders want their losses to be small and their winning trades to be big, but the obvious question is how do you do that? Chapter 22 addresses that question partially by showing you how to hedge your position to avoid the occasional drastic loss. This chapter focuses on how to minimize the normal, everyday losses that are a natural part of every successful trading method.

Some professional traders say that how you manage your losers and your risk is more important than how you manage your winners. However, I believe that managing both your winners and losers is critical, which is why the quote is, "Keep your losses small *and* let your winners run."

Traders often do exactly the opposite for the simple reason that they focus on making money rather than trading and trusting their rules. This adversely affects their behavior because by focusing on making money, they

✔ Take profits too soon out of fear of losing the unrealized gains they've accumulated.

✔ Can't bear the idea of locking in a loss if the market turns against them. Hoping the market will turn around, they keep their position open while the market continues to move farther away from their entry and increases their losses.

How you deal with losses, both technically and psychologically, is a huge factor in determining your success as a trader.

Placing Protective Stops to Minimize Losses When Trades Go South

A *protective stop* (sometimes called a *stop loss*) is a price point at which you exit your position when the market has turned against you. Using protective stops is an absolutely critical part of keeping your losses small.

You can use a protective stop to limit your loss or after the market has moved in your direction and you get into profit. In the latter case, you're using the stop to lock in profits at a certain level should the market turn against your profitable trade.

Determining your initial stop price

The initial stop you establish is the price at which you want to exit your trade if it goes against you. You make that decision before you enter the trade. In general, you place stops at a price level you wouldn't expect the market to reach if your trade is going to be successful.

You can determine where to place your initial stop on any of the following:

✔ A risk/reward ratio

✔ A fixed percentage of the price of the asset you're buying

✔ Below a support level

✔ Below a retrace or swing low

✔ Below bullish candlestick patterns

✔ Just outside of the market's average true range at the time

You make every trade for a reason. Your stop belongs at the price level where your reason for taking that trade is violated, meaning the trade setup you were taking is no longer valid. For example, in Figure 23-1, if my intention is to buy a cycle low in an uptrend and the market goes down below that cycle low, then my reason for buying that market is violated. Therefore, I place my protective stop one penny/pip/tick below the low of the cycle I'm buying.

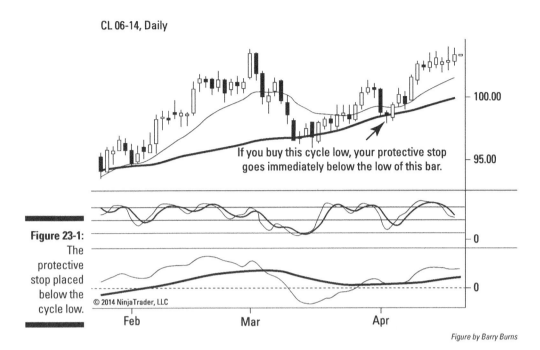

Figure 23-1:
The
protective
stop placed
below the
cycle low.

CL 06-14, Daily

If you buy this cycle low, your protective stop goes immediately below the low of this bar.

© 2014 NinjaTrader, LLC

Figure by Barry Burns

Figure 23-2 illustrates that when short selling a cycle high in a downtrend, I place my protective stop one penny/pip/tick above the cycle high.

Opting for hard stops versus mental stops

You can use stops by actually executing the stop orders in your broker's trading platform (hard stops), or you can keep the stop order price levels in your mind (mental stops). Each has its advantages and disadvantages:

- ✔ **Hard stops:** With hard stops, you place a stop order with your broker that is then automatically executed if the market reaches the price level of your stop.

- ✔ **Mental stops:** When using mental stops, you don't place the order to exit your position until the market reaches your stop price.

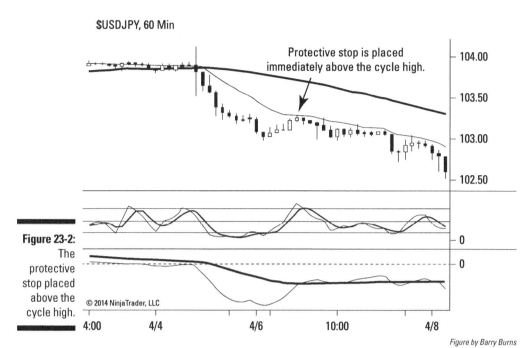

$USDJPY, 60 Min

Protective stop is placed immediately above the cycle high.

104.00

103.50

103.00

102.50

0

0

© 2014 NinjaTrader, LLC

Figure 23-2:
The protective stop placed above the cycle high.

4:00   4/4   4/6   10:00   4/8

Figure by Barry Burns

I'm a firm believer in using hard stops. If my trade setup (the reason I entered the trade) is broken and no longer valid, I want to be out immediately. I trade by objective rules, and when the rules of my trade setup are violated, I'm out.

Some traders use mental stops because it gives them the opportunity to evaluate the market again before they're stopped out. If they feel that the market may turn around in their direction soon, then they won't exit. However, I never use mental stops because I find no need to reevaluate the market at the moment my objective rule for entering the market is broken. Such an approach is too discretionary and subjective for my liking.

Mental stops have two other significant disadvantages:

 ✓ **They require discipline most traders don't have.** The natural tendency of people is to hang on to losing trades in the hope that the trades will turn into winners. It's psychologically challenging to lock in a loss.

✔ **Mental stops require time to evaluate and, therefore, cause hesitation.** That extra time spent analyzing the market before exiting typically results in getting out at a worse price.

Opting for limit orders or market orders

Another consideration in placing your stop orders is whether to use *limit orders* or *market orders*:

✔ **Stop-limit orders are filled at a given price, or price range.** They literally "limit" the price at which you'll be filled. The advantage is that you know the price and avoid any surprising slippage. You can also be filled at a more favorable price than you stipulate, but not at a worse price. The disadvantage is that if the market gaps, or is moving fast, you may not get filled at all. And your broker may charge more for limit orders.

✔ **Stop-market orders are filled at the best available price at the moment.** The advantage is that you're guaranteed to have your order filled. Also, your broker may charge less for market orders. The disadvantage is that you're not guaranteed to get filled at the price you want. If the market gaps, or is fast moving, you'll get filled at the best current price available, which could be quite far from the price you wanted.

I use stop orders to both enter and exit my trades. For entries, I prefer limit orders. Following the adage "Buy low, sell high," I don't want to get filled too far from my intended entry price. For exits, I prefer market orders. When I decide it's time to get out, I want out now! In a fast-moving market, I may not get the exact price I want, but at least I'll be out of the trade. If I use a limit order during a fast-moving market, I may not get out of the market at all, thus having a live position in a market that's continuing to nose dive against me.

Consult with your broker regarding what type of orders (limit and/or market) are available for trade entries and for stop losses.

Protecting Your Profits with Trailing Stops

Initial protective stops are designed to limit your loss when your setup fails and you're left with a losing trade. *Trailing protective stops* are designed to protect the profits of a winning trade.

Understanding how and when to use trailing stops

The idea of a trailing stop is to allow the market to continue to move in your direction but designate a price level at which you exit your winning trade if the market turns against your trade more than you like. Trailing stops include those that are

- Based on a fixed percentage of the price of the asset you're buying

- Below the most recent previous support level, retrace or swing low, or bullish candlestick patterns

- Just outside of the market's average true range at the time

- Below the trend line of the trend you're trading

- Below a moving average

- Fixed dollar amounts below the current price

- Indicators created for the purposes of providing a trailing stop (Some of these indicators accelerate their stop level — that is, moving closer to the current price — the longer the market move continues.)

After decades of trading experience, I've never found one perfect trailing stop strategy or indicator that works best. I've come to accept that the best that can be realistically achieved is to use a trailing stop that gives a *reasonable* profit based on historical performance. In trading, no one knows in advance how far a market will move on any given trade.

Trading isn't about predicting; it's about making money. If you're able to make good money in a trade and you exit with a profit that's reasonable based on an average trend length, then you've done as well as realistically possible.

Before I even begin employing a trailing stop, I exit part of my position at a target level. If I'm buying a cycle low, my first exit is at the next cycle high. Thus, the first leg of my trade lasts only for a half cycle and is essentially a scalp trade within my longer trade.

Figure 23-3 illustrates the short selling at a cycle high and covering part of the position at the cycle low. Notice that it's a very short-term move, but it has a dramatic effect on keeping losses small.

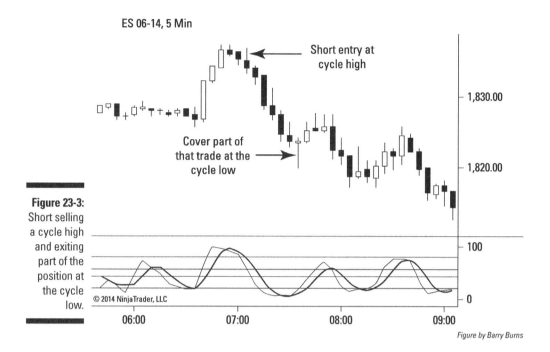

ES 06-14, 5 Min

Short entry at cycle high

1,830.00

Cover part of that trade at the cycle low

1,820.00

Figure 23-3: Short selling a cycle high and exiting part of the position at the cycle low.

© 2014 NinjaTrader, LLC

100

0

06:00   07:00   08:00   09:00

Figure by Barry Burns

Figure 23-4 shows the same thing with a long trade, this time buying a cycle low and exiting part of the trade at a cycle high.

This strategy is pure money management. When all five energies align and the cycle low has a mini-divergence pattern, the probability of that being the final cycle low before the next cycle high is extremely high. This part of the trade doesn't provide a great risk/reward ratio, but it does provide a tremendous win/loss ratio, and that's what scalp trades demand.

Here's a conservative example of how this technique dramatically adjusts the risk in the trade:

> You buy 400 shares of a stock at $100 so you have $40,000 invested. Your stop loss is $2 below your entry, meaning that your risk in the trade is $800 at the point of your protective stop. If the market goes up and makes a cycle high even just $1 above your entry price (conservatively assuming worse than 1:1 risk/reward ratio), and you sell 200 of your 400 shares, you make $200.

After that, if the market turns down and stops you out, you lose $2 per share, but you have only 200 shares left. Therefore, your loss is $400. Offsetting the $400 loss with the $200 you made on your first exit, you have a net loss of only $200 rather than your initial potential loss of $800.

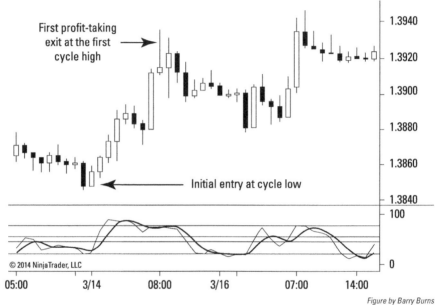

$EURUSD, 60 Min

First profit-taking exit at the first cycle high

Initial entry at cycle low

© 2014 NinjaTrader, LLC

Figure 23-4: Buying a cycle low and exiting part of the position at the cycle high.

Figure by Barry Burns

Remember, this example is intentionally very conservative, assuming the market moved up weakly, not even providing you a 1:1 risk/reward ratio. Often, your first exit will be at, or close to, a 1:1 risk/reward ratio, thereby reducing your losses even more. And this strategy is a way of keeping your losses small. You can survive a lot more $200 losses than you can $800 losses!

This strategy works only when the probability of making money on the first leg of that trade (from cycle low to cycle high) has an extremely high win/loss ratio, as it does with this trade setup.

Managing a trailing stop

I don't employ trailing stops until after that first exit. After that, it's time to let my winners run with a trailing stop! An example of how I commonly manage a trailing stop is simple.

For example, early in a new trend, I continue to move my stop up just below the previous cycle low. Every time a new higher cycle low is plotted, I move my stop below it. I consider an average trend to be five waves, so I tighten my stop as the market approaches the high of the fifth wave. At that time, I begin using a one-bar trailing stop, meaning I move my stop under the low of the previous closed bar.

Figure 23-5 marks the levels of the cycle lows, from left to right, that I'd use to move my trailing stop as the market continues to trend up. Notice that each low on the price bars designated by an arrow corresponds to a low on the cycle indicator in the lower panel of the chart.

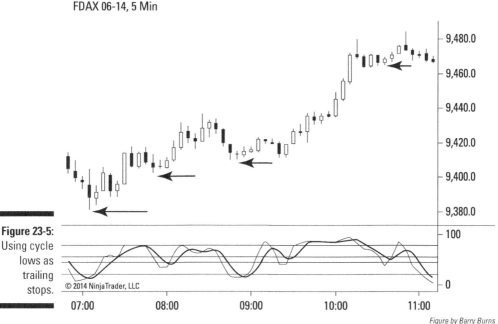

Figure 23-5: Using cycle lows as trailing stops.

FDAX 06-14, 5 Min

© 2014 NinjaTrader, LLC

Figure by Barry Burns

Figure 23-6 marks the levels of the cycle highs that could be used as trailing stops as the market continues to trend down.

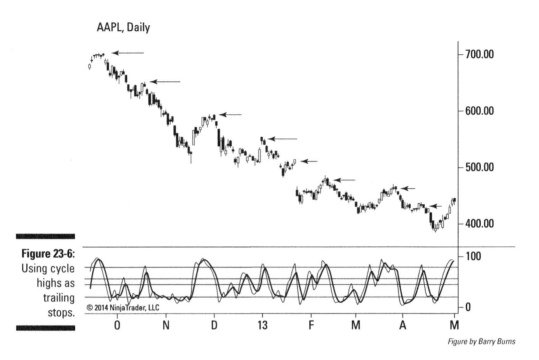

AAPL, Daily

Figure 23-6:
Using cycle
highs as
trailing
stops.

© 2014 NinjaTrader, LLC

Figure by Barry Burns

As the market moves into its fifth wave, I tighten my trailing stop, meaning that I place it closer to the current market price. By this time, I've made good money in the trade, and I'm expecting, based on historical averages, that the trend is nearing an end. Therefore, I don't want the market to make a large move against my position. I want to keep as much of the profits as I can.

Figure 23-7 shows an uptrend that has complete waves 1, 2, 3, and 4 and is approaching a resistance level. In this type of scenario, I'd tighten my trailing stop.

Figure 23-8 shows a downtrend that has complete waves 1, 2, 3, and 4 and is approaching a support level. In this type of scenario, I'd tighten my trailing stop.

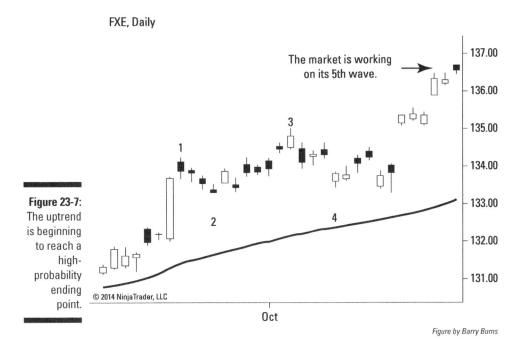

Figure 23-7: The uptrend is beginning to reach a high-probability ending point.

Figure by Barry Burns

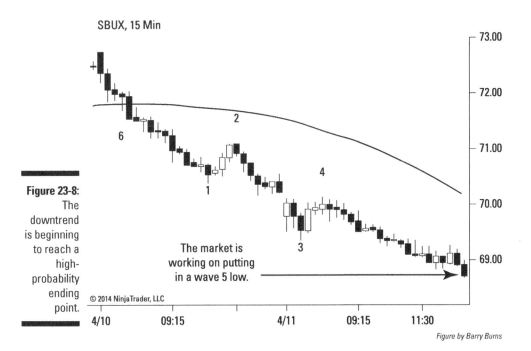

Figure 23-8: The downtrend is beginning to reach a high-probability ending point.

Figure by Barry Burns

On the other hand, I don't want to exit as long as the market is moving aggressively in my direction. Therefore, I begin using a *one-bar trailing stop,* which means I place my stop order below the low of the last closed bar, as illustrated in Figure 23-9.

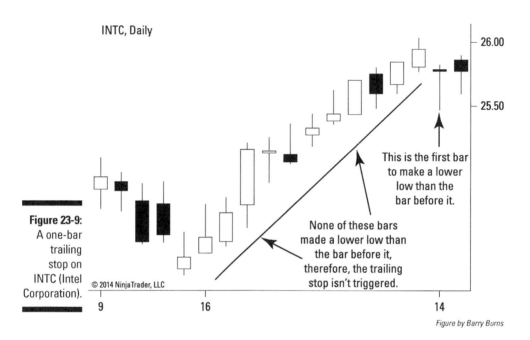

INTC, Daily

This is the first bar to make a lower low than the bar before it.

None of these bars made a lower low than the bar before it, therefore, the trailing stop isn't triggered.

© 2014 NinjaTrader, LLC

Figure 23-9: A one-bar trailing stop on INTC (Intel Corporation).

Figure by Barry Burns

Notice in Figure 23-9 how far the market moved without a bar making a lower low than the bar before it. Placing my stop one penny below the low of the previous closed bar would have kept me in that uptrend until INTC finally created a one bar lower low.

I could then implement a one-bar trailing stop in a downtrend by placing my stop just above the high of the most recently closed bar, as demonstrated in Figure 23-10.

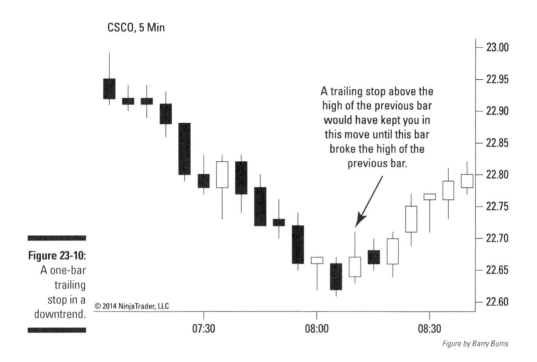

CSCO, 5 Min

A trailing stop above the high of the previous bar would have kept you in this move until this bar broke the high of the previous bar.

© 2014 NinjaTrader, LLC

07:30   08:00   08:30

23.00
22.95
22.90
22.85
22.80
22.75
22.70
22.65
22.60

Figure 23-10: A one-bar trailing stop in a downtrend.

Figure by Barry Burns

Utilizing Stops Each Day/Week/Month/Year

Just as you employ money management and risk management for each trade, you should also have rules for how much money you risk for each day, week, month, and year. Each trade you take has a stop loss, and each day, week, month, quarter, and year can also have a stop loss to help prevent you from taking quick, dramatic losses in a short period of time.

The best way to explain this technique is by way of illustration. (**Note:** I'm not recommending these exact numbers; I just want to communicate the ideas of this type of time-based money management.) For example, say that your trading account is $20,000. You decide that you'll trade two contracts on the YM (the DOW E-mini futures) with a maximum risk of ten points per trade. The contract is worth $5 per point, making your maximum risk $50 per contract or $100 per trade for your two contracts. And $100 is half of 1 percent of your $20,000 trading account.

Risking a very small percentage of your account on each trade is important, allowing you to financially survive *drawdowns* (a series of losing trades), which are a natural part of even good trading methods.

That percentage is the maximum risk per trade you'll allow in your money-management plan. Now, you need to set maximum risks for various time horizons. Here are some examples to demonstrate the point of the advantages of risk management:

- ✔ Maximum risk per day is 2 percent of account ($400).

- ✔ Maximum risk per week is 4 percent of account ($800).

- ✔ Maximum risk per month is 8 percent of account ($1,600).

- ✔ Maximum risk per quarter is 16 percent of account ($3,200).

- ✔ Maximum risk per year is 30 percent of account ($6,000).

Although you may not choose these exact numbers, your percentages should be small enough to keep you from losing a large part of your account quickly. (***Note:*** The percentages used for the large time frames aren't equal to the percentages used for the time frame before it. So even though the risk per day is 2 percent, and there are 5 days in a week, I didn't multiply 2 by 5 to designate a maximum risk of 10 percent per week. Rather, I designated 4 percent because I won't allow myself to consistently lose 2 percent per day.)

The point is that you should choose percentages and dollar amounts that, if hit, indicate something is consistently wrong. It may be that you're not in the right frame of mind, that you're not disciplined, that the market is in a chaotic pattern, or even that your trading method isn't viable.

Just as you use protective stops with these time frames, you can also attach trailing stops to each day, week, month, quarter, and year to protect your profits. Here's an example:

- ✔ If I'm in profit $500 in one day, I won't let my profits for the day drop less than $300.

- ✔ If I'm in profit $1,500 in one week, I won't let my profits for the week drop less than $900.

- ✔ If I'm in profit $5,000 in one month, I won't let my profits for the month drop less than $3,000.

"I blew out my entire account . . . for the third time"

It saddens me to hear of people who entered the trading arena and thereafter lost all the money in their trading account. Many reasons can contribute to their lack of success, including the following:

✔ A faulty trading method

✔ A bogus forex "robot" (automated trading software)

✔ The lack of discipline to keep their trading rules

✔ Not having trading rules (trading by "gut" feel)

✔ Lack of education and experience

Most all traders I know, including myself, were losing traders when they began. Trading is a profession, and like any profession, it requires education, study, diligence, hard work, and then a lot of experience before you become proficient. Sadly, you can find a lot of individuals and companies selling get-rich-quick trading schemes. Don't believe them.

To begin your trading career with losses is normal as you're going through your learning curve. For this reason, you want to utilize very conservative money-management principles. If you follow the rules I provide in this chapter, you could be a losing trader for an entire year and still not "blow out" your entire account. You'd lose only 30 percent of your funds after a terrible year of complete failure!

Better yet, after you get an excellent and thorough education on trading, I encourage you *not* to trade with real money, because the truth is, you'll likely lose it. Instead, begin trading on a simulator or a demo account in which no real money is used. Some trainers disagree with me on this point, saying you don't get the emotional impact of real trading when your money isn't on the line. Although that may be true, dealing with the emotional aspect of trading real money should come second to assuring yourself that you can trade your methodology successfully with play money. If you can't trade successfully on a simulator, then you won't trade successfully with real money, so why experiment with real money first?

Another benefit to trading with a demo account or simulator first is that after you prove to yourself that you can trade the methodology successfully and consistently over time, it will boost your confidence in your trading method. Then if you start trading with real money and you start losing (a common experience), you'll know that it's not the trading method that's faulty but rather your trading psychology. On the other hand, if you start trading with real money before using a simulator, you'll never know whether you're losing because the method is faulty or because your trading psychology needs work.

Finally, you may choose to have profit targets based on historically exceptionally winning days:

✔ If I'm in profit $1,000 in one day, I'll stop trading for the rest of the day.

✔ If I'm in profit $3,000 in one week, I'll stop trading for the rest of the week.

✔ If I'm in profit $9,000 in one month, I'll stop trading for the rest of the month.

Limiting your profits in this manner may seem counterintuitive, but those with experience know that an unusually good profitable run that defies the odds is often followed by giving some of the money back. When the market is uncharacteristically generous, it's usually temporary, so it may be wise to take your above-average winnings and go home.

Figuring out your personal numbers for average and above-average winning and losing time frames comes with experience. You must consider the market you're trading, the leverage at your disposal, and the chart time interval you trade. It's not my place to tell you what percentages you should use, but I can tell you that most traders tend to be overly optimistic. I encourage you to err on the side of being conservative.

Log all your trades in a journal so that over time you'll see what those numbers are for your personal trading.

Finally, keep in mind that these risk numbers are based on the dollar risk from your entry to your protective stop. They don't take into consideration gaps, catastrophic events, and companies going out of business. To help you with those issues, check out Chapter 22 on hedging and Chapter 21 on diversification.

Chapter 24

Documenting Your Trades and Printing Your Charts

In This Chapter

▶ Recording your trades

▶ Monitoring your thoughts and feelings

▶ Admitting your mistakes

▶ Viewing your charts on paper

A business lives and dies by its numbers. Business owners must know what their income and expenses are. Tracking where the money is spent, how to lower or eliminate those expenses, and how to increase income are all part of running a profitable business.

Trading is a simple, straightforward business. You don't have to worry about legal liabilities, underperforming employees, account receivables, mounds of paperwork, or being at the mercy of unreliable vendors. With trading, nearly 100 percent of your time is directly related toward making money. You rely on yourself. You succeed or fail on your own skill and ability.

Despite the simplicity of its business model, trading is still a business and must be treated as such. Part of that means documenting everything and monitoring your numbers to see where you can improve.

Trading is also performance-based, which makes it almost like a sport. In fact, I've found the field of sports psychology to be especially helpful for improving my trading psychology. Like a professional athlete, you should monitor your trading performance and continually look for places to improve your statistics. In this chapter, I show you how to document your performance. In Chapter 25, I explain how to use that documentation to improve your performance.

Documenting Your Entries, Exits, and Reasons for Taking a Trade

Traders commonly record their entries and exist in a trading log. They also use that log to record their profit or loss. That's a good practice, but you can easily get that information from your brokerage firm.

The type of documentation that's most useful is that which you can analyze to make you a better, more skilled trader. You begin your trading log by recording the following:

✔ Your entry time(s)

✔ Your entry price(s)

✔ The reason for taking a trade

Note: I indicate the possibility of multiple entries because you may choose to enter a position at various times and various price points (called *legging into a position*). Figure 24-1 shows an example of what this part of the trading log may look like.

Entry Time	Reason for Trade	Number of Contracts	Entry Price(s)	Number of Contracts
			Entry #1	
			Entry #2 if applicable	
			Entry #3 if applicable	

Figure 24-1: A simple spreadsheet for documenting entries.

Figure by Barry Burns

When the trade is over, you record your *exit price(s)* — your total dollar amount gain or loss for each of your entries, the total dollar amount gain or loss for the entire trade, and, finally, the reason you decided to close out your trade position. Figure 24-2 provides an example of this part of the trade log.

Exit Price(s)	$ Gain/Loss	Total Gain/ Loss	Reason for Final Exit
Exit #1	Dollar amount made/lost from exit #1	The total dollar amount made/lost from the entire trade	
Exit #2 if applicable	Dollar amount made/lost from exit #2		
Exit #3 if applicable	Dollar amount made/lost from exit #3		

Figure 24-2: A simple spreadsheet for documenting exits.

Figure by Barry Burns

Figure 24-3 shows how the log looks when combining the entry and exit portions of the trading log.

You list the entry and exit times so you can go back and review your trades, which is a vital part of becoming a successful trader, as I discuss in Chapter 25.

Note: The terminology in the trading log I use as an illustration is for trading futures. You can use this format for trading any type of market. Simply change the terms to fit the market of your choice.

Entry Time	Reason for Trade	Number of Contracts	Entry Price(s)	Number of Contracts	Exit Price(s)	$ Gain/Loss	Total Gain/ Loss	Reason for Final Exit

Figure 24-3: The trading log showing both entries and exits.

Figure by Barry Burns

This trade log is just a sample. Feel free to customize it to your needs. Some traders like to create the log in an actual spreadsheet and enter the information into the spreadsheet software. They even create simple formulas that automatically calculate the profits and losses after they type the entry and exit prices. Other traders prefer to print the blank trading log sheets and enter the information with a pen or pencil. I like to do this and keep copies that I refer back to on a consistent basis.

It's best to complete the trade entry part of the log immediately after entering the trade, especially if you're holding your trades for long periods of time.

If you're a short-term day trader holding positions for only minutes, you may find it challenging to take your trade, complete the trade entry part of this form, and monitor your trade all at the same time. But it's important to record an entire trade before moving on to the next trade.

If you're tempted to wait until the end of the day to document your trades, consider the following:

- If you take a lot of trades per day, by the end of the day you may forget the reasons you took each trade.
- Your thoughts and emotions regarding each trade are more clear and fresh as you're entering the trade and before you see the results of the trade.

✔ The mind has an uncanny ability to revise history when looking at your trades in hindsight. If you record your trade immediately, you're more likely to document accurate records.

Documenting your actual entry and exit prices over time gives you your actual risk-to-reward ratio, your real-world number. Some traders claim that they'll take only those trades that have a 1:3 risk-to-reward ratio, as if they know how far the market will move in their direction. That would be nice to know, but you have to trade the market as it is at any given time. Avoid imposing your own desire for a certain risk-to-reward ratio.

In addition to those numbers, you should also record your reason for entering the trade. This should be one of the objective setups in your trading plan, such as the first retrace in a trend in my five-energy methodology.

Being Aware of What You Think and Feel As You Trade

Moving beyond statistics, in this section, I delve into the factors that can improve your trading psychology, and that's where the real money is made.

More than anything else, traders struggle with the psychological aspects of trading. Money is a very emotional thing. The two primary emotions connected with money are fear and greed.

As part of my trading education, I was briefly mentored by a former floor trader at the Chicago Mercantile Exchange. He was the best trader for his brokerage firm and was given the task of training other traders. His methodology was making him so much money that not only was he teaching the traders at his firm, but he was also counseling traders from other firms at the exchange.

During my stay, I walked around looking at the profit and loss totals of his students, and consistently, day after day, most of them were in the red. How is it that this amazingly profitable trader was making so much money, but many of his students who were using his exact same method and technology, couldn't squeak out a profit? In talking with them, I concluded that they lacked emotional control to maintain strict discipline in keeping the rules he taught. Time after time, I found them straying from his trading rules because of the following excuses (er, reasons):

- ✔ A setup wasn't perfect, but "it looked pretty good."

- ✔ They were bored because no trades had set up for a long time.

- ✔ They tried some other trade setups they learned elsewhere.

- ✔ They jumped on a rumor.

- ✔ Someone at lunch told them about a "sure thing."

- ✔ They lost some money and were now trading frantically trying to get it back.

- ✔ They had made a lot of money last week and now felt like a trading god who could do no wrong. Their sense of being "gifted" caused them to feel they had a special intuition about the market.

If you find yourself struggling in this area, look for a coach who specializes in helping people with the psychology of trading. But also keep in mind that recording the trading logs in the manner I describe in this chapter and then using that information in the way I outline in Chapter 25 has been the most helpful tool to improve my own trading psychology.

Being aware of and documenting what I'm thinking and feeling while I take each trade is absolutely critical and has provided many revelations into myself that have dramatically improved my trading. Immediately after recording my entry time and price, I write down what I'm thinking about the trade at that moment while it's still fresh. (This has nothing to do with the reason for entering the trade because I've already recorded that.)

No right or wrong answers exist about what you're thinking when you're entering a trade as long as you're honest. Here are some examples of some of my thoughts while getting into trades:

- ✔ This setup is perfect based on my rules. If this trade doesn't make money, then I won't feel bad because it's a high-probability trade.

- ✔ I know I shouldn't take this trade, but it just looks good for some reason.

- ✔ The market has gone up far; it just can't go any higher.

- ✔ I know this isn't the best trade setup, but it's pretty close to my rules.

- ✔ The market has to go up on this new report that just came out.

- ✔ I think I've seen this setup before somewhere, so I'm going to try it.

The only time I consistently make money is if I'm thinking the first item in this list. The other thoughts are signals that I shouldn't take the trade. I know this now because I've documented my trades when I had these thoughts, and they most often become losing trades.

Recording my feelings has been even more revelatory. Emotions are the downfall of many traders. Controlling your emotions begins with being aware of them.

Here are some of the emotions I've recorded as I've entered trades:

- I feel very alert and confident.
- I'm anxious.
- I've lost more money than I'm comfortable with and now I'm mad. I've got to win it back, or I'll be in a bad mood all day.
- I'm excited that I've made so much money recently. I really have a special gift for trading. I have a special intuitive connection with the market.
- I'm tired.
- I'm bored.
- I'm sad over the fight with my wife last night.
- I'm tense.
- I'm scared.
- I'm starving.

Again, the only proper emotional state for trading is the first item. In fact, one of the rules in my trading plan is that I won't trade at all unless I'm in an alert, calm, centered, and confident emotional state.

Professional trading isn't only about monitoring the markets; it's also about monitoring yourself. By monitoring your thoughts and feelings over time, you see patterns develop. After doing this a long time, you see a consistent connection between certain thoughts and feelings and your profitability. Eventually, you'll be able to use that information as actual signals to keep you out of a trade, knowing that those particular thoughts and feelings lead to bad trades.

Recording Your Mistakes

One of the biggest revelations I've had about successful trading is that I do well when I simply avoid making mistakes. Therefore, I've added a section to my trading log where I record mistakes I made on a trade. I consider this the most important part of the log.

Mistakes are actions that violate the rules of my personal trading method and actions that violate generally accepted good trading practices. Violating the trading rules of your trading method is clear if you have an objective trading plan with written rules. The following are what I consider to be generally accepted good trading practices by most traders I know:

- Keep your losses small (see Chapters 21, 22, and 23).
- Don't chase a move. If you missed your optimal entry, let the market go without you and wait for the next setup.
- Don't get distracted and miss excellent trade setups. Stay focused on the market while you're trading.
- Don't trade against the dominant energy of the market (after all, you're a trend trader).
- Don't trade at all when the market is moving randomly with low volume and without any clear structure or trend.
- Avoid overtrading. Be patient and trade only the very best setups according to the rules of your methodology.
- Don't increase the dollar amount of your trades in an effort to recover losses more quickly.
- Don't micromanage trades. When the market is moving aggressively in your direction, don't exit your trade prematurely. Let your winners run.
- Never trade when you're not in a good emotional state. Don't trade out of anger, revenge, or frustration.

These things are easier said than done. However, using the trading log will help you do that over time. Figure 24-4 provides a complete view of the trading log with all the aspects I describe in this chapter.

Trading Log								Date: _____	
Entry Time	Reason for Trade	Number of Contracts	Entry Price(s)	Number of Contracts	Exit Price(s)	$ Gain/Loss	Total Gain/ Loss	Reason for Final Exit	
What I Was Thinking:				Mistakes:					
What I Was Feeling:									

Figure 24-4:
The complete trade log.

Figure by Barry Burns

Going Old School: Printing Your Trading Charts

One of my dear mentors taught me the practice of printing charts, and I thought he was nuts. He was an elderly man who had been trading for decades, long before computers were available to the common person. I'd already been studying and trading for quite a while before I asked him to mentor me. He was a local trading legend with a tremendous reputation, and I wanted to learn what his decades of experience had taught him.

I was fortunate that he took a liking to me. He adopted me as his protégé and stopped charging me. I would go to his girlfriend's house (yes, that feisty old codger had a young girlfriend!), and the three of us would trade the markets together.

Although I never fully adopted his trading method, one of the most helpful things I learned from him had nothing to do with indicators, price patterns, or secret market geometry. He insisted that I print my charts after trading every day. I resisted, telling him that I reviewed my trading every day on my monitors. There was no need to print the charts on paper. He pulled out a box filled with papers. Every page had the printout of a chart from a day he'd traded. Then he pointed to more boxes and said he still had the printout of every chart he ever traded (since he got a computer).

At first, I wasn't convinced, but he wouldn't take no for an answer. "You came to me and wanted to learn; well, then don't question me, just do what I say!"

At that moment, I remember thinking that he was absolutely right. Many of the best things I've learned in life as well as trading have been things I didn't think I needed. That's exactly why they remained lessons uncovered for me.

I immediately started printing my charts at the end of every trading day. To this day I'm still not sure exactly what it is, but printing the charts out on paper and looking at them in that way provides a different perspective than simply reviewing your trades on the computer screen.

Discovering how to print your charts

At the end of your trading day, print your charts out in color. If you're a short-term day trader and use very short interval charts, you may need to use several pieces of paper to print out the chart of the entire day. You can tape the sheets of paper together so you can see the entire day's chart, which is critically important to this exercise.

Some charting software has printing capability built in. Whether or not yours does and how you access the print function varies from one piece of software to another. Sometimes, you can simply right-click on the chart, and a menu appears, offering you the ability to print. You may also see a print function in the top toolbar or under the File menu.

Some charting programs allow you to copy a chart, in which case you can use the copy function and then paste the chart into a word processing program and print it from there.

If none of those capabilities are available, you can get a screen capture program. Type "free screen capture software" into the search field of your favorite search engine to find multiple options.

Screen capture software allows you to capture a portion of the screen of your monitor (in this case, your chart) and saves it as a file (often some type of image file). You can then paste the image into a word processor or possibly even print directly from the screen capture software.

Analyzing your printed charts

After you print your charts for the day, lay them out on a desk. Make sure you see the entire day's chart at a glance, even if you have to print out parts of the chart on separate pieces of paper and tape them together. Go through your trading log and mark every place you entered and exited a trade.

Now look at the big picture and take in the bird's-eye view of the trading day. (This alone has helped me see consistent overall patterns of a trading day.) Then, ask yourself these questions:

- ✔ Were the reasons I took the trades valid?

- ✔ Did I get out too soon? What did the market do after I exited each trade?

- ✔ Did I miss any good trades?

- ✔ What type of day was today: trending, consolidating, chaotic?

- ✔ Was I trading with the dominant direction of the day, or was I fighting it all day or part of the day?

These are just some questions to get you started. As you engage in this discipline day after day, week after week, month after month, you'll begin seeing things you've never seen before! There's something about printing your charts and reviewing the trading day on paper that provides a different perspective.

After you're done reviewing the charts, attach them to your trading logs for the day so you have a complete record of your trading for the day.

The ultimate, top-secret mystery of becoming a successful trader

When I started my education in technical analysis, I thought trading looked easy. I soon learned it's deceptively difficult. The markets provide no certainties or guarantees and are unpredictable. This fact is very uncomfortable to most people. People have a natural desire for security, and that requires some level of certainty.

The good news is that you can have that in trading, but it doesn't come from the market. The only certainty you can have is the certainty of your own behavior. The only guarantee you can enjoy is to guarantee yourself that you'll keep your trading rules. They only thing you can predict is that you'll act consistently and stick to the commonly accepted good trading practices.

All of this is within your control. There's no one else to blame. The Holy Grail of trading is self-control, self-discipline, and self-mastery.

Chapter 25

Reviewing Your Trades — Always!

*I*n Chapter 24, I show you how to document your trades. In this chapter, I show you how to use that information to turn yourself into a better trader.

Many traders are looking for the magic indicator or trading "robot" that will make them money. In reality, documenting your trades and doing the exercises associated with it will be the thing most likely to bring you success as a trader.

This documentation and review requires a bit of work that most people aren't willing to do, but your willingness to work harder than others is exactly what will bring you the profits that elude so many.

Looking for Your Mistake Patterns

Successful trading is largely a matter of not making mistakes. Although no one ever completely eliminates all mistakes, the closer you get to that ideal, the more profitable you become.

Your goal isn't to become perfect. Your goal is to find those mistakes you make habitually and reduce them dramatically. Those mistakes are the ones that are damaging your trading account. You can survive making mistakes here and there if you put an end to your habitual mistake patterns. I show you how in the following sections.

Taking a look in the mirror

The best tool I've used for overcoming trading mistakes is my weekly trading log. I go into detail about creating a daily trading log in Chapter 24. I use that to track and record the dynamics of every individual trade: the entry, the exit, the reason for the trade, what I was thinking, what I was feeling, and any mistakes I made.

That's where you begin, but having that information spread out over multitudes of pieces of paper doesn't give you the big picture. The information is too scattered.

This is where the weekly trade log comes in. The weekly trade log has five rows, one for each day of the week. At the end of each day, you add up the results of the entire day and summarize them on one row of the weekly trading log. At the end of a week and the end of a month, you can look at those summaries and see at a glance the patterns of your own trading results — the good, the bad, and the ugly. Looking at that weekly trade log is like looking into a mirror.

You may already have a general idea of the problems you have, but often, traders grossly underestimate how big those problems are and how often they make the same mistakes. When you summarize your trading behavior on paper and look at it over a significant period of time, you may be shocked to see how those mistakes occur. This revelation may be the first time you see how serious your trading mistakes are and how much money they're costing you. Don't run from this revelation; instead, learn from it.

Knowing that you're a uniquely flawed trader

Every trader is unique. Although traders as a group make similar errors, the issues you struggle with as an individual may be different than the issues other traders struggle with.

For example, one of my biggest challenges is overtrading. I love to trade as actively and as much as possible. As a result, I'm tempted to take trades that aren't optimal high-probability situations. On the other hand, a former trading partner of mine had the opposite problem. He was so afraid of losing money that he'd let even the best trading scenarios pass by without taking them.

Reading books on the psychology of trading can definitely be helpful, but at some point you need to make it personal and discover your unique trading challenges. No one can do this for you. It must come from your own trading results day in and day out.

Normally, after a week of trading every day (I'm referring to short-term day traders here), you start to see patterns you've been unaware of. In just five short days, you'll be surprised by how often you make the same one or two mistakes. Whether you're overtrading, being overly cautious and missing great trades, getting out of winning trades too soon, or moving your stops and taking big losses, you'll be surprised that you make certain trading errors more often than you think.

The best way to discover your individual trading struggles is to document them on paper. The cloudy awareness of your trading problems you hold in your mind become crystal clear when put down on paper.

Having worked through this process one-on-one with many trading students, I assure you that the issues you're aware of in your mind are much more serious and numerous than you imagine. When you put each incident on paper, that piece of paper becomes a mirror of self-awareness that will surprise you.

Comparing Your Actual Profits to Your "Perfect" Profits

Documenting the details of your entries and exits, your reason for taking a trade, your thoughts and emotions, and the mistakes you've made can help increase your self-awareness and may lead to changed behavior. But awareness doesn't always lead to change. So you have to add some more motivation.

On the weekly trading log, this motivator is the column with the heading *Net P/L without Mistakes*. Here, you see the difference between the actual money you made or lost with your current trading habits and behavior compared to the money you would have made if you didn't make any mistakes.

This alone is often enough motivation to get traders to change their behavior and start trading with more discipline. You can start being a consistently profitable trader right this moment by simply eliminating your mistakes!

Reviewing the Documents for Your Documentation

As I explain in Chapter 24, using a trading log, like the one in Figure 25-1, helps you keep track of your trades. You enter the summary of each day's trading logs into each of the five blank rows in the log. So by the end of the week, you have a summary of the data of your entire week's trading on one sheet of paper, thus enabling you to see the overall patterns without being distracted by the details.

Trade Log for the Week of _____ to _____									
Date	Win/Loss	Total P/L	Average $ Win/$Loss	Com-mission	Net P/L; % Acct	# Of Mis-takes	Net P/L w/o Mis-takes	Mistakes	
Week Totals									
Week Averages									

Figure 25-1:
Weekly trading log.

Figure by Barry Burns

Here's what you should record in each box and why (see Figure 25-2 for an illustration):

✔ **Losing and winning trades:** The number of losing trades compared to the number of winning trades provides your win/loss ratio for the day.

✔ **Money won and money lost:** The amount of money made on winning trades compared to the amount of money lost on losing trades helps you identify whether your winners are bigger than your losers on average.

✔ **Commissions:** When you record your total commissions for the day, alongside your profits and losses, you'll be surprised at the effect commissions have on your net profit for the day.

Figure 25-2: Calculating your win/loss ratio and the dollar size of your winners versus your losers.

Win/Loss		Total P/L		Average $ Win/Loss		Commission
# of winning trades	# of losing trades	Gross $ amount made with winning trades	Gross $ amount lost with losing trades	Gross $ winners divided by # of winning trades	Gross $ losers divided by # of losing trades	Total commissions for all trades this day

Figure by Barry Burns

In the rest of the boxes, record the following (and check out Figure 25-3 for an example):

✔ **Your net dollar amount profit or loss for the day after commissions:** Many traders don't take the cost of commissions into account and are surprised to find the dramatic effect that commissions can have on their profit or loss at the end of the day.

✔ **The total number of mistakes you made that day:** Your primary goal is to reduce this number as much as possible.

✔ **The net dollar amount profit or loss you would have made if you didn't make any mistakes:** This amount is almost always a huge difference than your actual profit or loss. Watching the disparity between how much you could be making if you eliminated mistakes against how much you're making or losing with mistakes is often the trigger that gets you to change your behavior.

✔ **A summary of the specific mistakes you made that day:** Don't be too concerned about a single mistake once in a while. What's important here is when you find yourself making the same mistake habitually.

Net P/L; % Acct		# Of Mistakes	Net P/L w/o Mistakes	Mistakes
Net profit after commission	Net loss after commission	Total # of mistakes made today	Your net $ amount P/L if you made no mistakes	3 times: overtraded 2 times: took profits too soon 5 times: traded against the trend 4 times: missed good trades because distracted
			↑ This # can be your best motiv- ation!	↑ Summary of your mistakes where you'll see your problem area patterns. You'll likely be surprised that you're making more mistakes than you previously realized.

Figure 25-3: Documenting your net profits and your mistakes.

Figure by Barry Burns

At the end of the week, tally your totals and enter them at the bottom of the weekly trade log. Then transfer that information to a row on the monthly trade log (see Figure 25-4) to see the big picture over a longer time frame.

Trade Log for the Month of _____									
Week	Win/Loss	Total P/L	Average $ Win/Loss		Com-mission	Net P/L; % Acct	# Of Mis-takes	Net P/L w/o Mis-takes	Mistakes
1									
2									
3									
4									
5									
Month Totals									
Month Averages									

Figure 25-4: Transfer the data from your weekly log to the monthly log.

Figure by Barry Burns

After you document everything, here's how to use it to change your awareness and your behavior:

- After every trading session, review that day's trading on the charts. Do this on the computer bar by bar, with each new bar on the right side of the screen so you can't see the next bar, as if you were trading in real time. Scroll through the entire day this way and review your trades.

- Print your charts and review them on paper.

- Transfer that day's trading summary to the weekly trading log.

- Every morning before trading, review the previous day's trade log and printed charts to remind yourself what you did right and wrong. Also review your weekly trading log for the previous four weeks to remind yourself of behavioral patterns (mistakes) that are causing you to lose money. You want that fresh in your mind before you begin trading each new day.

- Every weekend, transfer the entire week's trading logs to the monthly trade log. On Sunday, review every daily trade log from the previous week, the last four weeks of weekly trade logs, and as many monthly trade logs as you have.

Part VI
The Part of Tens

Check out a bonus tens list at www.dummies.com/extras/trendtrading for the ten commandments of disciplined trading.

In this part . . .

✔ Discover ten habits of highly effective trend traders so that you can follow in their footsteps.

✔ Find out the ten most common misconceptions about trend trading so that you can separate fact from fiction and make wise and successful trades.

Chapter 26

Ten Habits of Highly Effective Trend Traders

In This Chapter

▷ Looking for ways to continue to learn and improve as a trader

▷ Balancing your trading career and yourself

Trading is a performance-based profession. You're pitting your wits and skills against the market, which essentially means you're competing with other traders. Successful trading relies on personal development, self-control, and being constantly adaptable to varying market conditions.

Human beings are creatures of habit, and it's those habits that create the results you get in your personal life and professional life. This chapter focuses on ten habits that can lead to being a consistently profitable trader.

Being a Perpetual Student

As with any other profession, you must engage in continuing education if you're to remain relevant in the trading world. Rules and regulations, technology, and who is trading and how are constantly changing, and you must keep up with it all. You must continue to learn. No one knows everything about trading.

Even after all the time I've been trading, all the classes I've attended, all the books I've read, and all the mentors and coaches I've hired, I still make it a practice to take one new trading course every year. I don't learn much from most of them, but I know that if I learn even one small new distinction, I can leverage it over time to earn me tens of thousands — if not hundreds of thousands — more dollars over the years.

In addition to learning more about trading, there's always room for self-improvement in terms of your personal discipline, mindset, belief system, confidence, and self-control. These things are crucial to trading success.

Being Flexible

One of the most challenging aspects of trading is that you never know what's going to happen from one moment to the next. A famous saying among traders is, "The market can do anything at any time."

I keep the mindset of trading "bar by bar." With each new bar that forms, I reevaluate the situation. In this way, trading is like playing chess. The great chess masters think ahead a certain number of moves, but it all begins with the list of potential next moves their opponent can make. A chess master once told me that the entire game of chess comes down to this pattern: "If he does this, then I'll do that, but if he does this, then I'll do that, but if he does this, then I'll do that. . . ."

Trading is the same way. I look at the market and consider all the next moves (read: next bars) the market can make. I'm never guessing what the market may do, nor am I predicting what the market may do. I keep a flexible mind so I'm never surprised, and I'm always ready for any eventuality, knowing that "the market can do anything at any time."

One of the foundational principles of Darwin's theory of evolution supports this idea — "the survival of the fittest." Some interpret this to mean the survival of the "adaptable," meaning when the environment changes, it's those who can adapt to it that will survive. This is certainly important in the markets. As they change, you must be flexible enough to change with them.

Being Part of a Trading Community

Trading is an isolating experience for many who trade alone in their homes or offices. If you're able to be self-disciplined and focus when alone, then it can be an advantage. If you need other people around to provide accountability and keep you alert, then it's a disadvantage.

If you fit into the latter category, you may want to become part of a trading firm, or at the very least, join an online trading chat room. Personally, I find the online trading rooms to be distracting and often the sources of bad information that reinforces a negative mindset. Either way, it can be helpful to be part of a trading community, whether you participate during or after market hours.

One of the most enjoyable ways to participate in a trading community is to join a local trading club where traders congregate once a week. Often, such meetings will have a headline speaker, a question-and-answer session, informal discussion, and sometimes even socializing afterward.

Having Realistic Expectations

Like many money-making endeavors, a lot of hype surrounds the world of trading, especially on the Internet. Individuals and companies are always trying to sell the latest e-book, course, magic indicator, or forex robot with outrageous claims of instant and enormous profits.

It if sounds too good to be true, it probably is. Trading is a real, legitimate profession, not a get-rich-quick scheme. Profitable traders are those who have received a quality education, paid their dues, studied hard, practiced for a long period of time, and gained a lot of experience.

Being Disciplined

Money is very emotional for most people, and it's easy to get caught up in the emotions of fear or greed. Day traders especially can get overconfident and overly ambitious, which leads to overtrading and treating electronic trading like a video game.

Profitable traders are masters of self-control. They trade less than you probably think. For example, I'll stay out of the market for long periods of time, waiting for the next high-probability setup to come to me. While I wait, I also have to remain alert so I don't miss the high-probability trade I've been waiting for.

Working on Your Mindset

One of my trading rules is that I trade only when I'm in a good emotional mindset. If I had an argument with my wife (which is extremely rare!), am worried about my kids, or upset about anything at all, I simply don't trade.

I know a lot of traders who do one to two hours of preparation every morning before the market opens. They look over news that came out overnight, and they examine what the markets did in other countries while the U.S. markets were closed.

My preparation in the morning is more focused on my mindset than the markets. I meditate and perform a Tai Chi form outside before I turn on my computer. That gets me in the proper alert but calm and balanced mindset that helps me trade well.

You can choose whatever routine works best for you, as long as you're calm and focused before you begin your trading.

Going to Work as a Professional

Some day traders don't do any preparation before the markets open. They roll out of bed just minutes before the open, go into their home office in their pajamas, and start trading.

Although that may work for some, I suggest preparing yourself as if you're going to work — because you are! For example, I take a shower, do my grooming, wear nice business-casual clothes, have a light breakfast, and then go into my home office. Preparing myself as though I was going to a public office, rather than my private home office, puts me in the right state of mind for behaving as a professional, being alert, and treating my trading like a business.

Reviewing Your Performance and Applying What You Learn

After each trading day, review your daily trade log (refer to Chapter 25 for more on reviewing your trades). Tally your mistakes, the difference in your net profits for the day if you didn't make any mistakes, and then summarize it on your weekly chart. Print out your charts, and mark every place you entered and exited a trade.

Then, each morning before you begin trading, review your daily logs from the last several days, and also review your weekly and monthly logs to remind yourself of the lessons you've learned from the mistakes you made. Also review your printed charts.

You want to keep that all very fresh in your mind so you don't make the same mistakes in the future.

Focusing on Trading Mastery

Trading is a challenging profession. You can't just show up, punch the clock, and earn an hourly wage for being there. You don't get paid for your time. You get paid for your results and only your results.

In addition, you're trading in the same markets that some of the brightest minds in the world are trading. Wherever there's a lot of money to be made, there you'll find some of the smartest, sharpest people in the world. That's certainly true of the trading world.

You can't take trading lightly. Your goal can't be to become a "good" trader or to just make enough to live on. That level of motivation won't be enough to succeed against the stiff competition. You must be completely devoted to mastering the art and science of trading. That's the level you must aim for if you want to be successful.

Leading a Balanced Life

Trading is a lot of fun. You can make a lot of money trading. Trading is intellectually stimulating. When you become skilled, there's a state of "flow" that you experience, similar to a runner's high.

Although focusing on trading mastery is important, you must counterbalance that with not getting so intoxicated with trading that you sacrifice your health, your family, and other interests. In fact, leading a balanced life will actually help you be a better trader. For example:

- ✔ Having a good, loving family life will help you enjoy a good state of mind and put you in a good emotional place.
- ✔ Eating well, having good nutrition, exercising, and taking care of your body will also help with your trading. Physical discomfort, sluggishness, and illness are all distractions that can hurt your trading performance.

✔ Maintaining a good spiritual life will also keep you balanced and help you avoid the temptation of greed.

Choose a charity in which you strongly believe and commit to donate a certain percentage of your profits to that charity. This can serve as a motivator on the spiritual level to help you maintain discipline and succeed in your trading profession.

Chapter 27

Ten Common Misconceptions about Trend Trading

. . . .

In This Chapter

▶ Busting the myths about trading successfully

▶ Finding what works for you and sticking to it

. . . .

*T*rading is deceptively difficult. In other words, it looks easy when looking at charts from the past. You can look at a historical chart and easily identify the times it would have been best to enter and exit the market.

Hindsight is 20/20, and when looking back on charts, the signs for entries and exits seem obvious. Trading "on the hard right edge of the chart," where you have to make a decision in real time without the benefit of knowing what will happen in the future, is an extremely difficult thing to do.

One of the primary reasons traders fail is that their minds are filled with misconceptions about the reality of trading. Those misconceptions make trading seem easier than it is. In this chapter, I do you the favor of dispelling those misconceptions now so you can deal with the reality of the professional trading world.

If I Back Test Successfully, It Will Work in the Future

One of the popular approaches to creating a trading system is to begin with a certain idea, translate that into a charting concept that's mathematically measurable, and then back test it.

Back testing is usually done with a computer program designed for that purpose. You enter the parameters of your rules into the program and choose a period of time to apply those rules to the charts. The program automatically applies those rules and provides you with a report that shows how much money that system would have made or lost during that period. If the system wasn't profitable over the time of period chosen (which it usually won't be), you can change the rules and try again. You do this over and over, through a process of trial and error, until you finally get a supposedly profitable system.

Some back testing computer programs can save you time by automatically testing numerous variables of indicator inputs for you and thereafter provide a report of which indicator inputs performed the best. This approach alone isn't very helpful because you're simply curve-fitting the indicators to the period of time chosen. A more respected approach is to take a system, after it's successful in back testing, and conduct *out-of-sample testing* — that is, taking a trading system that traded profitably on the chosen historical data and then choosing a completely different time period of historical data and running the system on it.

The idea is that if it worked on both historical time periods, it's probably not just curve-fitting and is robust enough to be successful in the future. Such a practice may be more convincing. However, the problem is that this entire process assumes that what worked in the past will work in the future. This assumption isn't necessarily true. The Securities and Exchange Commission (SEC) requires funds to tell investors that "a fund's past performance does not necessarily predict future results."

The Market Is Out to Get Me

Many traders over the years have told me with complete confidence that they believed someone evil was watching their specific trades and intentionally trading against them personally. They often think their broker or some big trader is watching their account, every trade they take, and where they place their stops and willfully trying to destroy them financially.

When asked how much money they have in their account, they typically respond by saying they have a few thousand dollars. I have to tell them, "No offense, but I don't think your broker or anyone cares about your account enough to be trading against you!" They don't believe me, saying that it seems impossible that every trade they make is so wrong.

The reason such traders feel that someone in authority with big money must be taking the other side of their trade intentionally, singling them out to turn almost all their trades into losers is actually much more simple than that. The trader is simply doing everything wrong. Trading is unnatural, and therefore people are constantly doing the wrong thing by their very nature.

People are generally contrarian. So when the market is moving up, I've seen trader after trader shorting the market, always trading against the trend (but you know better than that, right?). Human beings also crave certainty because it gives people a feeling of security. Trading provides no certainty, and many people simply can't psychologically handle that. They therefore grasp onto an idea and won't let it go, which is why a lot of people move their stops when the market turns against them. They can't stand the idea of locking in a financial loss. They'd rather keep their hope alive that the market will turn back in their direction, even if there's no solid evidence that it will.

Trading Is Easy — Just Follow the Trend

One time, at a holiday party, I was asked what I did for a living. When I told the man I was a trader, he replied, "Oh, that's easy; all you have to do is follow the trend."

Of course, I know that trading isn't easy, and I was offended that he had diminished the skills I've worked so hard to gain over the years. I asked him, "Are you a trader, too?"

He replied, "I tried it, but I lost all my money!"

I got a bit of an attitude and said, "How could a smart guy like you lose all your money at something that's so easy?" He gave me a dirty look, turned, and went to talk to someone else.

Even though this book is about trend trading, being successful at trading isn't as simple as following the direction (trend) of the market. The trend of the market is indeed critical. In fact, it's so important that it's the first thing I look at when I view a chart.

Determining the trend of the market at any given moment is easy. What I really want to know is will the market continue to move in the direction of the trend after I buy in? To evaluate that, I also need to know the momentum of the market (how strong the trend is), how early I'm getting into the trend (has everyone already bought in, or are there still a lot of market participants with their money on the sidelines who could join the trend?), whether it's the right time to enter (cycles), whether I'm bouncing off a support level, and what the energy of momentum is on the higher scale.

Beyond all of that, trading still isn't easy even if you have a successful trading methodology, because the hardest part of trading is your self-discipline.

The Professionals Know a Secret That I Don't Have Access To

The trading world definitely holds a lot of secrets. High-frequency traders aren't going to give up their edge, and those who have successful computer trading models aren't likely to give them to you. However, there's no key secret that isn't accessible to you that keeps you from being profitable.

The biggest "secret" of successful trading is that it's more about self-management than managing the market. That's not a secret in the sense that the knowledge isn't available (you just read it here!). It's a secret only in the sense that most people refuse to believe it.

I'd Be Successful if I Just Had That One Special Indicator

It's often said that trading doesn't have a "Holy Grail." I agree with that. Trading is about developing a trading methodology that has enough variables that, when combined, provide a high-probability scenario that favors your profitability over a large sample of data.

No one single thing will make you money, especially not an indicator. Indicators do what they promise: They indicate. They can't tell the future. They're derivatives of price, volume, and/or other factors they measure, all put together in a mathematical format. That's it. There's nothing magical about them.

Commission Prices Aren't Important

Like any business, trading has expenses. The more you can lower your expenses, the more net profit you can make. Some things are worth spending money on because they make you money. If you're a day trader, for example, you want a fast computer and a fast Internet connection. Those are expenses that will make you money.

Commissions have come down tremendously since I started trading, and that alone makes it easier to become profitable. I've found excellent brokers who provide rock-bottom commissions. So I can get low commission rates without sacrificing anything I want.

Full-service brokers generally charge more for commissions. If you want a full-service broker for the extra services they provide, then you may want to go that way.

Personally, I'm not looking for recommendations or help from a broker other than to provide me a quick connection to the exchange, a readily available trade desk, and to be honest and stay in business.

It's Best to Follow the Advice of the Professionals

My father was my first trading instructor. The worst investments he took were often the ones referred to him by a broker. I've subscribed to many newsletters over the years. None of them have helped me make better decisions than I could on my own. I've followed analysts' recommendations on stocks and found them to be useless.

The only professionals that I've found to be helpful are the ones I paid to provide me private mentoring. They all provided me with something of value, even if I didn't end up using their methodology (and I never did!).

I Have a Gut Feeling for Where the Market Is Headed

I once was out of town for a meeting, and at one of the social gatherings, I met a man who said he was a trader. I asked him what type of approach he used for trading. He answered, "I just go by my gut. I can feel what the market is going to do. I have good intuition."

You probably know my next question: "So how did you do? Did you make a lot of money?" He said, "No, I lost everything, and my wife got very mad."

You don't have a special intuitive connection with the market. No one does. At times, you may make money for a while and start to believe you're special. That's not an unusual experience, but it's inevitably followed by a series of staggering losses.

I'll Be Successful if I Trade Exactly Like My Mentor

Just because some people are successful traders doesn't mean that you'll be successful if you follow their method. The first issue is that you may not have the same type of psychological disposition they do regarding discipline, keeping a cool head, and not getting overly emotional. The other issue is that their methodology may not suit your personality.

I have a friend who trades breakouts, and he does it very successfully. I've learned his method, but I can't trade it as profitably as he does simply because I'm not comfortable trading breakouts. I always feel that I'm getting into the market too late. I'm comfortable trading retraces in the trend. That's what resonates with me and fits my personality. He's not wrong, and I'm not wrong; we just have different trading styles that fit our different personalities.

I'd Be Profitable if I Could Find a Trading Method That Worked

Many people have successful trading methods, and they don't even know it. It may be because the method doesn't fit their personality. It may be because they're undisciplined and unfocused. It may be because they make too many mistakes, and they don't bother to record them on their trade log and correct them.

Many viable trade methodologies exist. In my work with traders, I've found that the problem with those who are unprofitable more often lies with them than with the methodology they're using.

Index

About the Author

Barry Burns has a doctorate in hypnotherapy and is a certified NLP practitioner; therefore, he's able to help people with the psychology of trading. He's also a businessman who's owned several small companies. His business background taught him to focus on the bottom line, so his study of the financial markets was for one purpose only: to make profits.

Barry started his study of the markets under the direction of his father, Patrick F. Burns, who became independently wealthy through trading and had more than 70 years of trading experience before passing away in 2005. Barry then furthered his education by reading more than 100 books on trading and investing and spending more than $50,000 in trading courses and education. In addition, he hired three professional traders to mentor him personally, including a former floor trader at the Chicago Mercantile Exchange.

All of this research and study resulted in insights, which led to Barry founding Top Dog Trading, to help students shorten their learning curves in becoming traders, and developing his own Top Dog Trading five-energy methodology (which now includes a plug-in for MetaStock).

Barry has been a seminar presenter for several exchanges, including the CME Group and Eurex, and at many wealth expos and traders expos; a headlining speaker at DayTradersUSA and Market Analysts of Southern California; a featured expert at Trader Kingdom; published many articles for various outlets, including eSignal Central; received several Readers' Choice Awards for "Technical Analysis Websites" and "Trading Schools" by *Technical Analysis of STOCKS & COMMODITIES* magazine; featured as a case study in the books *The Complete Guide to Using Candlestick Charting* and *The Complete Guide to Investing in Derivatives,* both by Alan Northcott (Atlantic Publishing Group, Inc.); developed a five-day course for WorldWideTraders; interviewed on the Robin Dayne "Elite Masters of Trading" Radio Show and on Otrader.com; and a lead moderator for FuturesTalk chat room, guiding listeners through the open and close of each trading day.

Dedication

This book is dedicated to my dear ol' dad, Patrick F. Burns, who inspired and educated me with his own passion for trading. You were my original teacher, not only in trading but also in life. I'll love you forever Daddy-O!

Author's Acknowledgments

First, I'd like to thank my daughters, Serena Kashmir and Anjalee Jasmine. We've gone through the hills and valleys together over the years. Your love, understanding, and kindness inspire me to be a better man. I love you with every cell of my being.

To my new best friend, lover, and soul mate, Sarah Anne. Although you may be a new addition to our family, you've brought love, laughter, and a righteous, fighting Irish spirit we so dearly needed. I've never loved, nor been loved, so deeply and completely. It was soul recognition from day one.

To my teachers and mentors who have liberally shared their decades of knowledge and who opened not only their wisdom but also their homes to me.

To my students who have taught me as much as I have taught them.

To my wonderful assistants Sheila Currie, Sheila Shea, and Barbara Holmes who have been loyal, trustworthy, and professional. You are very rare indeed, and I'm lucky to have you in my life. Thank you.

Last but not least, I thank all the people at Wiley. You were an absolute pleasure to work with.

Publisher's Acknowledgments

Acquisitions Editor: Stacy Kennedy

Senior Project Editor: Christina Guthrie

Copy Editor: Jennette ElNaggar

Technical Editor: Russell Rhoads

Art Coordinator: Alicia B. South

Project Coordinator: Melissa Cossell

Cover Image: ©iStock.com/Henrik5000

Notes

Notes

Notes

Notes

Apple & Mac

iPad For Dummies,
5th Edition
978-1-118-72306-7

iPhone For Dummies,
7th Edition
978-1-118-69083-3

Macs All-in-One
For Dummies, 4th Edition
978-1-118-82210-4

OS X Mavericks
For Dummies
978-1-118-69188-5

Blogging & Social Media

Facebook For Dummies,
5th Edition
978-1-118-63312-0

Social Media Engagement
For Dummies
978-1-118-53019-1

WordPress For Dummies,
6th Edition
978-1-118-79161-5

Business

Stock Investing
For Dummies, 4th Edition
978-1-118-37678-2

Investing For Dummies,
6th Edition
978-0-470-90545-6

Personal Finance
For Dummies, 7th Edition
978-1-118-11785-9

QuickBooks 2014
For Dummies
978-1-118-72005-9

Small Business Marketing
Kit For Dummies,
3rd Edition
978-1-118-31183-7

Careers

Job Interviews
For Dummies, 4th Edition
978-1-118-11290-8

Job Searching with Social
Media For Dummies,
2nd Edition
978-1-118-67856-5

Personal Branding
For Dummies
978-1-118-11792-7

Resumes For Dummies,
6th Edition
978-0-470-87361-8

Starting an Etsy Business
For Dummies, 2nd Edition
978-1-118-59024-9

Diet & Nutrition

Belly Fat Diet For Dummies
978-1-118-34585-6

Mediterranean Diet
For Dummies
978-1-118-71525-3

Nutrition For Dummies,
5th Edition
978-0-470-93231-5

Digital Photography

Digital SLR Photography
All-in-One For Dummies,
2nd Edition
978-1-118-59082-9

Digital SLR Video &
Filmmaking For Dummies
978-1-118-36598-4

Photoshop Elements 12
For Dummies
978-1-118-72714-0

Gardening

Herb Gardening
For Dummies, 2nd Edition
978-0-470-61778-6

Gardening with Free-Range
Chickens For Dummies
978-1-118-54754-0

Health

Boosting Your Immunity
For Dummies
978-1-118-40200-9

Diabetes For Dummies,
4th Edition
978-1-118-29447-5

Living Paleo For Dummies
978-1-118-29405-5

Big Data

Big Data For Dummies
978-1-118-50422-2

Data Visualization
For Dummies
978-1-118-50289-1

Hadoop For Dummies
978-1-118-60755-8

Language &
Foreign Language

500 Spanish Verbs
For Dummies
978-1-118-02382-2

English Grammar
For Dummies, 2nd Edition
978-0-470-54664-2

French All-in-One
For Dummies
978-1-118-22815-9

German Essentials
For Dummies
978-1-118-18422-6

Italian For Dummies,
2nd Edition
978-1-118-00465-4

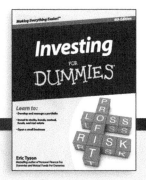 **Available in print and e-book formats.**

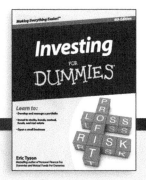

Available wherever books are sold. **For more information or to order direct visit www.dummies.com**

Math & Science

Algebra I For Dummies,
2nd Edition
978-0-470-55964-2

Anatomy and Physiology
For Dummies, 2nd Edition
978-0-470-92326-9

Astronomy For Dummies,
3rd Edition
978-1-118-37697-3

Biology For Dummies,
2nd Edition
978-0-470-59875-7

Chemistry For Dummies,
2nd Edition
978-1-118-00730-3

1001 Algebra II Practice
Problems For Dummies
978-1-118-44662-1

Microsoft Office

Excel 2013 For Dummies
978-1-118-51012-4

Office 2013 All-in-One
For Dummies
978-1-118-51636-2

PowerPoint 2013
For Dummies
978-1-118-50253-2

Word 2013 For Dummies
978-1-118-49123-2

Music

Blues Harmonica
For Dummies
978-1-118-25269-7

Guitar For Dummies,
3rd Edition
978-1-118-11554-1

iPod & iTunes
For Dummies, 10th Edition
978-1-118-50864-0

Programming

Beginning Programming
with C For Dummies
978-1-118-73763-7

Excel VBA Programming
For Dummies, 3rd Edition
978-1-118-49037-2

Java For Dummies,
6th Edition
978-1-118-40780-6

Religion & Inspiration

The Bible For Dummies
978-0-7645-5296-0

Buddhism For Dummies,
2nd Edition
978-1-118-02379-2

Catholicism For Dummies,
2nd Edition
978-1-118-07778-8

Self-Help & Relationships

Beating Sugar Addiction
For Dummies
978-1-118-54645-1

Meditation For Dummies,
3rd Edition
978-1-118-29144-3

Seniors

Laptops For Seniors
For Dummies, 3rd Edition
978-1-118-71105-7

Computers For Seniors
For Dummies, 3rd Edition
978-1-118-11553-4

iPad For Seniors
For Dummies, 6th Edition
978-1-118-72826-0

Social Security
For Dummies
978-1-118-20573-0

Smartphones & Tablets

Android Phones
For Dummies, 2nd Edition
978-1-118-72030-1

Nexus Tablets
For Dummies
978-1-118-77243-0

Samsung Galaxy S 4
For Dummies
978-1-118-64222-1

Samsung Galaxy Tabs
For Dummies
978-1-118-77294-2

Test Prep

ACT For Dummies,
5th Edition
978-1-118-01259-8

ASVAB For Dummies,
3rd Edition
978-0-470-63760-9

GRE For Dummies,
7th Edition
978-0-470-88921-3

Officer Candidate Tests
For Dummies
978-0-470-59876-4

Physician's Assistant Exam
For Dummies
978-1-118-11556-5

Series 7 Exam For Dummies
978-0-470-09932-2

Windows 8

Windows 8.1 All-in-One
For Dummies
978-1-118-82087-2

Windows 8.1 For Dummies
978-1-118-82121-3

Windows 8.1 For Dummies,
Book + DVD Bundle
978-1-118-82107-7

Available in print and e-book formats.

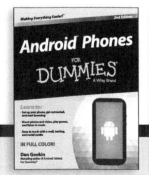

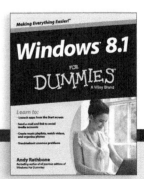

Available wherever books are sold. **For more information or to order direct visit www.dummies.com**

Take Dummies with you everywhere you go!

Whether you are excited about e-books, want more from the web, must have your mobile apps, or are swept up in social media, Dummies makes everything easier.

Leverage the Power

For Dummies is the global leader in the reference category and one of the most trusted and highly regarded brands in the world. No longer just focused on books, customers now have access to the For Dummies content they need in the format they want. Let us help you develop a solution that will fit your brand and help you connect with your customers.

Advertising & Sponsorships

Connect with an engaged audience on a powerful multimedia site, and position your message alongside expert how-to content.

Targeted ads • Video • Email marketing • Microsites • Sweepstakes sponsorship

21 Million Monthly Page Views & 13 Million Unique Visitors

# of For Dummies

Custom Publishing

Reach a global audience in any language by creating a solution that will differentiate you from competitors, amplify your message, and encourage customers to make a buying decision.

Apps • Books • eBooks • Video • Audio • Webinars

Brand Licensing & Content

Leverage the strength of the world's most popular reference brand to reach new audiences and channels of distribution.

For more information, visit www.Dummies.com/biz

Dummies products make life easier!

- DIY
- Consumer Electronics
- Crafts
- Software
- Cookware
- Hobbies
- Videos
- Music
- Games
- and More!

For more information, go to **Dummies.com**· and search the store by category.

FOR
DUMMIES
A Wiley Brand

Printed and bound by CPI Group (UK) Ltd, Croydon, CR0 4YY

09/06/2025

14685923-0002